KITCHENER PUBLIC LIBRARY

910
.4ᵒᵒ
C
F

W9-BDK-193

Unfinished woman : a memoir

UNFINISHED WOMAN

BY THE SAME AUTHOR

Tracks
Desert Places
Travelling Light
No Fixed Address: Nomads and the Fate of the Planet
The Picador Book of Journeys

UNFINISHED WOMAN

ROBYN DAVIDSON

A Memoir

BLOOMSBURY PUBLISHING

NEW YORK · LONDON · OXFORD · NEW DELHI · SYDNEY

BLOOMSBURY PUBLISHING
Bloomsbury Publishing Plc
1385 Broadway, New York, NY 10018, USA

BLOOMSBURY, BLOOMSBURY PUBLISHING and the Diana logo are
trademarks of Bloomsbury Publishing Plc

First published in 2023 in Great Britain
First published in the United States 2023

Copyright © Robyn Davidson, 2023

Extract from *View with a Grain of Sand* by Wisława Szymborska,
published by kind permission of Faber and Faber Ltd.

Extract from *Collected Poems* by Sylvia Path published by kind permission of
Faber and Faber Ltd.

Lyrics from "You Are My Sunshine"; words and music by Jimmie Davis
© 1940 Peer International Corporation

All rights reserved. No part of this publication may be reproduced or transmitted in
any form or by any means, electronic or mechanical, including photocopying,
recording, or any information storage or retrieval system, without prior
permission in writing from the publishers

ISBN: HB: 978-1-62040-162-0; EBOOK: 978-1-62040-163-7

Library of Congress Cataloging-in-Publication Data is available.

2 4 6 8 10 9 7 5 3 1

Typeset by Newgen KnowledgeWorks Pvt. Ltd., Chennai, India
Printed and bound in the U.S.A.

To find out more about our authors and books visit www.bloomsbury.com
and sign up for our newsletters.

Bloomsbury books may be purchased for business or promotional use. For information on
bulk purchases please contact Macmillan Corporate and Premium Sales Department
at specialmarkets@macmillan.com.

The distortion of a text is not unlike a murder. The difficulty lies not in the execution of the deed but in doing away with the traces.

Sigmund Freud

Philosophy is really homesickness. The desire to be at home everywhere.

Novalis

May my dead be patient with the way my memories fade. My apologies to time for all the world I overlook each second.

Wisława Szymborska

Prelude

When I was eleven years old, my mother gave me a pair of gold sandals. These were for 'best', and not at all suitable for school. In all my life so far I had worn socks and sensible lace-ups to school. Other children were allowed to run around barefoot – there was cow shit between their toes, and their feet splayed out like thick T-bone steaks. But they were 'common' and the Davidsons were not.

What could it have been about that morning in particular, that gave me the courage to end my mother's dominion over me, to dress not only in the gold sandals but in a gathered green poplin skirt with rope petticoat, rather than the pleated tartan that was customary? Children mocking at first breasts, perhaps. Or a boy sending love notes across the classroom. Loyalty to a future self conflicted with loyalty to my mother's realm. The old bindings had to be cut.

I came down the wrought-iron staircase inside our house. My mother stood below me, more a force than a person. She held my blue plastic lunchbox; I clutched my school port. We argued and it seemed this had never happened before. I knew that I would wear these clothes, these sandals. I had already won the battle inside my own will.

'Aren't you even going to kiss me goodbye?' she said.

Not guilt nor love nor fear must be allowed to weaken the momentum of victory. Without turning around, I flounced through the kitchen and out the front door. 'No, I won't.'

When I came home that afternoon, my mother was dead.

This could be the beginning of a memoir – a curtain drawn aside to reveal the theatre of life as it exists inside my mind and no one else's. But although I know the gold sandals were real, that I wore them on a particular day and this led to an altercation with my mother on the stairs, these facts exist as no more than an instant of sense perception filed in memory and encased as a kind of seed. The other details in the picture – the skirt, port, lunchbox; the duration in which the scene unfolds; the walk through the kitchen; the inference that I understood, at the time, the import of my actions – these have been furnished by imagination. If I continued with the story, it would unfurl out of that seed, that moment, and its relationship to what-really-happened would become increasingly obscure.

But factual truth is the least of my worries here. What I have written is inauthentic in a much more profound sense. The confrontation over the gold sandals had nothing to do with my mother's death, either in reality or in the depths of my own conscience. Or rather, it may have had something to do with it, perhaps even a lot to do with it, but not in the way I have intimated here.

I have been trying to write about my mother for years. Some attempts attained a considerable length, others didn't struggle beyond five pages before being tossed in the bin.

Each beginning was different in style from every other beginning. There was an awkward attempt to write short 'meditations', each precipitated out of an object from the past. My mother would emerge from these meditations as a whole piece of music is created from individual phrases. It wasn't long before I admitted to myself that this was too contrived.

Another described my surroundings at the time – a small room in India. Through the window I saw boulders and jungle. A langur sat on the veranda parapet, swinging its leg. But I wasn't actually in India when I wrote it, I was in Australia.

In yet another I placed myself at a London literary high table, and pulled the scene to bits – its pretensions, its mediocrity, its envy, its insecurities – using the scene as a 'how did I get here?' device.

But in judging those imaginary characters at the dinner table, I was failing in my job. An author's job is never to judge her characters, but to understand them. Which is the same as saying, to love them.

All of these beginnings could probably have gone on to become books. But not THE book. Not the RIGHT book.

But why the unease after so many attempts? Why should I be so shy of reaching the lode-bearing stratum that the moment I think I might be anywhere near it, I shoot back up to the surface?

My mother hanged herself from the rafters of our garage, using the cord of our electrical kettle.

Where can I go with a sentence like that? How do I unfurl the story of her life (a life rendered retrospectively tragic by that sentence) without descending into melodrama?

My first book, *Tracks*, was an account of a journey I made, alone, across the Australian deserts. The person who made that journey – myself – became the central character in the book. This character/narrator/self did nothing factually different from what I did in reality. That is to say, the account contains no lies.

Yet it is deceiving. That 'fictional' 'me' seems to have a greater authenticity than the flux of contradictions, mental disappearances, memories and self-talk that must have constituted my inner life at the time. The fictionalising of myself was instinctive, guileless and completely candid.

And I did not doubt that I had a right to speak.

But I now know that memory is shot through and through with falsehood; that published words are powerful, and while one has a responsibility to try to get at the truth, one has also to remember that one person's version of it can bury another's.

My sister's take on my mother's story is so different from mine that it is as if we emerged from different wombs. Up to now my sister has owned the copyright on my mother's story. Our story. If I tell it another way, I am breaking a kind of familial law.

★

I don't feel any emotion when I think of my mother's death. I have imagined the act, what it required to do it, but I imagine it as one sees a scene in a film. It seems to hold no special significance for me. Perhaps by the time she killed herself I was already quite far away. In any case, when I touch the area around that day, I can feel only callus.

The day opens for me at about 3.30 p.m. This must be the time, because I have just left the school grounds and am looking down the street towards our house. The port is in my right hand. We have only lived here for a year or two, having moved from the country. All of us, in our different ways, struggle against suburban life like trapped birds. I loathe the Moreton Bay beaches just a half-mile from our house. The water is waveless and opaque and it contains jellyfish. There are mangrove swamps and moaning casuarina forests. The beaches are narrow and lonely. I hate swimming in the shark enclosure with the kids from school because my mother has bought me transparent Speedos, and you can see my bottom through them when they are wet.

Summer afternoon. Cotton frock. (No rope petticoat or gold sandals.) Right hand clasping handle of school port. I am standing still, looking down the street to our house, which is different from all the other houses. Our house is two-storey with 'patios'. Built by an *Italian*. My mother says it's vulgar. Inside the house, every room is filled with thick dark misery, even though there is plenty of suburban light pouring through the venetian blinds. My mother, unable to get out of bed one day, told me God had come to her through the venetians and held her hand. Greg Hamilton, who passes me notes in school, reckons the house is unlucky.

It's as if I am on an escalator from which it is impossible to get off. Dread. I can feel it now. A swooning sensation, and the stomach revolving. Occasionally in my life I have wondered about the intensity of this dread. This wish to fall down where I stand, for some miracle to intervene and cancel the inevitability of that journey to our house. I have wondered if perhaps I already knew my mother was dead, if perhaps I had sneaked home at lunchtime and found her. But there was no psychic foreseeing, no blocked memory to be tweezered out later by some crank shrink. The more appalling truth is that this was how I must have felt every day, when I looked down the street towards our house.

As I approach I see that there is a police car outside our house. My father is standing at the front of our house in his khakis. It appears someone has thrown a bucket of water over him. Next to him is our neighbour, Mrs Wallace. My father is trembling all over, and weeping. As I walk towards him he bends down to take me in his arms, something he has never ever done before. He says, 'Mummy's dead, darling.' I reject him and go to our neighbour, Mrs Wallace. I cry but only because this is expected. Later, my mother's mother is leading me through the kitchen. Her bony hand is gripping mine but she doesn't seem all that aware of me. She shows me the electrical kettle and says something about my mother and the cord. I did not understand her because her voice was odd and high. I thought that my mother had tried to electrocute herself, and failed, so had to choose another method. I seem already to know that she has hanged herself, but I don't remember who told me. There are no details at that time. The garage rafters, the torn fingernails, my father giving her mouth-to-mouth resuscitation, these embellishments came later, from my sister.

The next memory is being out on the golf course behind the house with Mrs Wallace. She says comforting things. I know it is difficult for her to find things to say that match the occasion. What she says in fact bears no relation to me, as if she and I inhabit different zones. My dog, Goldie, is there. I feel I should be with someone else, not Mrs Wallace, though I can't think who that might be. I still don't feel as I believe I should feel – I don't feel sad or grief-stricken, for example. But there is still that dread in my body. Not pain pain, but numb pain. It's not pain being done to you, it's pain that IS you.

Later, I am in the back of a taxi with my sister, who is seventeen; that is, six years older than me. Or perhaps we are in the police car. She looks as if someone has slapped her in the face. I would like to wrap my arms around her but my body is out of time with my thoughts, as if it had stiffened. She is taking control of things. Our father doesn't seem to be involved. I am to go and live with my father's twin sister on Tamborine Mountain. This is to save me from the worse fate of living with our grandmother in the pigeon-box house she shares with our grandfather. But I won't be allowed to take my dog.

Those are the seeds embedded from that day. I can go back to them, just as I went back to that memory of the gold sandals, crack them all open, and from each one I could fashion a deluge, an infinitude of memoirs.

But would they be true? Would they be *fair*? As dispassionately as I've tried to describe the residue of that day, the whole passage is still hopelessly skewed by the first-person pronoun. Especially the bit about the dog. I don't deny that to dispose of the pet of a child whose mother has just hanged herself is a strange thing to do. But the interesting thing about it is precisely that – that it is a strange thing to do. Not that it happened to *me*. But if I leave out the dog, where does the leaving-out end? Whom do I erase from the scene of that day?

My mother died when she was forty-six. It never crossed my mind to write about her, indeed even to think about her, until I approached the same age. Then that erased, safely buried woman came back with, literally, a vengeance. It was as if she were imprecating me to release her from the prison of other people's stories. It was my duty to do so. There was no one else who could or would. She had been misrepresented, dishonoured, *murdered*.

My mother always overestimated my talents. The job she gave me is beyond them. I have failed her as consistently as Hamlet failed his ghost.

But were I to write again about the day of my mother's death, I might not mention the walk home from school, or the dog, or my poor father and sister. I might leave out entirely that impassable sentence – 'my mother hanged herself …' I might try, instead, to focus on the kettle. It was one of those yellow, chunky kettles with a black, flip-up lid. Bakelite, I should think. A fifties kettle. From that kettle, which sits on the Laminex counter next to our new electric fry pan, I might describe 1961 as it was in a kitchen in an Australian suburb. And from that year might unfurl previous years – Mooloolah siding on the North Coast Line, where my sister rode her horse to school and sometimes let me double behind her, where my dad sheared sheep by hand while my sister and I stamped the wool in the wool press and the big green carpet snake stared down from the rafters above us, where I got stomach ache after stealing mad Valerie's peaches, where my mother and father flicked each other with tea towels in the kitchen and laughed till the tears ran, where the kids at school had cow shit between their toes, where I couldn't bear to see my sister teased, where I saw my father punishing the horse with his stock whip, where I was frightened of my sister's anger, where the Gripskies' bull chased Grandy and me up a tree, where mirrors watched us impassively from the walls of Malabah house. And before Malabah there was Stanley Park, the cattle station where I was born, the buggy by the barbed-wire fence, picking harebells along the dirt track, sing-songs around the piano. And before that there was a war during which my mother and father fell in love, and before that war there was a Depression, and before that there was another war, and my parents' worlds contained the seeds of these events, so that although the kettle is common to all of us, nevertheless coded in it are all these other memories that existed before I was born and that I have inherited.

My mother is as close to me, and as hidden from me, as my own face …

One

In the beginning is Stanley Park. It consists of a few glimmers in the darkness of infancy, sense memories lodged in the brain by some unknown law, unremarkable in themselves, yet as essential to the formation of character as rocks are to the building of a coral reef. Gradually the glimmers move closer together illuminating scenes around which stories gather. Trateggios of the real and the imagined, legitimate and contestable, stolen memories and my own.

My mother is sitting up in bed, wearing a blue crocheted bed jacket tied with silk ribbon. It is morning, and through the doors leading on to a little veranda, the sky is immaculate, not a stroke of cloud.

My father sits beside the bed. He is wearing his Sunday best – sports coat with an RSL pin in the lapel, gaberdine trousers, fat tie, broad-brimmed grazier's hat. He takes off the hat, leans forward with his elbows on his knees, and turns the hat round and round in his hands. It is a habit of shyness, or feeling.

Dr Charlton (or possibly Dr Forster) wheels in a chipped enamel cot. Inside it is an unnaturally large baby – me – eleven pounds, two ounces – dragged by forceps from a woman who doesn't reach five feet, who has shoulders like a perched bird. The baby's ears are as crushed as a boxer's, and the head is deformed from the forceps.

These malformations do not penetrate the mother's love-blindness, however. Later, she would say, 'When you were born I wanted to stand on the roof of the hospital and shout for joy.'

And, 'I love you so much I could *eat* you.'

My sister, nearly six years old, peers into the cot. Her auburn hair is in ringlets tied up with bows. She looks up and says, 'I love my mummy and my daddy, but I love my little sister more.' The adults laugh and praise her and the phrase enters family legend.

There is no record of the time of birth, and those who might remember are gone.

Outside, heat rises off the corrugated-iron roofs of a small country town bisected by a gravel road. There are a couple of tillies parked outside the pub, but there are no people around. The road vanishes into scrub in both directions – eucalyptus and boxwood, the trees powdered with pale bulldust. The drought is already three years long.

Twenty or thirty miles along the road, past Giligulgul, past Guluguba siding, past our neighbour who has 'diabetes', are the gates of Stanley Park. Two perfectly spherical stones, bigger than heads, adorn the tops of the posts. At the side, a horizontal drum acts as mailbox. From there, a two-wheel track leads to the clump of trees hiding the house, a windmill limping in the air, some cattle yards and a hay shed. Along that track are harebells that wilt the moment they are picked.

It is a small Queensland cattle station, a mere fifteen thousand acres, on the western edge of the Darling Downs, a long way west of the strip of lushness on the eastern side of the Great Dividing Range which protects the seaboard from the incalculably old heart of the country. My father inherited the property from his family. He has returned from Africa and from the war. He has brought his city-bred wife here. They have been 'making a go of it' for almost a decade.

The house is wood. The paint is rust-coloured, peeling. There is a veranda at the back, a corrugated-iron tank beside it; a blue cattle dog, Wilga, under the tank stand, panting. This Wilga is one of a succession of Wilgas – blue heeler or kelpie dogs used for mustering stock, barking at strangers and snakes.

There will probably be a cat around and it will be called 'Chittle', though my dad doesn't like cats. They kill too many native birds. When he strokes the ears of the dog, he croons, '*thwetulaa thwetulaa*', in a sing-songy voice. It is a Swahili word.

It is probably with the arrival of this second baby that my mother becomes 'Little Mummy' in his lexicon, rather than 'Gwen', or 'Sweetheart', or 'Sweetheart Darling'. Little Mummy is indeed tiny. He is six foot one.

There is a swing near the veranda that he has made. There is a mandarin tree and somewhere, though I can't place it, a mulberry tree. My mother grows silver beet and a few hardy flowers – hydrangea, gaillardia, a rose bush.

The house has no electricity yet, the mail comes once a fortnight, and the lavatory is outside, quite a distance from the veranda steps.

When she takes her children to the lav at night, she shines the torch nervously on the path in case a copperhead, western brown or taipan should slither across, and she shines it under the wooden seat to see if any redback spiders are clustered there. Beside the seat is a box of sawdust and a tin scoop.

She reigns over the inside of the house, and is afraid of the outside, which is her husband's realm. His boots, hat and stock whip live at the border between the two – the back veranda. She scrubs and polishes the ragged lino of the kitchen, starches the doilies, the children's dresses, presses the bed linen. She uses beeswax on the furniture that came with her from Before. She bakes sponges and scones in the Kooka wood stove, simmers salt beef on the hotplate. She washes everything by hand in cement tubs on Monday, and hangs it out (wooden pegs in her mouth) on long lines, where it whips and flaps. She damps down the clothes on Tuesday, ready to be ironed on Wednesday, using two flat irons which she heats on top of the Kooka. She presses his khaki work clothes. The good aroma of sweat and Sunshine soap rises out of them. She wears pretty summer sun-frocks, and is careful of her appearance. She teaches her oldest daughter correspondence school. The lessons come by pedal wireless. School of the Air. She sews her daughters' clothes on a treadle Singer sewing machine – pintucks, lace, bows at the back, puffed sleeves – organza, lawn, poplin and the just-new thing, nylon. We stand on the kitchen table for our fittings. She holds pins between her lips and mumbles at us to stand still. The outside she is afraid of comes inside in the form of poisonous snakes, bulldust, and loneliness.

Looking out from the veranda, past the swing and the mandarin tree, past the creek bed lined with river red gums, their leaves turned edgewise to the sun – the land spreads out silent and empty. White blossom on a gum tree explodes into screeching corellas, but the noise only intensifies the silence absorbing it. Everything is dry. The white sand of the creek bed, the eucalyptus leaves, the grass, the piss ants ceaselessly streaming up and down the trunks from which bark hangs as if flayed.

Not so very long before, less than a hundred years, some Aborigines were murdered somewhere along this creek.

One night my father is so certain he can smell lion, he dresses and goes outside with a loaded rifle. He hasn't been in Africa for fifteen years.

Once, when my mother is alone at the house, and he is far away ringbarking the brigalow, a stranger arrives looking for bit work. The stranger says, 'So you're all alone, eh? Your husband won't be back till nightfall, eh?'

'Oh no, he'll be back any minute. Why don't you go over to the yards and wait for him there.' She takes Wilga off the chain, and holds him by the collar. The dog growls at the stranger. This is one of the stories she will recount later, making a joke of it, mimicking his leer, her breezy response and false courage, impressing townies. Other men arrive who are not threatening. They 'hump' their 'swags' around, unable or unwilling to settle, leftovers from the Depression, from the war. There is always tea and food for them.

Up in the brigalow forest, my father whistles to himself, and enjoys heaving the axe. He has ridden the big chestnut mare up here, Val. She has a white blaze down her Roman face. He will boil the billy soon, on a brigalow campfire, and eat the sandwiches Little Mummy has prepared. He will sit alone in the bush feeling a sweet contentment.

One day, Val shies and bolts through the brigalow. Before he can rein her in, he has careened into a hornets' nest. He comes home with a head twice its size. Little Mummy doctors him, just as she does when he suffers yet another strangulation hernia. These stories are cause for laughter later, when the danger has dissipated.

I am little, and therefore frightened of the gekkos that walk upside down on the ceiling above my bed. I often go to my parents' bed at night, because of the gekkos. Usually they let me cuddle up between them. I recite what my father has said to reassure me. 'Dere's no need to be fightened ob de gekkos, dey only eat de 'piders and de fies.' There are lots of 'piders and fies at Stanley Park. Big huntsman spiders the size of a man's fist, running around the walls. Poisonous redbacks, under the house, under the lavatory lid, under beds. Golden orb weaver spiders up in the brigalow, buttery fat abdomens at the centre of webs as strong as wire, strung between the trees. And flies of course, zillions of them, the little black bush flies that cluster in the eyes, or on a patch of sweat-stained khaki, or the house flies and blowies, waiting for the gauze doors to open so they can zoom into the kitchen and land on Little Mummy's sponge cakes.

Sunday mornings, the sleeping-in day. We two children cuddle up against our mother's body in bed. I throw my legs over my mother's legs. We all lie together in sensual bliss, she stroking our limbs, our backs, our tummies. She sometimes reads a Penguin paperback posted from the city. (One of them is covered in brown paper and kept on a hidden shelf. It is an expurgated edition of *Lady Chatterley's Lover*, the only version allowed in Australia at that time.) Daddy comes in with a tray. He has made big piles of toast dripping with butter, Vegemite, peanut paste and marmalade. A big brown teapot with a cosy. Milk jug covered against flies, sugar bowl, big cups with saucers. He pours the tea, and clang clang clangs the spoon in the cup to dissolve the sugar. He gets into bed with us. The adults read, and talk.

I don't remember much about my sister from the Stanley Park time. But I know she plays down in the dry creek bed, with stones and twigs and her duckling, Auburn. She is rounding up imaginary horses and putting them in stock yards made of leaves and sticks. Who is watching over her there? Is my father around? Doing some work, perhaps?

I also know that one day she declares that she is going to run away from home, and our mother says, 'Are you, darling? Oh well, let me make you some things to take with you so you won't get hungry.' And she ties some food up in a cloth and ties that to the end of a stick, and off my big sister goes with her little stick over her shoulder, and her little bundle at the end of it. Not very far, it turns out.

One Sunday morning our father doesn't climb into bed with us, but stands staring out the window, at the drought – six years now, and there is no money left. Our mother slides out of bed quietly, sneaks up behind him and rips the string out of his pyjama trousers, which fall around his feet. They laugh like storms.

All four of us are standing outside under a blue sky. But instead of withered grass and dust, the whole earth is white and the air is strangely cold and polished. Hailstones, some as big as tennis balls, others like pearls, lie a foot thick where the storm has drifted them. We children cannot cram enough of the little spheres in our mouths. Everyone gathers them up and puts them in old jam tins.

Sometime after the hailstorm, it rains so heavily that a wave of brown water comes roaring down the creek bed, eating away whole trees and chunks of bank so that the river moves closer to the house. The great drought of the fifties has broken, but there is no money left to shore up the river bank. If the creek floods again, it might take the house with it.

★

One day Little Mummy says to her youngest child, who totters beside her in the garden, "'Mary Mary quite contrary, how does your garden grow? With silver bells and cockle shells …'"

And suddenly I remember so vividly, as if a spotlight has fallen on a stage, illuminating us … I am close to my mother as she digs in the narrow flower bed behind the laundry. The extraordinary, unprecedented idea: 'cockle shells'.

When I remember my mother gardening, I remember it from inside my body; that is to say, I don't see myself in the scene, I *am* myself. But in another scene I am slightly to the left of, and slightly behind, myself. And that is the position from which I recall most of the things that have happened to me. What is that trick of memory? Do we all remember ourselves as actors of our own lives?

Another room. A brownish place, shadow corners and some gleaming things. Other objects almost completely black, sunken back into darkness. I am sitting at the head of a long table, in a high chair. Down the sides of the table are faces whose attention is fixed on me. They are as big as moons hanging in the sky. In front of me is a cake.

The same room, my mother is sitting at her piano, singing. The room is shadowy and golden-brown. It smells of beeswax and dry air. She gets up, lifts the lid of the piano and places inside it, next to the strings, a tin of water. Then I am down on the floor, watching her foot working the pedal. I must be quite small, as her foot seems huge to me.

Another vivid memory is of being on the swing and composing a 'symphony'. I am delighted with myself, and run to the back stairs to tell my mother. I have to climb those enormous steps like a monkey, using my hands.

And finally: she is standing on the veranda, at the top of the same back steps. I cannot hear her voice, but I know she says, 'Don't you poke your tongue out at me.' I could describe the scene – the house, the tank stand, the dry grass, the smell of the mandarin tree and the itchy smell of dust, somewhere the clanking of a windmill, sheets flapping on a clothesline. I know these things are present but it would be incorrect to say that I can discern any of them from this image which has darkened over the years, like a painting. And yet I am aware of a supersaturation of light, a torrent of brightness containing us.

It's hard to say precisely what I remember other than that she is up there at the top of the steps, looking down and across at me where I stand at the gate, down and across to where I sit, sixty years later, in a place on the other side of the earth, which she will never see. She has falsely accused me. I did not poke my tongue at her. My lips were dry and I was licking them. Perhaps this awareness of her was engraved because, in understanding that she was capable of misjudging me, I saw that she must be Other than me.

Stanley Park exists in infant time, before history takes hold. I was four years old when the drought and worry prised us loose from there, and pushed us over the Great Divide.

To Malabah.

Two

Bring forth, from your inner vision, the island-continent of Australia. It is pink (for historical reasons) and completely encircled by blue. It may even stand out from the blue, if you have added little cliffs in such a way as to give the illusion of a three-dimensional object raised off the page; that is, above sea level. Of all the shapes on the globe, this surely is the most arresting and intriguing; the only one which seems the product of aesthetic vision rather than contingent geological forces. To belong to such a place is to inherit a sense of being MEANT.

Now superimpose the state boundary lines. Most are conceptual and therefore straight as rulers – dot dash, dot dash – though some wiggle, following rivers. Go to the top right-hand state – Queensland, the Sunshine State. It takes up half of the Great Dividing Range, which can be drawn with the flat of a pencil starting way up in Cape York Peninsula, coming down parallel and close to the coastline, then swooping to a hooked conclusion at the bottom of the island-continent, in Victoria. The Great Dividing Range protects the east, of which there is a narrow fertile strip of rain-shadow, from the west, of which there is everything else.

The lower right-hand corner of the state is known as the South East Corner and its right to a designation lies in the fact that it contains the capital, Brisbane. You may wish to mark a black line with crosses in it to indicate the railway line linking Brisbane to all the coastal towns right back up to Cape York, the names of which you will have learnt during your second year at school, as a two-four prosodic chant which goes: '*Bris*bane, *Gym*pie, *Mary*borough, *Bun*daberg, *Glad*stone, Rock*hamp*ton, Mack*aaaaaay*.'

Notice that by far the greater density of place names occurs over on the right-hand side of the Great Divide – the strip referred to above, and known as Coastal Queensland – while the left-hand side, known as, yes, Western Queensland, contains a great deal of emptiness on which are stamped little pictures of emus, kangaroos, sheep and cattle, mines and Aborigines standing on one leg clutching spears. These are our 'primary products'.

Now, put your finger on the segment of black line running between Brisbane and Gympie, and you will have found, more or less, the most important place on earth between the years 1954 and 1959.

Malabah, Mooloolah, North Coast Line, Queensland, Australia, The Earth, The Solar System, The Milky Way, The Universe, locates you with greater precision in space. The time, as I said, is that chunk of it between my fourth year of existence (1954), and my ninth.

In 1954, we, the Davidsons, crossed the Great Dividing Range from west to east. My father drove the tilly and my sister and I were wedged between him and our mother. The only reminiscence on record of that portentous journey is that I kicked my sister with my little shoes.

I myself remember nothing of it, but I imagine the tilly appearing at the brink of the Great Divide as if disgorged from a mirage which rolls over the parched country behind us, rolls back over the lonely place where I was born, rolls on west into shimmering myth. In that instant when, for the little family in the tilly, west becomes east, the mirage crystallises into History, and we are successfully delivered into Time.

Day one. An old-fashioned utility car, with a front cabin for passengers and a flat open back for things like rope and fencing wire, is approaching a railway crossing. Mark Davidson is driving. Gwen, his wife, is clasping their four-year-old, Robyn, in her lap. Margaret, the older child, sits between Mummy and Daddy, fending off her little sister's shoes, and looking like thunder.

The back of the tilly is packed expertly with such possessions as could not be entrusted to the furniture van – the Leichhardt tree, Mark's elephant gun, Gwen's crystal – then lashed down under a tarp. I'm not sure if the tilly is a Holden. Holdens may have come later. And I don't know if the road is bitumen yet. If not, then dust barrels out behind the tilly as it approaches the North Coast Line which will become so familiar but which now is a cause for excitement and relief.

They have driven hundreds of miles, unconscionably far in those days when 50 mph was considered reckless even on bitumen, and most of the roads were gravel. They are cramped, hot and bored.

All the way from Stanley Park they have rallied themselves by singing, 'Pack up your troubles in your old kitbag and smile, smile, smile,' or, 'Life is GREAT in the

Sunshine State,' or stopping for tea from a Thermos, and a wee, behind trees. Then cleaning the windscreen of its thick crust of insects.

When the rallies peter out, they sink down into their own thoughts again, as the scrub rolls on and on past their windows. Sometimes they are jolted out of reveries by a kangaroo leaping in front of them, or an emu charging along beside the car. Or, spotting a funnel of dust way off on the horizon, someone will say, 'There's something coming,' and when, a long time later, the oncoming vehicle slows down to pass them, both drivers lift a hand to acknowledge the other. Drivers who don't wave are probably from the city, and don't know any better.

Once the tilly is on the eastern side of the range, it is noted that quite a few drivers don't wave – confirmation of the moral decline that accompanies overpopulation. In the bush, the population is about right: one person per few thousand square miles. Even Gwen, who was once a city girl, follows disapprovingly with her eyes those cars containing people who don't wave.

But here they come, mustering their enthusiasm for the last few miles. The strains of 'How MUCH is that doggie in the window' comes from the cabin, then Gwen points to the sign on the left, Mooloolah, telling her children to sit up and stop grizzling because we're there. She tells them to put out their tongues so she can dampen the corner of her hanky and rub their faces with it. Then she takes a powder compact out of her handbag (from which a Helena Rubinstein waft escapes), opens it and surveys her face which frowns back at her from the little round mirror. She pushes at her hair, dabs lipstick (titivating, as my father calls it), then clicks shut the compact, replaces it, clicks shut the handbag, smooths creases from her skirt and clasps her hands in her lap. But her fingers resist discipline, twisting at rings, twitching because somewhere in her head she is playing the piano, or typing the tail ends of thoughts which rise in her mind like fish surfacing into the light, then vanishing back into deep water. They come and go unbidden, directed by some unknown principle which seems not to belong to her will. She is barely aware of them, yet they constitute her truest life.

I am, in large part, their continuation.

The railway crossing has gates that close once a week to allow for the passage of the Sunlander diesel which charges importantly north to Gympie, Maryborough, Bundaberg … Not even coming to full rest in Mooloolah siding, but merely slowing down so that its conductor can exchange batons and mail with our station master, Mr Stevens. Then the Sunlander blares its horn all over the valley, and when it is well on its way north again, Mr Stevens will stroll up to open the gates – a white swing post across four metal lines.

On the other side of the gates, a dirt track leads left and down to the sawmill – an open-sided shed employing a couple of men in navy singlets. Another goes straight, to the school and the School of Arts hall, of which more later, and the third turns right – that is, north – to Malabah. But I'm getting ahead of myself.

The tilly slows down as it approaches the crossing (the gates are open today), stops, changes into first gear (synchromesh has not yet been invented), and we drive straight across the famous North Coast Line, bump bump pause, bump bump, coming to rest in front of the store/

post office/telephone exchange that is Harry Crack's establishment and ganglion of Mooloolah village.

Let's pause here to describe the Davidsons as they must have appeared then. Mark: six foot one, cheek skin smooth and smelling of Old Spice shaving cream. Springing, curly auburn hair cut short back and sides, aristocratic nose, thin lips, bright blue eyes, Errol Flynn moustache. He is in his mid-fifties though appears younger. Dressed in khakis, elegantly faded and pressed, sleeves rolled to the elbow, a plaited kangaroo-skin belt sitting comfortably under the stomach. A gloriously handsome man whose beauty is marred by a small balding spot at the crown of his head where the hair is as fine as a baby's. The thumb of his left hand is missing, and one toe. He is very slightly deaf because he was with the 2nd Anti-Tank during the war and the blast of artillery damaged the nerves in his ears.

Gwen: four foot eleven, thin as a harebell, with shoulders like a perched bird. She has hazel eyes and light brown hair, cut and permed in the fashion of the day à la The House of Windsor. Very little make-up, a stylish cotton frock that she has made herself but you would never guess, sandals, bare brown legs unshaved because shaving is vulgar, half-moons showing on neat nails, dabs of eau de cologne behind ears and in crooks of elbows. In spite of the long journey, she might have just stepped out of the pages of a pattern book. She is pretty, but not only that. She is … noticeable. How to put it? She has *flair*. There are two dimples in her face and her teeth are ever so slightly bucked. The dimples are like inverted commas calling attention to her vivacity and charm. It is a spirited face, made for and by laughter. She laughs in the same way that she sings — to give people pleasure and, thereby, to be loved. She is seventeen years younger than her husband.

Children: Margaret, the oldest, has masses of auburn ringlets tied up in bows. A burnishing of russet lights through thick brown gloss – fabulous Davidson hair. She is chubby and watchful. Youngest: plump and bonny with a cliché of blonde curls and baby-blue eyes. Both are beautifully dressed and both wear black patent-leather court shoes with ankle socks.

It is obvious that a lot of work goes into this family, into its presentation and confidence. The fifties could have produced nothing more representative of its best.

It is an unusual family, but not too unusual. Just unusual enough.

One of the things said of Gwen at the time is that she was 'highly strung', and an example of this tensility in her character was her dread of snakes. In fact, one of the reasons we left the west, it was said, was her phobia of the copperheads, western browns, king browns, mulga snakes and taipans – all of them deadly – which treated our house as if they were the owners and we were the blow-ins which, I suppose, was true. By day they settled in the corners of her kitchen; at night they lay across the path to the lav, scaring the 'living daylights' out of her as she took us for a last wee before bedtime, shining her kero lamp all around and shepherding us, with quick little steps and quick little breaths, into safe patches of light. My father, on the other hand, was so fond of snakes (of all things wild) that he refused to kill them, and instead would pick them up behind the head so that they wrapped around his arm. He would present them to his cowering wife saying,

'Poor old joe-blake, you've given him quite a scare,' before releasing them far away from the house, into the dry grass.

When my mother entered Harry Crack's establishment to introduce herself on that first day, she asked what Mooloolah meant.

'And what does Mooloolah actually mean, Mr Crack, does anyone know?' She would have asked this engagingly, willing him to like her, and everyone in the village would have known, within an hour of our arrival, that the newcomers had 'tickets on 'emselves'. Harry Crack leant sideways on the counter, all angles and levers of sinew and bone, and took his time. 'Abbo word. They reckon it means red-bellied black snake. Poisonous buggers.' It was a story my mother would tell against herself, wryly, raising her eyes heavenward.

Here, then, are the coordinates of Mooloolah village: Harry Crack's store. Mr Stevens's siding. Mr Jeays's schoolhouse. The School of Arts hall. The open-air sawmill. Railway lines with gate. And parallel to them, in a northerly direction, the road leading home.

My father had bought Malabah sight unseen. From the drought country, it had sounded like a paradise, where the creeks contained water rather than sand, where there were patches of rainforest rather than brigalow scrub. There were 240 acres of green kikuyu pasture for Romney Marsh and Border Leicester sheep – refined, English sheep, not the hard-bitten Merinos upon whose back Australia was said to ride. Instead of Hereford cattle bellowing through cumuli of dust, stock whip cracking above them, withers banging and crashing along stock-yard rails, eyes rolled to the whites, here we had moist milking cows whom you could pat. Malabah cows did not bellow, they *lowed*.

So it was difficult to interpret the inflexion in my mother's voice when, not long after our arrival, she called Malabah the 'white elephant'. It was a fair description of the house which stood four-square on its hill, different from and grander than the other houses in the district. It was white tongue-in-groove with a bottle-green corrugated-iron roof, a bottle-green corrugated-iron tank, and yellow wooden shutters on the outside of the windows. An allamanda vine climbed all over the front, matching both roof and shutters. Creosoted stumps capped with tin elevated the house from the hot earth and white ants, so that it brought to mind a lady lifting her skirts. Underneath (between the lady's legs) was parked the tilly in gear and unlocked; a cubby house with downscaled furniture and miniature window; my mother's laundry (three big cement tubs with a hand-wringer); my father's workbenches and tools; a bunch of Lady Finger bananas ripening at the rate of a hand a day; the suspended net of eggs rubbed with Keep Egg; a parade of black rubber boots in ascending sizes, which had to be checked for centipedes before being worn; antlion funnels in the dirt, and the tracks of red-bellied black snakes.

The unearthly image of a 'white elephant' nicely captured Malabah's atmosphere too. The mats of passion-fruit vine smothering the back quarter were as enigmatic and brooding as the briars surrounding Sleeping Beauty's castle. And the ox-heart mango tree could easily be substituted for the Grimm Brothers' linden: 'Shake, shake, mango tree, gold and silver over me ...' Malabah drew you into itself, and kept you for itself.

In short, Malabah was enchanted. At night, the little bedroom I shared with my sister would expand and melt away to reveal ballrooms made of gold and crystal, where women wore dresses spun from sunbeams and starlight. There were palaces of agate glimpsed through jungle, cities of tall, crooked houses where snow wheeled in sooty air, and chimney sweeps in top hats climbed over 'parapets'. There were foggy marshes and quicksand bogs, where children fled from wicked soldiers. There were strange sounds, strange weathers, strange beasts, plants, words – linden tree, chimney sweep, parapet, Amazon … Until sleep came and took it all away.

At the front of the house was a high hedge of bougainvillea whose magenta bracts contained three white flowercules in succeeding stages of openness. The boundary was completed by a white paling fence which was magnified, over the driveway, into a rectangular arch from which swung the sign, MALABAH, in green and white. Our driveway turned off the corrugated gravel road which followed the ghost of the Cobb and Co. coach route which had faded out fifty years before along with Gympie gold. This was the road we took to Nambour once a fortnight, for supplies and music lessons, or to Eudlo, once in a blue moon, for the pictures, and over which, once a year, the council could sometimes be persuaded to pass its grader. There were rain gutters gouged in the clay on either side of the road, then blady grass and sclerophyll scrub as far as you'd care to think about.

Blady grass. Groundsel. Paterson's curse. Lantana. Khaki burr. Cobbler's pegs. Stinking Roger. Thickets of escape raspberries. Stinging Gympie trees along the creek. Wait-a-while vines. Flayed eucalyptus. Humidity. Heat. And refined, English sheep.

They suffered from foot rot, worm and pink eye. Blowflies settled under their tails and ate their flesh. Floods washed them away; bushfires roasted them or stampeded them into the creek. Dingos and feral dogs tore out their entrails. One night 80 per cent of our flock was lost in this fashion, and my father had to 'finish them off' with his rifle the next morning. He suffered six more strangulation hernias erecting dingo-proof netting all around the property. But our neighbours on the east side, the Gripskies, were no-hopers who left our gates open. And the dogs were cunning, finding places along the creek where they could dig beneath the netting in order to tear the guts out of our bank balance the moment it poked its nose above the red. My father laid traps by the holes in the netting, and saw a dog chewing its own foot off to get free. The sheep, living up to their reputation for stupidity, lambed during the winter wet. Off my father would go each frosty morning with his rifle to finish off the dead ewes and collect the orphaned lambs, eager little things who butted the bottles we gave them to suck, and wiggled their tails, and who quickly grew from adorable to dull, at which point they were reintroduced to the flock, and forgot the names and the love we had given them.

I suppose I knew that my father was making no more of 'a go of it' on Malabah than he had on Stanley Park; was dogged by the same 'rotten damn luck'. And no doubt I had already absorbed from my mother the notion that luck is related to character. But the white elephant's problems were adult concerns and the adult world floated close to, but discrete from, my own.

And my own was the first day of creation.

Every child is a mystic. That is, immersed in a state of wonder unsullied by blight of comparison, by tug of history or pull of consequence. Phenomena and perception are seamlessly aligned and consciousness is in perpetual rapture at the miracle of its own existence.

The light that drenched each Malabah day was always dazzling and new. No one had used it or dimmed its colours with too much seeing. No blue was as deep as the Malabah sky, no green as green as the grasshoppers I caught in the paspalum grass around the house. The bright fur of a chick, ripe loquats fallen from the tree, the insides of mangos exposed by the fruit bats, these sent out the shine of the sun itself. Malabah time did not hurry or harass. It did not intrude upon the attention paid to a grasshopper's eyes, the tiny saws along its legs, nor distract from the intense love for these other forms of life. Time billowed around us all, and held us safe, so that we could be still.

When I picture life after Malabah it is as if curtains have been pulled across a window somewhere. Only once, many years later, when I walked into the desert alone, did I recapture something of childhood's vision. Then too, for just a moment, I entered the first day of creation, and the wide open spaces of time.

Of course, famously, mystical insight demands solitude. Its light is eclipsed when Other People are around. Other People require an entirely different kind of attention, at once more superficial and more exacting. Other People have separate selves which make you aware that you, too, are a separate self, strung out along time's line, somewhere between history's tug and the pull of consequence.

And once you are aware of time's line, you are also aware of endings.

'"Now I lay me down to sleep, I pray the Lord my soul to keep. / If I should die before I wake, I pray the Lord my soul to take." God bless Mummy and Daddy and Marg, and Prince and Bertha and Yellow Eyes and Thumper and the black cat ...'

The black cat was a skinny creature who refused to be tamed. She had her litters in the old overgrown sheep race – curled balls of fluff which were tied in a sack by my father, to be drowned in the creek, before they had opened their eyes. My father would have liked to get rid of the black cat, but was restrained by his children's protests. He was not, however, about to cave in when it came to Bertha and Yellow Eyes who ended up on our dinner table, their names having provided them no protection from the chopping block. My sister and I sulked, but the smell of roasting chicken, a culinary luxury beyond compare in those days, caved us morally in.

We built elaborate graves for any dead animal we found, reserving especial tenderness for the chicks who died beneath their mothers' feathers.

I pondered the phenomenon of death and its implications, but became convinced that death was a failure of will. One simply decided not to die and then naturally – that is to say, in a straightforward sort of way – one would not. This was as evident to me as the evidence of my body. I would think, close your hand, and my hand would close. Similarly, I would simply say, 'Do not die.' It should perhaps have seemed odd that so many before me had not resorted to this technique, but I was certain that a personal capacity for inviolability was there, ready to be called into play when the time came. Thus death anxiety was put away, like winter clothes in summer. At least for myself. About my parents and sister I was not so sure.

During the first year at Malabah, before I was delivered to the educational talents of Mr Jeays, the socialising process was limited to the immediate family. We laughed and joked, played and teased in an idiom that belonged to us alone. It granted us the illusion of unity, belying the fact that behind each set of eyes were barricaded hordes of strangers.

But then any human head is a bedlam, if you care to look.

Three

Only the rosy glasses of motherhood could have rendered my childhood self anything other than plain. I had two buck teeth, and ears sticking out of my head like a taxi cab with the doors open, as my sister succinctly put it. It was extremely unlikely that I would evolve into anything but a plain grown-up. And yet, often in my adult life, people have commented on my beauty. I have found this disconcerting because if it is so, I can neither see it nor, more to the point, enjoy it or use it. Of course, like most women I have learnt how to enhance what features I have. I am not pretending innocence in matters of physical improvement. But when the make-up comes off and I confront that face in a mirror, I cannot, for the life of me, see what others claim to see, and the discomfort is something to do with the suspicion that they are therefore not seeing *me* at all.

Malabah house contained a respectable number of mirrors for a family our size. There was a small bathroom mirror, though only half sketched in memory. I corroborate its existence with the fact that my father must have shaved into something. Memory has no trouble with the queen mirror – an ovoid plate of silvered glass clasped by delicate curving wood, which swivelled in the hinges of the silky-oak Rosenstengel dressing table which had accompanied my mother from her previous life. The mirror's perfection was sullied in one small patch where the backing silver had crisped, but this only added to its glamour. It was consecrated to my mother's feminine practices, and to stare at one's own face in it seemed like profanity. Close to itself, the mirror reflected a crystal bottle of eau de cologne, a crystal plate with crystal hairbrush on it, and a round crystal bowl with lid. There was a crystal jug with silver neck which sometimes held flowers. Beyond these, the mirror contained a room in which sat the rest of the Rosenstengel suite – elegant daddy wardrobe and dainty daughter chest of drawers – a little family of silky-oak beings who had fallen on hard times, and were maintaining a certain reserve in the presence of the large double bed with whom they were forced to share cramped quarters.

Other objects, beside the Rosenstengel furniture and the crystal, had tumbled with my mother through marriage's entry port. A German upright piano, a camphor linen press, a silver fox fur, a modest clutch of jewels. Ball gowns too, stuffed into a wooden chest on the veranda.

Was there a mirror in the spare room off the veranda? That was a peculiar room, not fully integrated into the rest of the house, like a lodger no one notices. In that room I saw the bare legs of the wife of the minister, next to her husband's trousered legs, while they were having an afternoon nap. The legs were facing each other. My mother put me in that room when my eardrum almost burst. Why there and not in the bedroom I shared with my sister? Perhaps she imagined that room as a quarantined ship moored offshore. Certainly my father stayed in there when he nearly died of chickenpox. And whenever he was recovering from yet another strangulation hernia. There was once a cot in there too, because I remember the outrage of being in it. I suppose the cot must have been discarded later, when my parents were certain there'd be no further need for it. In any case, I'm pretty sure that, mirror-wise, that room was blind, which is just as well, as that was the room in which my sister and I got up to shenanigans which I was told never to tell, on pain of being bashed up. As if I *would*.

And then there was the small square mirror on the wall beside my bed.

By the time I was six, I had developed a habit of studying this mirror. I thought to myself that no matter how many times I saw that face amongst others in, say, the streets of Nambour, I would not recognise it. There was nothing distinctive there, which might snag attention. I was not invisible, but I receded from notice so quickly that I would not 'take' on the memory of others as more than a sort of smudge.

The indeterminacy did not trouble me, it was a fact that I accepted with the stoicism of innocence – that is, the lack of experience by which to judge one's thoughts, to have second thoughts. No one would notice or remember me, so the mirror asserted. It is possible that a kind of precocious wisdom lay at the core of such self-effacement. If no one notices you, you are somewhat protected from the evil eye of envy. And behind the protection of smudginess you can form, in your mind, a kind of cave to shelter in while safely observing what goes on outside.

Whatever-it-was-that-wasn't-there tugged me back up on to my bed to study it – right side, front on, left side – a metaphysical tendency of mind which was leavened by a robust and conventional vanity. I gathered my hair up into a fountain on top of my head, tied a rubber band around it, and called attention to myself by announcing the new 'palm-tree fashion'. This raised a laugh, which was one of my principal duties in the household. Of all the laughs harvested from my family, laughs from my mother were the least valuable because the most reliable. From my father laughs were valuable mainly because he was usually down in the paddocks, and unavailable as an audience. However, making my sister laugh …

My father once told a story about the war. The Australians and the 'poor old Ities' (eye-ties) had been dutifully shelling each other, but on Christmas Day the men from both sides climbed out of their bunkers, walked on to no man's land, shook hands with each other and shared rations, before returning to mutual slaughter. Sometimes, my sister and I met like that, in the armistice of comedy.

Another mirror event bursts into memory. My mother is stationed in front of her dressing table, at night. She is wearing a hairnet. Slapping on Pond's cold cream. Making her mouth into shapes – oooo eeeee.

From there, suddenly I see her ironing in the kitchen: thump down the iron goes, on the clothes that have been washed by hand, starched, then 'damped down' and rolled up in the reed basket. Now she is playing the piano, dabbing iodine on my knee, hugging me when I howl, tucking her violin under her chin, cooking pikelets and sponges. I am in bed with her, my little-girl leg tossed over her thigh. 'You kick me in your sleep, Rob, I'm black and blue,' but she laughs and cuddles me up. Her delicious musky smell. She places her hand on my forehead when I am ill. She brings half an aspirin to the spare room when my eardrum threatens to burst, ahead of time because the pain is unendurable. She is handing me a plate of bread and Vegemite after school. She is pinning a new dress for a 'fitting', pins in her mouth. 'Don't fidget.' The crisp poplin slips down my upstretched arms – such pretty new dresses, only natural to feel vain and special. And I am running, leaping up into her arms, my legs cinching around her waist – our double act performed away from my sister's gaze.

In my fifth year, my infant curls grew mousy and lank. With dressings of Curlypet, with wet comb and bobby pins, she set to defying what time had done. And nature did give way to her will. My hair began to grow in patchy spirals out of my scalp. The moment I think of Curlypet, I see the half-sketched bathroom mirror very clearly. Green. With a cabinet behind containing a bottle of Curlypet and the exotic paraphernalia of male vanity – shaving cream (Old Spice) and stand-up brush.

Another memory suddenly bobs to the surface: it occurred sometime during the outright declaration of hostilities between my sister and my mother, hostilities which, if we are to credit those unexpressed thoughts that rise out of families like miasma, began at birth, as if mother and child took one look at each other and continued an enmity begun lifetimes before.

There is a more plausible explanation for the friction between my sister and our mother: me.

I find myself in that spare room off the veranda. My sister is standing in front of a mirror. (So there IS a mirror in that room! Odd how it has hung there all along in some cellular cluster, just waiting for a neighbouring neuronal firing to illuminate it.) She is wearing a watermelon-pink bubble nylon dress with gathered skirt and cross-over bodice. She has breasts. Under the dress I know she is wearing a suspender belt and stockings. And possibly, though this may have come later, a rubber corset. The top of the stockings will be cutting into her flesh, I've seen that and it has made me squirm in empathy. My mother has sewn the dress. It is pretty. My sister hates it. Hates the cream court shoes with the one-inch heel. Hates most of all her hair which has just been dressed, I guess, by our mother. Why else the fury in that room, so powerful it curdles the air and makes me want to drop where I stand. I have come in here to stand by my sister, to side with her. I know that her fury is the visible part of unhappiness, and our mother has been unfair.

My sister tells me to reset her hair with the wet comb and the bobby pins. I have to stand on my toes to reach her head. I reach up, but my fingers cannot twist those thick waves, and the pins fall out. She turns and I know what's coming, because it has come so often before. Her nails dig into my arm, the air goes out of my stomach, and the sneering, loathing refrain pours down: 'useless, ugly, stupid'.

Where do they come from – useless ugly stupid? Do they descend from one mouth to the following generations of mouths, down the long long line until someone refuses to utter them? Or are they in the air, unacknowledged, looking for a mouth to give them sound?

I know (do we all know?) that her anger arises out of my usurping her place. I can leap into my mother's arms. She is too big for such things and 'wears her mother out'. I am the rose. She is the gaillardia. It is an anger beyond consolation, and bad things happen when it swamps her reason. It forms a habit, like flood rains coursing down the clay runnels beside the road, carving them out, deepening them.

The rose and gaillardia. It is a story my sister tells, and it has stuck in her heart like a splinter of ice, for a lifetime. It happened when we lived out bush, on Stanley Park, before I was conscious enough to verify it. Seemingly our mother, who slaved to make a garden in that recalcitrant earth, said to Margaret one day, 'You are like my gaillardia flowers, you're tough and you'll thrive anywhere. But your little sister Robyn is like the rose.' That she could say such a thing has been taken as an illustration of her favouritism. Everyone knows that in the horticultural order, roses rank higher than gaillardias.

But are second thoughts possible here?

For the first six years of my life I suffered from recurrent attacks of croup. Ear and throat infections followed. I remember my mother tying kerosene-soaked cloth around my neck at night. The closest medical practitioner to Stanley Park was many hours away over a rough dirt road. And the telephone – a black box on the wall, which connected us via the 'party line' to an exchange – came later, along with electricity. When I was an infant, my mother walked me up and down the corridors of the house, night after sleepless night, willing me to breathe. Perhaps, in order to explain to the older child the extra attention that was going to the baby, she used this metaphor of the garden. A parental blunder, maybe, but not meant to wound.

But wound it did, and became an emblem of the subterranean causes of my sister's rage with our mother and therefore with me.

A stronger case for favouritism could perhaps be made for the musical box, given to me by my mother (nominally my parents) after I had my tonsils out. It was a tiny Tyrolean house with rocks on the roof to protect it from snow. Tiny gardens surrounded it and a fir tree stood by the front door. The roof lifted to reveal a little container for precious things. And from beneath this compartment came the tune, 'You are my sunshine, my only sunshine, / you keep me happy when skies are grey, / you'll never know, dear, how much I love you, / please don't take my sunshine away.' We all knew the words of that song.

I hesitate to write about my sister's anger for everything has reasons and explanations behind it. We are all conglomerates of habits, thematic sequences set in motion by circumstances we had no hand in. And who is it who really masters these habits? How many can appraise them and search for alternatives? There isn't much will involved when it comes to the human passions. Another thought occurs to me. That my sister's envy has saved me from carrying too much of the same ingredient. It's as if she took up all the envying available. Such a limited number of ingredients, which chance and circumstance chuck into the developmental pot. I have other evils that my sister lacks (cowardly retreat, for example) which I do not wish to conceal. The caveat being, of course, those that I conceal from myself.

But just as my birth left its effect in my sister's development, so her contempt marked my unfurling ego (unfurling used here as that most obvious metaphor – the butterfly emerging from its chrysalis. Any glitch in the chancy process will deform a wing, leaving it useless as a claw). It is with me still, that malformation – a habit of worthlessness – and it has governed much of my fate. I have accepted as normal that deep love from someone can be mixed with a desire to obliterate. On the other hand, I must also have internalised my mother's opposing view of my inherent value. Whether maternal affection for me inflamed my sister's mockery, and vice versa, is impossible to say. Either way, one must never forget the crucial importance of point of view.

In some ways, deeper ways, my sister and I are of the same substance. We share the contents of dreams. Tidal waves routinely engulf us. Huge snakes, talking lions, flesh-eating parrots meet us in the lands of sleep. Though I don't think she encounters the devil in hers. In mine he is implacable, inescapable; no matter how fast or far I run, or how cleverly I outwit him, his powers always defeat my own. His lip curls, he laughs with scorn, he adores his power to dominate and torment, and is incapable of mercy.

Reflected back from Malabah's mirrors, I can see my father's face, my sister's face, but my mother's face is indistinct. Sometimes I think I can glimpse it, as it was, animated by her thoughts. But then it disintegrates and I realise I never possessed it; I was thinking of a photograph, perhaps, something flat, milky and still. In my memory, there are bits of her floating around in a kind of fog – hands, smells, veins, phrases, shoes, a crocodile-skin handbag and its contents, the smell of Helena Rubinstein lipstick, a gold tooth, fine pale hairs on her arms, goosebumps, a crystal stopper being dabbed in the crook of an elbow, nervy fingers twisting rings, fingers twitching as she holds my hand (she is typing or playing piano in her mind, exactly as I still do), the pores in the skin of her back between the straps of her sun-frock the day I sat behind her in our new Holden 'sedan'; a shiny straw hat which she clamps on in front of the queen mirror when we are going to Brisbane; a black feather cocktail hat with net fascinator which she wears with the silver fox fur; long black kid gloves; and there she is standing by the gardenia tree she was so proud of. 'Don't touch the petals, you'll bruise them.' She is wearing the cotton dress with big green and blue flowers on it, and a cowl neck. And in the back dining room, after she has thrown boiling water on a red-bellied black snake sunning itself out on the passion-fruit vines, I absorb from her the thrill of loathing. But these elements don't cohere, they have floated beyond gravitational pull. I suppose she died before making the transition from mother to person, and the locus of a person is a face. She was known by my body as it knows itself – nothing closer, yet never possessed by its own senses as others are able to possess it.

She stands in front of her queen mirror. She is winding her hair into a roll. All her vitality is gathered in order to attack her own hair, to venomously brush it into this severe, old-maid's style. But her anger doesn't come out of her as it comes out of my sister, coursing through me into the earth. Instead, it turns near the surface and goes straight back in, like light at the event horizon of a black hole.

'But why are you changing your hair, Mummy? It doesn't look nice.'

Her lips tighten to hold back the pressure of that tremendous gravity. Then a little wisp of something escapes.

'I have to match your father.' I know she is saying a great deal more than this because I can feel it down in my stomach. I don't know what it is but I know for sure that no one has to 'match' a father. Fathers all have the same haircut, they all dress the same, and they never ever titivate in front of mirrors.

But I see that I have been caught up in the underneath of things without properly exploring the shallows. If the success of a family unit can be gauged by how much laughter it generates, and how often its members sing together, and how much love resides in each heart, then we weren't doing too badly. Yes, ours was a happy family, then, and what happy family doesn't have underneaths?

Four

Lying in the bath one evening, in London, suddenly, for no reason at all, the words to 'Alice Blue Gown' came back to me. I was in my forties then, and these mysterious little geysers of memory had begun to spurt into consciousness, disturbing the surface.

In my sweet little Alice blue gown,
When I first wandered down into town,
I was both proud and shy, as I felt every eye,
And in every shop window, I'd primp [pause for a coy glance over my left shoulder], passing by ...

'Alice Blue Gown' had been my stage debut at the Mooloolah concert when I was about seven years old.

My mother had coached me to pronounce town as 'taaaooon' rather than the Australian 'tairn'. The 'gown' ('gaaooon') was blue seersucker, printed with sprays of pink flowers. My mother was a fine seamstress, but the dress, and matching parasol, had warranted the greater talents of her brother's wife, a professional dressmaker in Brisbane. The skirt was tiered around a hoop, and ruched with forget-me-nots. Ditto the brolly.

In the middle of my act, the parasol had fallen apart, but without missing a beat, I had bent while singing, picked it up, put it back together, and continued my dance steps. After my bows and the roar of applause from the Mooloolah assembled, my mother's arms were waiting for me. I knew for certain at that moment that I had made her truly happy. But then I had to go and vomit, presaging a performance anxiety that would, many years later, arrest my career as a pianist.

Georgina Parker, who could crumple her chin to lure boys, and whose mother had murdered her husband, sang 'Tan Shoes and Pink Shoelaces'. My sister, I think, sang 'Vilia, oh Vilia, the Witch of the Wood'. A spoon-player had come all the way from Eudlo, and it might have been Larry Roach's father who accompanied him on a saw.

The School of Arts hall was a weatherboard building with a tin roof across the road from the school. It contained a small stage, on which stood an out-of-tune piano, a dance floor on which was sprinkled Pops Dancing Dust to make it slippery, and a side veranda enclosed in glass louvres – the 'supper room'. The ladies had made butterfly cakes, pikelets, scones, sponges, lamingtons, and little triangular sandwiches with shredded lettuce on them, all of which were laid out on long trestle tables, along with big white teacups and saucers, and huge aluminium teapots. The day before, all the children from school, under the direction of the principal, Mr Jeays, had decorated the hall with crushed milk-bottle tops threaded on string, after which we had done a final run-through of our ballroom dancing steps, culminating in the 'Hokey Pokey', in preparation for the big night.

I see the Sunday-school teacher dancing with his wife. He is in a wide-lapelled, navy striped suit, shiny with age and pressing. His hair is brilliantined. His raw, dairy farmer's hand, pitted and etched with black, holds a white handkerchief sensitively against his wife's back, to prevent any marks on her frock. They are good dancers and they know it. They twirl around the slippery dance floor, others giving way to their superior talents. They dance a waltz to my mother's piano, the spoons and the saw. Proudly. Unaware that I am watching them from the future, pulling them out of the meaning of their present. They are as serious and happy as birds.

That present: how to convey its flavour. The trauma of war still lingering but never spoken of, recognisable in the refusal to buy Japanese products, or the occasional muted reference to some 'poor blighter' with 'shell shock'. Immigrants arriving in Australia, partly as an outflow from the great global disturbance, partly to build the infrastructures of the post-war boom. Italians and Greeks were beginning to come, to be treated with the easy-going contempt of white Australians who christened them Dagos, Wogs, Reffos, Ities, Gyppos. I recognised the casual racism later. But at the time there seemed to be no such rancour in our little community. Everyone got on, more or less. Helped each other out, more or less. Everyone was more or less poor. Every purchase was saved for, cared for. Clothes mended, socks darned. Almost nothing was thrown away. My dad tried to convince neighbours that insurance was a good thing, worth the money. To be insured against catastrophe was a new idea, and quite alien to the self-reliance of hardship-hardened farmers. The only time I can remember absorbing a sense of 'otherness' was when the Gypsies came to Mooloolah. Again, no specific warning was given; it was simply understood that you did not go near their encampment. They disappeared quickly and never returned. I often wonder where they went, how they integrated themselves into a country so taken over by the rule of the fence. As for Aboriginal people, it was as if they had never existed. My mother had pined for a more cultured life, but again, in this rural backwater, there was little to assuage her isolation. People were decent to each other but there was no one for her to open her heart to. And perhaps I remember this particular concert clearly because my mother participated in it, indeed was the key artistic director of its theatrical productions of which 'Alice Blue Gown' was the star turn.

At the end of the evening, after the children have hauled each other, sled fashion, along the Pops Dancing Dusted floor, now abandoned by the adults, who are having grown-up conversations in the supper room about weather and dairying and the Common Market, everyone comes together again to join hands and sing: 'Should auld acquaintance be forgot, / And never brought to mind ...'

Ted and Bunty would have been there; in fact, I can see their faces below the stage, laughing up at me as I fix my umbrella.

Ted (Edmund Augustonauwitz) was my first exogamous love. He was a Polish war veteran who had bought the pineapple farm next door. My parents took him under their wing, and when his wife, Bunty, arrived later from Scotland, my mother's heart 'bled for her'. Bunty was a lady, and she and my mother hit it off immediately.

Ted and Bunty met when Ted was on furlough in Edinburgh – that war again, that turned everything upside down and made for unlikely couples – and they don't get more unlikely than Ted and Bunty. Ted spoke no English when he arrived in Australia, and never got anywhere near proficient. But sweetness radiated out of him, at least to me, and language is hardly necessary where love is concerned. He brought me pineapples, and made me pineapple juice. He christened me his 'Pineapple Queen'. I overheard my father saying that he, Ted, had seen too many terrible things in the war ever to want to return to Europe. He seemed to have no family.

Bunty had pure-white hair, and the softest skin imaginable. Softer than a hibiscus petal. And like our English sheep, she suffered.

The house Ted built for her, which we all visited when it was complete, to congratulate him, was a one-room wooden shack on hard white earth, with a little corrugated-iron tank outside. No electricity, no running water. Yet how prettily he had done it up inside. A clock, probably purchased from Harry Crack's store. A double bed with crocheted blanket. Pineapple crates turned upside down for seats. I thought it was the best cubby house I'd ever seen and was, I think, dismayed that someone else should live in it with Ted.

All around the shack were the tops of pineapples rooting for replanting. And around that, the dismal scrub that was nothing like Scotland or, for that matter, Poland. Ted's only asset, apart from the farm, was an old green Land Rover which Bunty referred to, later, as 'that breadbox of Edmund's'.

Pineapple farming … Imagine, first, clearing hard straggly gum trees and saplings and blady grass from steep slopes. By hand. Then imagine preparing the compacted sterile ground by digging. By hand. Then planting the tops of pineapples, whose leaves are like long saws tipped in poison. After that, waiting for rain, but not too much, or it will wash channels into the newly cleared earth, and destroy your planting. But enough to counter the threat of bushfires roaring up your slopes and destroying everything you've got. After that, imagine walking along the rows of pines, chipping weeds. With a hoe. Miles of rows. In the subtropical sun. The leaves slicing your legs as you go. Then picking the thorny fruits. Then packing them in crates. Then loading them in the breadbox and driving them to Mooloolah siding to be stacked on to a goods train heading for the Golden Circle pineapple cannery in Brisbane. And imagine the prices for pineapples going down and down, so that you get less and less return for more and more labour. And imagine living in the all-pervading stench of fermenting pineapples in a one-room shack with no running water and a husband who doesn't speak English.

The cuts and mosquito bites on Bunty's legs soon turned to ulcers. So it can be seen that, under the circumstances, her voluble, constant and unabashed criticism of 'Edmund', of all things Edmund-ish; of Australia and all things Australian (with the exception of the Davidsons) was forgivable.

I remember going for a 'Sunday drive' with my parents and Bunty. We drove around the coastal hinterland, and up to the soft green hills. My mother said, encouragingly, 'Now, isn't this pretty country, Bunty?' to which Bunty, staring stubbornly ahead, replied, 'Only if ye've never been to Scotland.'

But somehow Ted and Bunty made 'a go of it', he grinning whenever she criticised him, refusing to change in the slightest. Eventually they built a new house, with two rooms, glass louvres, a small veranda and lino on the floor. They also adopted a couple of musical dogs. Bunty would start to howl, and the dogs would join in, then Ted would howl, and the dogs would howl even louder, and then everyone would laugh. My mother said that the dogs were their 'children'.

Should old acquaintance be forgot ... How could I forget Ted and Bunty coming around of a Sunday evening, to be audience to the plays my sister and I put on? We charged a penny entrance fee. Or our sing-songs around the German upright. When we sang together it was as if we all breathed an eternal air of friendship and goodwill. Each of us felt the boundaries of our solipsisms dissolve and we were one with each other and all things.

In the afterglow we offered our solos. My mother, a Schubert song. My sister, 'Vilia, oh Vilia' in a warm voice that would develop into a rich mezzo. My red-letter moment arrived with 'I heard a robin singing' in quavering soprano. It was touch and go whether I would hit that top A (for which a gulped breath was necessary), or land a good halftone below it.

Then it was my father's turn. He was self-conscious standing there beside his wife, with his pipe clutched in his right hand, singing 'Sarie Marais' in what was probably bad Afrikaans. But no one was allowed to be too shy to sing. My mother got everyone up, even Ted, who mouthed along to words he didn't understand – 'Speak to me only with thine eyes' sung in harmonic parts – grinning as ever, but close to tears.

I watch us gathered there, through the transfiguring light of years. It is the late fifties. The colours are a little muddy. There is a new seventeen-inch-screen television in the corner which will gradually erode our sing-songs. Big changes are on the way – my growth spurt after a tonsillectomy, my sister's abandonment of me for boarding school, our mother's decline. But for now, it's 'Roll out the barrel' and 'Bimbo, Bimbo, where you going to go-e-o', and 'Life is GREAT in the Sunshine State', and everyone has forgotten their worries and sorrows and is warmed through.

Five

Hearing, they say, is the first sense to arise in the womb. For a certain time inside our mothers' bodies the entire universe is a soundscape; nothing else exists.

As soon as we are delivered into the world, our mothers begin to speak to us in a special lilting way – helping us to develop the prosodic features of speech long before we are capable of words. Perhaps, back in the shadows of deep time, such exchanges formed the root of music, which morphed into speech, the first lying beneath the later – gatekeeper to more primal realms.

For something that played such an important part in the family, music received very little of my curiosity. It was just there. An accompaniment weaving in and out of our lives, as unremarkable as breathing. Yet one of my first uncontestable memories is being on the swing in the back yard of Stanley Park composing a 'symphony'. I would have been less than four. The event exists as a series of seed memories – the swing my father had built for us, a hot sunny day, crackly parched grass and the smell of dust, the awe and exhilaration of creation as if my chest might burst, followed by the enormous scale of the back veranda steps as I struggle up them to inform my mother. I hear her words, 'Hum it for me.' But when I listened for the melody again in my mind, it had vanished. I was inconsolable. She laughed and hugged me to her legs.

My musical ambitions, such as they were, were abandoned when I was nineteen; something I have not for a moment regretted. I had briefly attended a conservatorium in Sydney, but realised that I did not have the staying power, dedication or temperament of a performer. But when, many years later, in London, I went to see a film about Glenn Gould, I was ambushed by an extraordinary sadness. Regret, I assumed, for a road not taken. What else could it be?

The sense of loss stayed with me. It would bubble up into the life I had made, causing disturbances that I did not know how to interpret. There had been losses in my life, of course, catastrophic ones, but I had dealt with them, or thought I had. And while it was true that that period of my life was full of complication and stress – a radical instability – this seemed to be something different. Eventually I bought a Blüthner grand piano, huge and black, built at the turn of the century, and with a sound as mellow and rich as expensive Bordeaux.

I was in my forties then, and at that time, I would say, I had few memories of my childhood, almost none of my mother. Or perhaps it is more correct to say that I contained a stockpile but had never bothered to haul them up. I had used a kind of scorched-earth policy in regard to my past: I threw bombs over my shoulder, and seeds ahead of me, into the future, on the assumption that when I arrived there, something would be growing.

If I thought about it at all, I imagined my earlier life as lying under a thick layer of cement, from which poked a few dilapidated markers. I travelled constantly at that time, the past being the only country that held no interest for me.

I hired a teacher to help me relax when playing. Tension kills everything at the keyboard. I picked up a Brahms rhapsody that had defeated me in performance when I was young. The teacher helped me to overcome those blocks, and eventually suggested that I should play in front of people – an idea that sent me into a sick panic for days. But I managed it in the end. I invited twenty people to my flat, performed a few pieces including the thundering Brahms – thus, I thought, overcoming any painful residue from giving up music in the first place.

But the sadness did not dissipate. There was something moving beneath the cement. I would sit down in front of the keys, begin to play, but be interrupted by the smell of beeswax and dust, or hear, in my mind, my mother's voice singing 'Funiculì, funiculà'... Songs came back to me, and it was as if the songs cast light on to a dark background, so that I could begin to make out what lay there. Pale light blooming then disappearing. Very dim at first. And completely random.

Mr Jeays teaching us ballroom dancing down amongst the tin-capped stumps holding up Mooloolah school. Above us, a wind-up gramophone playing 'Roll out the barrel' and 'Oh dear! What can the matter be?', as we clumped and shuffled the Gypsy Tap, the Pride of Erin, the Progressive Barn Dance. And then, the one everyone liked best because you could shout the last line:

You put your left foot in,
you put your left foot out,

you put your left foot in and shake it all about,
You do the hokey pokey and you turn around
THAT'S WHAT IT'S ALL A-BOUT.

From there, I noticed other pools of light illuminating those early years, one memory seeming to ignite another.

I would have been five when I entered grade one of Mooloolah State School under the tutelage of the head teacher Mr Jeays and his serial apprentices. Attendance at the school varied from twenty to forty depending on weather, and how much work had to be done on the surrounding dairy farms. We pupils were divided into eight classes: four in one room, four in the other. That is, the little-kids' section and the big-kids' section. Mr Jeays chewed chalk and spat it out the window on to the corrugated-iron tank where it accumulated like guano. He held a cane in both hands behind his shoulders as he paced the big-kids' half of the weatherboard schoolhouse. He also chewed PK and Juicy Fruit gum, and there were two small wire trays on his desk, containing used gobbets of gum.

The Gripsky boys were particularly galling to Mr Jeays. They turned up in batches, and stayed away in batches. When they did attend, the veins in Mr Jeays's neck became prominent and once he chased Robert Gripsky around the room, flailing at him with the cane.

He instructed the big kids beneath a picture of the Queen wearing a crown and a blue sash. With his cane he pointed to chalk scrawl on the blackboard. The little kids came under the care of a succession of female teacher trainees who had been sent out to bush schools as a way of paying back their bond to the education department.

Much is written these days about the accoutrements necessary to good schooling: libraries, labs, music rooms, facilities ... But in the fifties, the only teachers' aids available in country schools were chalk, grey plasticine, grey slates and heroic dedication. I believe Mr Jeays would have tried his best on our behalf even without the yearly visits of the government school inspector, of whom he seemed afraid. He was perpetually teetering on the edge of nervous collapse, but he and his trainees sent all of us, even Maxine and Colette l'Estrange, even the Gripsky boys, out into the world literate and numerate.

Every morning we would line up in front of the flag, hands on hearts, declaring our love for Country and Queen. Then a needle dropped on to the record on the wind-up gramophone on the veranda. Six years of the daily repetition of 'Colonel Bogey' has tattooed it indelibly on to memory ... da da, dadada dit dit da. We marched into the rooms, shuffled into the long desks – three on each side of the room, and each containing four inkwells – whereupon Mr Jeays began the day's assignation with knowledge, chalk already showing at the corners of his fruity lips. He instructed us in mental arithmetic, spelling, multiplication, crayon drawing, cartography (blue cliffs around the coastline, stamps of Aborigines with one leg lifted), copybook running-writing, social studies, essays on topics, woodwork and metalwork for the boys, embroidery stitches on grubby samplers for the girls, geography (Brisbane, Gympie, Maryborough, Bundaberg ...). And whenever the school inspector visited, Mr Jeays, though nervous and fawning in front of his superior, smiled, incredibly, as if he were proud of us.

I was his pet. I came top and wore pressed dresses and lace-up shoes to school. I could play 'La Cascade' on the piano very fast without a mistake. Jennifer Garbutt was my only serious competitor which was against the natural order because she lived in a house with cardboard windows.

I never visited the Gripsky family, even though they were our immediate neighbours. I was not forbidden to go near them, it was assumed that I would not. Their fences were hopeless. They left our gates open. Their Jersey bull chased my grandfather and me up a tree. Although I did not hear anyone speak about them, I nevertheless knew that Ma Gripsky slept in a bath out the front of their house.

The first thing we did upon arrival at 8.30 a.m. was to go underneath the school to sharpen our slate pencils on the cement around the creosote stumps. (That was during the first four years as a 'little kid'. When we reached grade five we became big kids, and moved into the next room. There we graduated to pencils or, on copybook days, pen and ink.) At 'little lunch' (10.30 a.m.), we lined up where the saddles were kept under the schoolhouse, to drink, gagging, the tepid, government-provided milk. At big lunch, after eating our smelly sandwiches, girls and boys separated. Girls played tig, or blind man's bluff, or vigoro, or What's the Time, Mr Wolf?, or built cubby houses out of pine needles, or skipped with a big slapping rope – 'one o'clock, two o'clock, three o'clock, four [pause], five o'clock, six o'clock, seven o'clock, more'. Sometimes we sat in a circle facing each other and played Drop the Hanky. If you are chosen as 'it', you have to hold the hanky and run around the outside of the circle, surreptitiously dropping the hanky behind one of your fellows. That girl must realise she's been targeted, leap up, grab the hanky and tear around the circle after you. You must get back to your empty spot in the circle before she catches you. If you do get caught, you must go another round. Having that hanky dropped behind you is an unpleasant experience, like being marked for sacrifice. You will do anything to pass the threat on to another, and return to the safety of the group.

Then there was a clapping game called Mary Mac. 'Mary Mac, dressed in black, silver buttons down her back [which the rude boys changed to "crack"], she likes coffee, she likes tea, she likes sitting on a black fella's knee.' The boys seemed to be forever chasing each other and tumbling and throwing cricket balls, or going down the creek (against the rules) to catch yabbies. They tied the long paspalum grass in the schoolground into knots, so that when you ran through it you were snagged and fell on your face. There were of course the unselfish sharings of mumps, warts, nits, worms and chickenpox; there were free polio shots and occasionally a medical van from Nambour visited to check for ruptured eardrums and rickets.

Susan Stevens was my first best friend and she wore rope petticoats. My mother thought rope petticoats were common, but eventually was persuaded to buy me one. It was nowhere near as voluminous as Susan's, but I loved it and wanted to wear it every day instead of just for 'best'. When the bullies threatened Susan, she said her uncle was a policeman and even though everyone knew it wasn't true, the bullies backed off. And when Larry Roach chased the girls to kiss them, she didn't run or flinch. I cannot imagine, for example, that she was ever wakened in horror by a nightmare in which she is sharpening her slate pencil under the school, and looks down to find herself naked. Nor did she suffer the sickness and remorse that afflicted me after a gang of us bashed up Jennifer Garbutt after school.

It was Jennifer Garbutt who, one day, drew little blue cliffs on her map of Australia so that it looked like it was standing off the page. Yet she had thick bare feet, and once when she asked Mr Jeays to be excused (to go to the dunny), she left threepenny bits of urine on the wooden form we shared. The animus I felt towards her was akin to the loathing my mother felt towards the black snakes she tortured. An exhilarating, illicit wickedness that smothers pity. I had felt it myself in regard to the large cockroaches that flew into our house at night. Once I found one in the handbasin, and forced it down the plughole with boiling water. So I was not innocent of sadistic lust. I had simply never transferred it from cockroaches to humans.

We surrounded her, outside the school gates, four or five of us. I would have been seven or eight, perhaps. But I felt myself to be on the verge of some new territory, precipitous and a little frightening. There was a queasy feeling in my throat, but then I thought of her coming top, and got in a pinch. Above her elbow, in pliable flesh. For an instant my body thrilled at its power to dominate, to mortify. But that power had a kickback stronger than my father's elephant gun.

The road home from school was a couple of miles long, over Mooloolah River bridge, under the North Coast Line railway bridge, past the McPhersons' and mad Valerie, past the Bonnys' slaughter yards, up the hill, through Malabah's gates and thence to my mother in the kitchen. That day

I did not go to my mother in the kitchen, I went straight to the darkness of the mango tree. The remorse, a sensation that flooded both body and mind, inoculated me for ever against that indifference to the suffering one causes, which is the most durable of human cruelties. After that, I could not even bring myself to torture a cockroach. It is possibly to Jennifer Garbutt that I owe a habit of being: my fear of being the cause of another's suffering is so intense that I will allow myself to be persecuted by them instead. (That is, when the only choice is between the two. The third option is to make oneself unavailable as either perpetrator or victim. To leave.)

Usually I walked home alone from school, via Harry Crack's store. I'd buy a ha'penny cordial ice-block wrapped in a square of greaseproof paper, and suck it to paleness while dawdling on the bridge throwing leaf boats into the creek. But when my father bought our new Holden sedan, he came to pick me up as a surprise. The car smelt better than a new book. He treated the gear stick as if it were made of blown glass, and paused carefully in the middle of changing it, so the cogs would not grind. And when he had to do something dexterous, like guide the car between two posts, he leant forward a little and softly whistled 'Little children, little children, who love their redeemer' through his teeth, without realising he was doing so. He tried to teach our mother to drive but she was nervous and he made her more so, and if ever she ground a gear he'd say, 'Aw, for gawd's sake … here, give it to me.' And she would get out of the car, close to tears. It is possible that my parents thought even two-tone Holdens were ostentatious. So when Robin Waters's father started showing off around Mooloolah in a two-tone cream and mustard Ford Customline, we remained faithful to monotone Holdens and the industrial output of our country. It was one thing to be grateful to the Yanks for saving us during the war, quite another to succumb to their flashy tastes.

Three children rode ponies to school; my sister was one of them. There was a paddock to keep the ponies in, and a place for their saddlery under the school. I barely remember my sister in class times, as she was far ahead of me, and the division between big and little kids was as fundamental as caste. She only comes into focus in the afternoons, when we children dispersed to go home. Sometimes she gave me a double-back home on Prince. He would be goaded into a trot, not the best gait from my point of view. Then, with the threat of a picked stick to the withers, into a reluctant canter. I wrapped my arms around my beloved sister's waist and off we would fly, over Mooloolah Creek, past the track where the Andersons lived (they called one of their sons 'Jesus'), under the North Coast Line bridge, past Neville McPherson's and mad Valerie's house, past Stephen Bonny's father's slaughterhouse, and in through the Malabah gates. Once, Prince propped at Mooloolah River bridge. The girth and surcingle had loosened, and my sister and I, as one, rolled slowly to the left side, and landed on the ground. Prince lowered his head to us where we lay – rose and gaillardia – helpless with laughter.

Six

If I were the blatantly favoured child, whence might such bad mothering have come?

Nanna, my mother's mother, was regarded by some as a person of mischief – a pernicious mother and a worse mother-in-law. (I once whacked her over the head with my vigoro bat, sincerely believing that I was ridding the world of a witch. I got into trouble for this, but afterwards noticed that my father smiled to himself.) To be fair, Nanna did look like a witch. Thin, slightly stooped, a large pale mole on her chin, grey hair tied in a bun. She had an array of potions and pills beside her bed because she was the sickest well person alive. She often required smelling salts. Something seemed to ail her, but whatever it was was unrevealed. Perhaps it was a very common and impossible-to-treat affliction back then – 'nerves'. When we went to stay with our grandparents, I was forced to sleep between them. Nanna stroked me with a bony hand, not the addictive and delicious tickling supplied by my mother, but something weak and vaguely unpleasant, like insects crawling over your skin. And sometimes I had to brush her hair. Long grey strands got trapped in the brush. When we visited, she gave us spoonsful of cod liver oil to 'clean us out', even though our mother was against it. Once, she told me, long before I knew what periods were, that if I had a bath or went out into the cold when I had them, the blood would go to my head and kill me.

My grandfather, Grandy, was a Jew, though at Easter, when Bach's music came over the radio, he joined in, singing the bass parts. He emptied Nanna's commode each morning in the lavatory down the back. At Christmas time he left money in there for the 'night-soil man'. Grandy also listened to cricket on the radio. The sound was as soporific as the buzz of blowflies. Sometimes he let me ride on his foot, as we recited together, 'Ride a cock horse to Banbury Cross, to see a fine lady upon a white horse ...'

Nanna had once been a beauty, to which the hand-tinted photograph hanging above the dining table attested. In it, her exquisite head was crowned with a ton of lustrous hair, the finger of her right hand was poised on her cheek, and the rest of her was garlanded in roses and tulle. Her predecessors, the McKenzies, hailed from the hills of Scotland. The Australian branch (Nanna's siblings) consisted of Auntie Pol, who came to visit us on Stanley Park to help my mother with the children. My father referred to her as a 'good stick' or 'the best of the lot' or 'good old Pol'. Uncle Son was a professional sick person, who took to his bed in youth and never left it. Uncle Don and Auntie Em lived in a dim house which smelt like over-ripe loquats. It was Uncle Don who had sent Cooktown orchids to my mother for her wedding. She had not wanted to wear them, but was too kind to refuse.

Then there was Nanna's 'Cousin May' – a milliner who had green false teeth that clacked. My father died laughing every time he told the story of Cousin May farting at one of Nanna's interminable lunches, then going to the kitchen to get Flit insect spray which she pumped under the table. (I need hardly say that my father would never have used the word 'fart' in front of us. He would have said, 'She broke wind.')

My grandmother hated sex, and my father.

I do not know how I knew that Nanna hated sex, or that Grandy was a Jew. 'Sex' and 'Jew' were two words never spoken in our household. Though they no doubt played significant parts in our family drama. Nor can I know whether Grandy's Jewishness had anything to do with my desire to become a 'Wandering Dew'.

In that long quiet moment between wakefulness and sleep, when the everyday world is gradually left alone, I would design and redesign a cassock for myself – soft brown flannelette, with a strong silk cord like the one in my father's dressing gown. The costume would have to be the last word in practicality, comfort and durability. Other than the cassock I would have no possessions whatsoever. The world would look after me if I opened myself completely to it, if, in every moment, I were not afraid. I've no idea who would have spoken the words 'Wandering Jew'. But somehow it conveyed the notion of going forth into transcendent freedom and, at the same time, being completely at home. Home would be wherever one was.

The fantasy took me through the surroundings of my childhood – the road to Mooloolah, the North Coast Line crossing – and into the still-mysterious border zone where the known revolves into its reverse. Beyond that zone I sensed there lay the anxiety of not being able to imagine what happens next, the point at which one's courage is tested, but before I reached it, the fantasy dissolved into sleep.

As for sex, let the Rosenstengel furniture, and my mother's pink nylon nightie with spaghetti straps, retain their secrets. I do not doubt that my parents were passionately in love when they married. You couldn't fake the look of mutual adoration in the wedding photo – he, Errol Flynn handsome in his army uniform, gazing down at her; she, exquisite in her crêpe suit, Cooktown orchids and jaunty little hat, gazing up at him through a fascinator, their hands tightly clasped, her dimples semaphoring joy.

But families generate sexual atmospheres. A tribute to my mother's child-rearing practices (her own instincts mediated by Dr Spock) was her tolerant attitude to a singular practice of mine which was named 'jiggity jig'. I had been jiggity-jigging all my life; in fact, I sometimes think I was jiggity-jigging in the womb, so natural was the habit. If babies can suck thumbs in there, why not masturbation? I do not remember when the fantasies began, or whether jiggity jig and fantasies went together then or not. I suspect they were quite separate; that the imaginative sexual life meandered along a different stream to the physical, only to join up later.

The fantasy which satisfied me most took, as its setting, a war. Bombs were falling, and men and women had to descend deep into the earth, to hide in cement bunkers. There, they went to sleep, wrapped up in blankets, all the men lined up at one end, and the women at the other. However, inevitably, the man at the end of the men's line was forced to sleep right next to, pressed up against, the lady at the end of her line. There wasn't enough room in the bunker for seemly separation. This man and woman did not do anything, but the desire in that woman's body, my body, was titanic, though I would not have had a clue to its meaning. In fact, when it came to knowledge of the 'facts of life' I was a late developer, and did not make the connection between what chooks and roosters did, and what men and women might do. When I was told, years later, I found it scarcely credible.

But Eros there was. In the shenanigans with my sister, in fantasy, and with any available visiting cousins, including Cousin Barbara whose *coup de grâce* in any argument was to pull her pants down and poke her bottom at you. I remember climbing into bed with Cousin Barbara and tying one of my mother's chiffon scarves around her nipples, then salaciously peeling it off. Later I found out that Cousin Barbara *told*. Then, too, there was my ache of longing for Neville McPherson, mad Valerie's nephew. He was a year older than me. His hair was as black as a crow. I would sit out on the lawn, gazing across the paddocks to the McPhersons', and imagine sitting on the toilet while Neville knelt in front of me and asked me to marry him. Often still, fifty years on, I sit on some lavatory and hear a phantom voice, 'Will you marry me?'

A bedlam, if you care to look.

Thus my erotic life continued to thrive until one unhappy night in about my seventh year. I had said my prayers and was happily jiggity-jigging away, when I felt a presence at the door. It was my father, in his dressing gown. This in itself was unusual enough to cause alarm. He said, 'For God's sake, cut it out, we can hear you all over the house.'

The shame seared through every organ, along every axon. God himself could not have done a better job. Devastating though his words were, certainly worth a couple of verses in the litany of parental crimes, they did not disincline me from the habit.

Which brings me to my father. Antil Guilford Montgomerie Lindsay Nugent Davidson, otherwise known as Mark, or Boy, was heroic in both the Greek and the Romantic senses. But perhaps it's easier here to refer to certain photographs of my father, taken in his youth.

A rainforest with waterfall and deep pool, located on Tamborine Mountain in Queensland. Three nineteen-year-old boys are standing on the rocks, smiling at the camera, naked but for huge cunjevoi leaves hiding their private parts. My father is the tallest and the handsomest and his leaf is the biggest. Four years prior to that moment, he had tried to enlist in the First World War by lying about his age.

Africa: pre-Second World War, probably the late twenties/early thirties. Jungle bank. Murky water in the foreground. My father is standing behind an enormous crocodile. In one hand he is holding a harpoon, the other end of which sticks out of the still thrashing croc, which must be about fifteen feet long. My father is wearing a pith helmet and khakis. There is another, smaller man beside him looking horrified but enthralled. The story attached to this photograph is as follows: word got out in Tanganyika that a young Australian was hand-harpooning crocodiles up in the jungle. A newspaper photographer wished to record this case of lunatic courage. My father conceded. The photographer brought a companion (the smaller man in the photo). A second after the photograph was snapped, the croc sank a tooth into the leg of the smaller man, and opened it, groin to ankle. They had no medical supplies, so my father poured a bottle of whisky on the wound, bound it up, and he and the photographer carried the man back to civilisation.

Same photo session. Murky water containing reeds. The receding back of my father, up to his chest in water and lily pads, pith helmet on, harpoon raised.

In Africa, my father prospected for gold and diamonds, and shot elephants for ivory. He had in his possession a torn photograph, frail as membrane, of the Grosventine gold rush – hundreds, possibly thousands of transparent sepia men running from the right side to the left side of the image, waving their claim stakes. He hunted lion and leopard. Once, on safari, he got blackwater fever so badly that he couldn't move and had to watch bush rats gnawing his feet. His friend died in the camp bed opposite him. But his 'boys' (African porters) turned up to tend him, and he recovered.

When it seemed that the Second World War was inevitable, he sailed a forty-foot ketch back from Madagascar to Queensland, in order to join the army. He refused an officer's commission, wanting to be closer to his 'men', and remained a warrant officer. It seems his 'men' were very fond of him and regarded him as something of a hero. They called him 'Trader Horn', and once, when they saw a letter addressed to him from his family, called him 'Antbed Guildhall Montgumboil Linseed Davidson'.

He was picked to join a group of six men led by Ivan Lyons for a secret operation (Operation Hornbill) sticking limpet mines on Jap subs in Singapore Harbour. He was eventually prevented from joining them because of his strangulation hernias. Ivan and his companions were all beheaded.

I grew up with these stories, not told to me personally, but to adults who requested them – visitors who leant forward absorbed and reverent. My father in his armchair, looking down at his hands, stacking his pipe with the stub of his missing thumb, taking a good long draw, then, as if reluctantly, in a voice constrained by shyness, and somewhat forced because of premeditation, beginning the amusing story about the time ... he would talk about the fineness of his 'boys'; the courage and humour of his 'men'. Bravery, daring-do – stories told always in a self-effacing, endearing manner in which pretty much everyone was a 'damn fine bloke' or a 'marvellous chap'.

On the wall of our lounge room were the photographs taken in Africa, some spears, a few rifles, including the elephant gun. (I see him cleaning and oiling them, checking down the barrels.) A warthog tusk. On recessed shelves were geological specimens he had found, including nuggets of gold still imprisoned in their quartz, a collection of prehistoric hand axes, fossils, a barnacle from a whale's back, pearl-shell plates and other arcane objects which he had collected on his travels. Nor should I forget the objects he made himself. A dinner gong fashioned from brass artillery shells. The outer shell was carved into a helix of leaves from the top of which dangled the inner shell. There were two letter-openers carved from bone. A metal serviette ring with scalloped edges – all around the surface of the ring were images pricked out as if with a needle.

A sailing boat, a kookaburra sitting on a boomerang, two palm trees on an island circled by two gulls, and a heraldic shield with the words 'Gwen 23 Apl 1942' written across it.

My mother's birthday.

It did not strike me at the time that not one of his stories contained, or could have contained, a female. His life before tumbling through marriage's entry port was a forty-five-year-long *Boy's Own* adventure, unhampered by emotional ties or family responsibilities. Yet there must have *been* females, tucked away behind those stories somewhere, aware of my father's moustache, his grin, his largest leaf, just as I was tucked away, listening, loving, but not in the picture.

My father's gaze was a romantic gaze. It was directed at the horizon. It contained distances.

'Can I come down the paddocks with you this-arvo?'

'Hmm?' I have brought him back from his distances.

'Oh. Rye-choo-ah [right you are], darling. But you'd better ask Mummy, eh?' And I would ask Mummy, and Mummy would say no, not today, because Daddy has a lot of work to do, and shouldn't I be practising the piano? Or reading the books she has sent away for – improving books about Mozart and ballet. 'Go and do your practice, then we'll see.'

But by the time she had a chance to 'see' – that is, by the time she had prepared our dinner, cleaned up after herself, scrubbed and polished, ironed, stitched, wrung and hung out and folded and dug and planted and baked – it would be dusk, and my father would have returned from the paddocks, and would be underneath the house having a shower in the laundry because he was always too dirty to come upstairs to our bathroom, where our mother would be having her ablutions efficiently and with a minimum of titivating. Then we would all sit down to dinner and my mother would place my father at the head of the table.

'Elbows off the table, and eat up all your pumpkin, and if you don't behave yourselves your father will give you the stick.' My mother insisted he keep a riding crop within reach, by means of which she hoped he might yet accept his role as the 'disciplinarian'. It was ever a source of contention between them – that he refused his parental responsibilities. Yes, he failed – our kind, faraway dad, who not once in his life could be persuaded to raise a hand against us, so that the disciplining, such as it was, fell to my mother, and never amounted to more than an exasperated, nervy 'smack' when she had finally 'reached the end of her tether' or 'had enough of you two'. Our father's authority inhered in him more subtly – by having the right to disappear to some vast inner place unavailable to us. That is what set him above us, like sky above land.

Seven

I must have been thirty-eight or so when I bought the flat in London. It marked the third era of my London life: the first was when I wrote *Tracks*; the second was taken up with the catastrophic love affair; and this final third was to be a settling down, a commitment to England. The flat would be my first anchor after years of wandering (friends gave up putting me in their address books: the entries took up pages). I had lived outside of Australia for so long that, even though I returned every year or two, even though I still considered it my heartland, I was nervous about returning to live there, so far away from everything, though what constituted 'everything' was hard to put into words. Perhaps it was no more than the lingering anxiety so many young Australians of my era experienced; world history was being made elsewhere, any deep intellectual and artistic engagement with that making was hindered in our homeland, and getting out of Australia was both very difficult (prohibitively expensive) and absolutely vital.

Besides, those previous periods in London, which stretched over two decades, were formative. I had written my first book there. Important events had occurred, important connections made. So London it was, and although bad times would eventually reveal the shallowness of my roots there – that I was not, as I had imagined, a perennial capable of sustaining a drought, but an annual that withered in demanding weather – nevertheless, for a handful of years, the apartment gave me a sense, almost, of being placed. It was as close to belonging as I had yet experienced, outside of the desert. And if there is one thing a residence can give you, that the road cannot, it is the privacy to dream in peace.

There was a third reason for choosing London. A stubborn refusal to let the difficulties I had experienced there rule my future. Had I settled anywhere else, I would have felt that I had left with my tail between my legs.

At that time it was important to me that my possessions be gathered around me. Objects inherited from people long dead, or chosen by previous selves long forgotten, came to rest like pieces of rock in a comet's tail. Australian paintings, oriental textiles, geological and archaeological specimens, shells, fossils, a barnacle off a whale's back, hand axes, an opal dinosaur tooth that my father and I found on a fossicking trip. There were walls of books, photographs of my family's properties, in which predecessor women in Victorian dresses sat on glossy horses, and Aboriginal women in Victorian dresses stood with their stockmen husbands beside their humpies, in a glade of gum trees. There were daguerreotypes of forebears, one of whom looked decidedly Indian in spite of her crinolines. There were photos of my father harpooning a crocodile. Of my mother at twelve, dressed as Isadora Duncan, dancing. Of my aunt shaking hands with a horse. Of myself at three, dressed as a fairy, posed under a river red gum in front of a barbed-wire fence. Of myself as a baby, held in my little mother's arms, my sister beside her on the other side, cut in half by the photograph's frame.

The flat was a huge room on the third floor of what once had been a Victorian shoe factory. Friends lived in apartments on other floors, or across the courtyard. We had bought the factory together, turning it into dwellings and studios for ourselves, thus forming another of those ad hoc 'families' whose ethics and values derived from the late sixties. I had been invited to join the group by a dear friend. She was a very famous actress but I had never seen one of her movies when we met, and so the distorting field surrounding celebrities was lost on me. Our connection was instant and deep. Through her I met the other people involved, film-makers and artists, all united in a willingness to live a different way. All of us had decided not to have children, and none of us were married. Some thought it would be too difficult to balance dedication to children with dedication to work/art. In my own case, I knew that I wasn't mature enough to do that most important thing – bring entities into the world and mother them well. Nor, at that time, did I have a stable partner. It bewildered me to see how casually people replicated themselves, without thinking about their fitness for the job or the future happiness of the child. Besides, I was in love with my nieces, particularly the oldest, Onnie, who had come to live with me for a while.

The East End was unfashionable then. I suppose we were among the first of incoming waves of artist types, clearing the way for gentrification and money. At that time, the only café within walking distance sold eggs floating in a puddle of grease, and big mugs of tea. There was a fish shop selling winkles and eels. One of the pubs had a notice keeping out 'Travellers', meaning Gypsies. The streets were cobbled. Gangs of kids from the surrounding council flats roamed those streets at night, like predator cubs.

Along three sides of the room, industrial windows threw long London light across the floor, up white walls, tinging everything in blue or gold. From across the street, voices of children playing in a schoolyard drifted up, reminding me of a Queensland rainforest. The main view was south and west towards the city whose skyline changed, as if an eraser and pencil had been brought to it, whenever I returned from Elsewhere. Sometimes, when I returned, the factory would be full of life, and we would all be in each other's apartments, sharing meals and conversations. At other times, in those drear winters that only London can produce, I would return to find the place deserted. Living there, at those times, required a hunkering down into yourself. Hunkering down, and dreaming.

At that time an old melancholy, a temperamental strain that I accepted as being as much part of me as my vital organs, was gaining ground over an otherwise sunny disposition. Partly this was due to the disorder and uncertainty of constant upheaval, of having had no safe place to retreat into; partly it was to do with the ordinary loneliness of always being an outsider; and partly it was the residuum of the love affair.

It was a beautiful room to dream in, as big as a church, and the objects, too, were pleasing. But they held a purpose only I knew. Possessions are proof that you have existed, coherently, somewhere in time. Possessions contain phrases of a narrative.

Without the chronological or narrative memories that others seemed to have, the objects took on the importance of tokens. Quartz laced with gold and fool's gold, a green hand axe smooth and cool as skin, a barnacle off a whale's back …

★

Sometimes I was allowed to go down the paddocks with my father and I remember those times as being radiant with a special kind of joy. I held his thumb, and babbled to keep his attention. Should I become an astronomer, or geologist, or geographer, or oceanographer or anthropologist, or zoologist or botanist?

'… hmm?'

'Should I be an astronomer when I grow up?'

'Astronomy, eh, Robbitybob?' and, when pressed, he would tell me, again, about infinity, and how blue stars were hotter and red ones cooler. He would explain the difference between planets and stars, and describe interstellar dust and Magellanic patches, and why the Milky Way looked as it did to us, because we were stuck out near the edge of the rim of the galaxy, and were looking through the dense part of it. Sometimes, as we walked through the tall grass, we might pass a snake, and he would tell me not to be afraid of it, because it was just a harmless old grass snake, and if you left it alone, it would leave you alone. If I mentioned my desire to be a geologist after all, rather than an astronomer, he would tell me about igneous and sedimentary rocks, about the inconceivable aeons of time that it had taken to make the earth, and how once it had been a molten mass, and was still like that at its core; the forces that had churned it into mountains and oceans, ground the mountains to stumps, thrust ocean beds up until they became plateaux, and how the seas had come and gone and come again, leaving fossilised shells like the ones we had at home. Our dear earth, so stable and firm, was really a slow convulsion of torturing forces – crushing, buckling, grinding, transforming. I could see all this as if from the height of the moon. Far above our miserly scale I saw mountains worn down to sand by ice and wind so that, for ever more, when I picked up a smooth stone, I would see it as a piece of ancient star, ground to its shape by time, carried down rivers long emptied, worn to its smoothness by a cosmic tumbler, like the one on my dad's workbench that he used to polish the agate and other stones he had gathered. And as I stumbled beside him through the kikuyu and paspalum, I was tantalised by all the areas of knowledge there were, far too many to encompass in one paltry lifetime.

Thus, by example rather than instruction, he taught me to be unafraid: of snakes, spiders, cyclones, ocean waves, gekkos, solitude and the dark. He taught me how to listen to the silence of nature so that its silences opened all the way out to the rim of our exploding universe.

There was no doubt in my mind or – I took it for granted – in my father's, that I would be a scientist. Back at Malabah house I would turn over the fossils, peer into the grains of petrified wood, feel the pleasing heft of the cool green hand axe, its texture as smooth as a cheek, run water over the opalised sandstone which, when taken into the sunlight, looked as if coloured lights had been turned on inside it. At those moments, geology and anthropology claimed me, but the moment I chose them, I grieved for all the other continents of knowledge I would have to forgo. I named a tiny tributary of our river 'Botany Creek' and would wander along its meagre gully, hunting for 'botanical specimens' – leaves – which were then pasted into an exercise book purchased from Harry Crack's store. It was obvious then that my future lay in botany after all, and astronomy geology geography gemology anthropology oceanography palaeontology and zoology would have to be secondary pursuits. When I grew up, I would explore every country, starting with the Amazon, where Mr Humboldt had been, and there would be no end to fascination as I encountered nature's immeasurable store of foliate forms. It was their prodigality – infinite variations on a theme – that introduced me to the satisfactions of taxonomy. Classification provided a kind of map by which to manage the unmanageable profusion, the hopeless infinity, of things.

Only collectors will be able to understand my ecstasy when a case of pears arrived via the Sunlander. I had seen a pear before, but never with a wizened leaf stuck to its woody peg. An exotic new form! And my most prized leaf amongst such quotidian exhibits as *Monstera deliciosa*, loquat, lilly pilly, frangipani, cunjevoi, bunya pine and wait-a-while vine.

My mother sent away for books about composers and dancers, but how could they compete with *Marvels of the Universe*, or *Customs of the World*, big bound door-stopper encyclopedias of the fabulous, published in the early part of the century, and containing coloured plates of such things as radiolaria, peridots, tiger iron, fish with electric lights in them, naked people with towers of feathers on their heads, snow crystals? To think that no two snow crystals were alike in an infinity of snow crystals! How could anyone knowing that fact not be made almost ill with the desire to understand? Because knowing a fact and understanding a fact are very different things.

I once asked my father to explain what wind was. It was obviously atoms, air, but why couldn't you see it? If it was so materially dense that you could feel it battering your face as you leant out the car window, so unequivocally there that it could, during a cyclone, lift sheets of iron off our roof, or impale pieces of straw into wooden telephone poles, you should be able to see it. I can't remember his answer, but whatever it was did not satisfy, and the problem of invisible matter continued to be troublesome.

It wasn't that I didn't understand thinness and density. Air was rarefied matter, faces were dense matter. But why, if matter was inherently invisible, should it become visible when it was thicker? And what about the point at which one kind of matter met another kind? For example, what was it that kept the atoms of face in their place, and the atoms of air in theirs? Why didn't they cross over, until eventually everything cancelled out into a soup of sameness? There were many conundrums left to be solved.

God was not mentioned in discussions with my father. I don't think he lacked belief necessarily, but his background was high C of E which meant that he was happy to let God exist or not exist, as He chose. However, although he had no time for 'wowsers', he accompanied Gwen to the Methodist church once a month when the minister visited

Mooloolah. Gwen played the little organ at the back, and Mark went to sleep in the pew and embarrassed us by snoring while my sister and I squirmed and itched under our hot hats and longed for the excruciating boredom to be over.

God leant more towards my mother's side. She gave me a Bible, which smelt good and contained pictures of lambs, skies and a wistful-looking Jesus. The pages were of impossibly thin paper edged with gold, and there were gold indents indicating where to open at the 'chapters'. But I don't think I understood, then, that she took God personally – a living presence who listens to prayers. Perhaps her faith in such a god only came later, when other kinds of faith had failed.

God, for me, was a bit like Santa Claus. I knew Santa was really my father, and that leaving a glass of rum out for him on Christmas Eve was done to humour the grown-ups. Religion was a convention one upheld. But although God died early for me, a certain longing was left intact. Science could take you a long way into reality, further and further into it, but ultimately, it stranded you there. There was something beyond the reach of its understanding, something neglected by it, and while that seemed to be all right for my father, it wasn't all right for me. It was in that region where science bled into mystery that the most tantalising questions lived. Questions like: If my father had gone with Ivan Lyons into Singapore Harbour, and been beheaded by the Japs, who would I be? What comes after infinity? If you add one to infinity, does it mean that the original infinity wasn't infinite after all? Why is green, green? Photosynthesis, chlorophyll, my father might have said. But that didn't explain greenness in itself. And might there exist colours of which we were not aware? When a grasshopper looks back at you, what does it see? Does it see itself as green? If you keep splitting atoms in half, could you go on doing it for ever? What actually happens at the moment a chook is beheaded? Does it, for just a moment, know? And is it really all right to then eat it? What is the reason things are the way they are? And if you follow that question all the way back, you come up against a question that forms a kind of barrier. What is the reason there are things at all?

What was it about my parents, about their parenting, that inclined me to philosophy? I think it was because, in the best sense, they left me alone. I cannot remember a single instance of either of my parents playing with me in child-world. We laughed and joked and sang together in the evening, when all the work was done; they read or sang to me before I went to sleep, but they did not enter my world as participants, nor would I have wished them to. Nor did they expect me to take part in theirs. From their grown-ups' Olympus, they loved, they provided, but down on earth, I had to figure things out for myself.

If this led to a feeling of being a little estranged in the world – that is, if I felt myself to be alone in a place where a sister might play with you or kill you, where neighbours could be deranged or so poor as to sleep in a bath, where people were so different from me that they never gave invisible air a thought – then in order to understand such a place, I had to ask questions about it: not of my parents, or grown-ups, or God, or even of my sister, but of myself.

Mummies and daddies and babies in prams did not feature in either my sister's games or my own. Our fantasies were peopled by female isolates, coping with extreme situations. If we played in the cubby house, it was because the wicked soldiers were after us, and it became necessary for one of us to poke a rifle out the miniature window and into the blizzard, while the other cooked mud pies from our rapidly diminishing supplies of food. My sister, being six years older than me, was boss of these games and the possibility of my being boss never even occurred to me. Sometimes it happened that a fight would break out. From my vantage, my sister was a giantess. Boomph, the air would go out of my lungs, and I would be left doubled up, wondering if, this time, I would die before breath came back. But I was not helpless in these exchanges. I had three stratagems which I used in ascending order of desperation. The first was to lie on my back and rotate my legs and arms in the air, thus protecting the soft target of my belly. The next was to feint until I could lay a punch on one of my sister's developing breasts, rarely resorted to because I believed her when she said this would lead to cancer, and guilt takes the fun out of winning. The third, and final, option was going to Mummy. I would be in tears, not from the punches, but from the words. Or perhaps it wasn't even the words, it was the *tone*. The sneering, annihilating tone which reduced me to sobs, so that Mummy's pet would run to Mummy, and Mummy would tell my sister to stop bullying me, a response which, while effective in the short term, only made things worse in the long run, because it proved my sister right.

And yet, playing with my sister, for all its hazards, was the ultimate of play. She was the heroine who grew ahead of me and brought back news of the future. She called me Rathead and I called her Cadbury. I could do comedy routines that made her laugh. She could dream up plays for Sunday nights, and games about wicked soldiers chasing us through snowy forests. Where my knowledge was limited to *Marvels of the Universe* and the Grimm Brothers, she had something called 'general knowledge' from the *Children's Encyclopedia* Dad had been talked into buying from a travelling salesman way out on Stanley Park – a place she could remember clearly and I could not.

If parents are the gods, only rarely getting mixed up in earthly affairs, siblings are down here below, made of the same dirt.

Eight

Hunkering down. Playing the piano. Remembering.

I say it was the music that summoned my mother, but perhaps she would have come forth anyway. I was approaching the age at which she died – forty-six – and that alone might have made her restless. The London flat had been a base for several years, and even though I was commuting between London and India, London and Tibet, London and Australia, London and Anywhere in order to avoid it, the past was approaching closer and closer.

I was aware that the life I had constructed had shaky foundations. So much was obvious. But I had taken that as a given, and not something to focus on. People survive much worse than having mothers who commit suicide. And scratching around in the landscape behind you, looking for terrible things, has always struck me as being … indulgent. Better to thank the gods for their beneficence so far.

But why had the affair been so destructive? I must have believed that I could not really be harmed, deep at the core where it counted. But that is precisely where the harm had been done. An evisceration.

It was Love, of course. Not ordinary love, but one of those spiritually costly passions that rips away pride, common sense, intelligence. Deep love and deep sex, for which we have to emerge from our hiding places, exposed, vulnerable and blind as grubs.

Because of the circumstances in which I met him, I had thought myself safe. He was committed to another life on the far side of the planet – a life I had no wish to enter. As well, the situation was contained by a limited period of time. A *coup de foudre* tucked inside parentheses.

So I gave myself to him completely. I would like to leave it at that, but as it was one of those events around which an existence turns, I must explain more, even though, in essence, it was like any other grand passion – full of melodrama and narcissism as well as soaring joy. At its best, the sensation of flying, of being met, and matched, of never having to slow down. As if you've found the twin you've been searching for all your life. A cocktail of delusion and truth.

I was back in Australia at that time, an interregnum between the first and second periods of living in London. We met on the phone, through a mutual friend. He was reading my book, he said. He would be in Sydney for a few days, on his way home, he said. It was strange that we hadn't met in London, as we had friends and publishers in common, he said. Yes, he would come by for dinner on his way through, he said.

And both of us knew …

I had been living with a partner for years, but that had ended, and I had moved away. I did not want to be with anyone else. I was enjoying being on my own. But an affair … a safely contained, impossible-to-go-anywhere affair … There would be a safety net over which to test my wings – the net of no commitment, of never-to-be-seen-again.

In all my previous loves, something (one could almost use the word 'soul' here) had been withheld. Now, inside the security of those parentheses, I could risk revealing that essence, or core. When our time was up, I walked away happier with myself than I could remember, and with this person whom I would not meet again. To have been seen, and found loveable, that was enough. That was everything.

But a couple of weeks after he left, I received a letter. His marriage had ended a long time ago. He had been separating just as I had. He was coming back to me.

At such a moment of blindsiding joy, how could anyone worry about the breach of that concluding bracket?

He flew from London. We were together about three weeks. Nothing of such intensity had happened to either of us before. In that state of mutual disarmament, trust is as essential as it is between trapeze artists flying into each other's arms. If one or the other refuses the catch …

Already insecurities, uncertainties had begun to show themselves, first in one, then in the other, and it was as if these ripples of disturbance oscillated at an ever increasing amplitude, as synchronised steps can shatter a bridge.

An overwhelming intensity of love and desire, followed by fear and withdrawal. One night, he said, 'I'm leaving. I'm going back to my wife.'

I lay on the floor, with the sensation that I had been opened from throat to pelvis. I would do anything, anything at all to make that sensation go away. I thought, I can stand this much, but if it gets worse, I will not survive it.

I abased myself. If he left now survival wasn't possible. But he did leave. He went to a hotel. The next morning he returned. We had sex and the pain subsided. So the pattern was set – abandonment and return, to be repeated over and over until there was nothing left.

I understood dimly, even then, that the devastation was too enormous to be the result of abandonment by a lover. This had to be what had lain beneath the callus all those years – the long-delayed shock of a more essential loss.

He went back to London, returned again, left again. Eventually we agreed that I should go to London to live with him.

He left his wife. He bought a house in Islington for us. I dismantled my life in Australia and followed him a few months later.

It should have been obvious that there had been no time in which to recover, in which to build a solid footing capable of supporting the added stress load of entering someone else's life.

The London I had known before was not like this one. This London was more socially ambitious, more competitive. It was nourished on gossip, and we were nothing if not gossip fodder. He enjoyed the attention; for me it was like being paraded naked.

Nor did I think of myself as a *writer*; that is to say, it did not form my identity. I had come to writing in such an unlikely way, in my own mind I had simply pulled another rabbit out of a hat. As I had done all my life, with everything.

His identity, on the other hand, was entirely taken up by his work, by the wish to be acknowledged and loved for it.

The gnawing sensation of being out of place, placeless, was reflected in the house. It was comfortable, but it did not contain a room for me into which I could retreat, where I might regain my stability, gather myself. As well, it was beige from floor to ceiling. Wherever you looked you were greeted by deathly beige. I suggested that I paint it – as a way, I suppose, of making it our home; that is to say, as much mine as his. But that would have disrupted his work so beige it remained.

There was no secure ground for me, it seemed, either in the house or in his life outside the house.

Yet within the universe of two, we were in other ways profoundly united. We finished each other's thoughts, each other's sentences, even completed each other's dreams at night. But just as ecstasy leaves the self behind to fuse with something larger, so such psychic merging can be befuddling, can cut you off from your own good sense.

Two damaged children each with a different bedlam inside their heads.

An older friend, fond of us both, said, when she first saw us together, 'You will have to learn to mother each other.' It goes without saying that we never did.

I remained with him longer than I should have, a couple of years, because I could not understand the reason for the upheavals, for the abandonments. There had to be something in me, in my behaviour, that caused them. If I could find out what that was, then the oscillations would cease, and only love would remain. Such is the dementing effect of desire on intelligence. Any idiot could see that this was not the nature of the beast. My childhood loves primed me to assume that any anger coming my way had to be my fault, my responsibility.

Towards the end (by which time the oscillations were off the scale), I had sent for my furniture in Australia. I don't know what had been in my mind. Perhaps I thought the presence of my 'things' in the house might encourage a sense of belonging there. But by the time it all arrived, I was in the throes of leaving him. This might have been a more drawn-out process had it not been for the poem.

It was left on the pillow on my side of the bed. It was a poem addressed to me in the form of a curse.

One does not have to believe in the power of curses for the curses to wing their way inside the target and do their damage there. I walked away eventually, but I was a different being.

Think of a cup which has been cracked but so successfully mended that you cannot see the fault line. The cup seems perfect and entire but is structurally weakened so that, if it is dropped a second time, it shatters along that invisible flaw – splintering and crazing into bits.

So ... a calamity. Stupid years of shock followed by aftershock. The awfulness of the ending was not just the end of an affair, but something much more damaging. Annihilation was its goal. When I left him, the final time, knowing I would not go back, I dreamt that I was a cigarette he was smoking. I was turned to ash, then stubbed out.

'Love must not touch the marrow of the soul,' said Phaedra's nurse. But what, ultimately, was it all about? All that *Sturm und Drang*. And how will I evaluate those years from a longer perspective, when I am able to discern more clearly what they gave rise to? And what is he to me now? Neither friend nor foe. An indifference. Yet through him I touched something mythical and primal, outside of individuality. An ecstatic infant love gone nuclear.

★

I went to America, to Australia, to Europe, but outward change changed little within. I had to finish a book. It is hard to write without your core. It is hard to live without it.

Eventually I returned to London and bought the flat with my friends. I bought the piano, I gathered my possessions around me. One might ignore or forget a past, but possessions proved it was *somewhere*.

Later, when memory became more available, the objects lost their importance. They, too, were temporary residents. When I died they would tumble through time to arrive at other addresses, lend themselves to new, equally fleeting coherencies. We are not the owners of anything, not even our thoughts, that rise to the surface like deep-water fish.

My mother at the upright, singing. (If I squint and concentrate, I see gold lettering – *Berlin Dresden Posen* – emerge on the wood above the keys. She stands up, opens the lid of the piano, and places a tin of water down beside the strings.)

"'Funiculee, funiculaa, funiculee, funiculaa, echoes sound afar, funiculee, funiculaa ...'"

We are standing around the piano in the lounge in Malabah. Green Axminster carpet with worn thread. Up on the bookcase there is a tiny royal coach pulled by horses. I am not supposed to touch it because of 'lead poisoning'. I see the little coach in my mind, then remember being in a crowd, holding up a flag and waving at a woman in a hat who sits in an open black car. It is 1954, the Queen's first visit to her favourite colony after the war. On the same shelf as the little coach is an Aboriginal 'bone' for pointing at people to kill them. The shelf below displays hand axes worn smooth by thousands of years of use. Somewhere there's a bullroarer that my father tried once, down in the paddocks.

Illogically, that memory sets off another memory, of our Guy Fawkes Nights every fifth of November, when Ted and Bunty came over for fireworks. The excitement of choosing the fireworks in Nambour. Drinking milk in Nambour through a chocolate straw or a strawberry straw. It was the flavoured straw or a Paddle Pop, we weren't allowed both. Driving home in the back of the ute, under the tarp, after swimming at Caloundra. Salty skin and sand in our togs. My sister and I fighting or giggling in the back seat of the new Holden sedan on Sunday-afternoon drives. Hanging out the car window feeling invisible matter drumming my cheeks flat. Ted and my father lighting the fireworks – pinwheels, bottle rockets. My sister and I write in the air with sparklers while we sit on the back stairs. From there I notice the golf holes my father made in the grounds of Malabah, old jam tins inserted into the lawn. IXL melon and ginger jam tins. How cross he was when bandicoots dug up the lawn leaving cones of dirt. 'Gawd stone the crows, look what the blighters have done, damn-n-blast it ...' There were native animals everywhere then – so plentiful we could consider them pests. They are rare now, many gone for ever.

Nambour was our nearest proper town, with a proper main street, pubs and shops, stock and station agent, a milk bar which sold the just-new things – Paddle Pops and flavoured straws. I bought my first gift in the Nambour department store. All by myself. A birthday card for my mother. We went to Nambour for doctors, dentists, supplies and piano lessons with Sister Augusta. She lived in a big building on the hill. Red brick with white trim, a cross on top, spooky rooms with heavy furniture. Along a side veranda, two or three piano rooms. When my mother and I first visited, Sister invited us into a dark inner sanctum. My mother said, 'Give Sister Augusta a kiss.' I took a running leap, cinched my legs around her habited waist, flung my arms around her starched neck and squeezed her, as I did with my mother. The two women laughed, my mother apologised (after a moment's dismay I knew the unorthodox greeting had won favour) and thus began the friendship between them. I was very pleased at this friendship, it seemed to bring my mother more alive. They laughed and talked animatedly together, and Sister was encouraged to unbutton the white wimple in the soggy heat, away from the gaze of Mother Superior. It was Sister who taught me 'La Cascade' – a showy piece that used most octaves of the piano, but wasn't all that difficult to play.

The dentist: fifties dentistry was a primitive science. It was assumed that adults should have most of their healthy teeth extracted and replaced with a 'plate', to save them future trouble. Thus it happened that one day my mother appeared with a delicate little silver wire contraption along the bottom row of teeth, to match her gold filling. And my father came home with hardly any teeth at all, smiling in a stunned sort of way, and pale as a corpse.

But he did not complain. He was too manly. He of the missing thumb and the missing toe. The first he lost when he jumped a gate on his horse, came out of the saddle, and landed on his hand. Shrapnel took the toe off during the war, but losing a toe was not even worth noticing when there were so many 'poor devils' worse off than yourself.

Like most men of that time, he did not speak about what he had seen during the war. Only once, years later, when we got to know each other better, he described shelling a tank and seeing a soldier come out of it on fire: '... poor devil, poor devil ...' And long after my father died, an old mate of his from the army days sent me a letter, and a photograph. He said that my father had cared deeply about the men under his command, looked after them, and had been very popular. (The photo shows him in the centre of these men, somewhere near Tel Aviv, and you can see the love, care and concern amongst them, my dad laughing, his hand on the shoulder of a kneeling young man – a child, really.) And that he had planned to go back to Africa after the war, and walk down the Rift Valley. Obviously marriage had knocked that idea on the head. If it is true that we live out our parents' unfulfilled wishes, then my walk across the desert contained a desire of my father's that I knew nothing about at the time.

And my mother's unfulfilled wishes? In a more complicated way, hers were also about freedom. From being 'under the thumb'. Freedom, perhaps, to develop her talents beyond mere 'accomplishments' – the gifts you bring to a marriage, like a dowry. Freedom to be a person, rather than daughter, wife or mother.

Sometimes I have imagined her making a blind leap into the unknown – picking me up and running, or just running on her own, ditching us all and saving herself. If I do harbour any anger towards her (people assure me that the children of suicides are always angry, but for the life of me I can't locate it), it's because she did not save herself before all other exits closed. But where could she have gone? What work could she have found? She had no money of her own. A woman then could not sign a cheque without male authority, could not open a bank account without a husband's signature. Mortgages were not available to women, hire purchase agreements could not be signed by women. Divorce would put her beyond the pale in any society she knew. You have to be able to imagine freedom to make a bid for it.

In that era, in that circumstance, at her age, with her background, it would have been possible only if she were prepared to live as a homeless pariah.

Or with Nanna.

Nine

Swan Lake arrived in Brisbane. There we are, sitting in a row, my parents, my grandparents and me. My sister must be there too, though I am not aware of her. On my left is my father, his long legs awkward in the theatre seats. He is not so much bored as incongruent. On my right, my mother, anxious that everyone should enjoy the treat as much as she does. That we should understand why she enjoys it. As if our enjoyment of the ballet will add heft to her side of the marriage.

Nanna sits beside my mother. Perhaps, wishing to please my mother, I say, 'I want to be a dancer when I grow up,' which draws a most unexpected reaction from Nanna. She leans across my mother and hisses, 'What! And get those big fat calves on your legs? What man would want to marry you if you had big muscles like that!' I sense that this derision is aimed at my mother, that it intimidates her. Had my mother wished to be a dancer? Like Isadora Duncan?

During the second half, my father eats peanuts that get stuck under his plate so that he makes sucking noises that can be heard at least three rows ahead.

These small irruptions confirm what I already know: that the two sides of our family tree – that is, the maternal and the paternal branches that met to form our very own little nuclear unit of four – were not of the same wood.

My father's tastes were less self-conscious than my mother's. He knew what he liked. He liked P. G. Wodehouse, Zane Grey and geology tomes. He grew up uninterested in the beautiful objects surrounding him. They were part of the overall aesthetic of a privileged life, which included dust and wide verandas, comfortable old chairs and good horses, though never adequate cash. His family were members of the squattocracy. Descended from the British upper class, they had 'pioneered' grazing land in Queensland and New South Wales during the previous century. The women of the line tended towards eccentricity, imperiousness and jealousy; the men towards evasiveness and good nature. They were all tall and strong and good-looking and led marvellously free lives. Indoors was where you resentfully went when you couldn't be outdoors, galloping bareback down a beach, or going for picnics in the first T-Model Ford in the state, or flying in the first aeroplane with Kingsford Smith, or mustering cattle or sheep on some vast holding. They looked down comfortably from an elevation that was moral and social as well as physical. It was not, after all, Aboriginal people of which they were scornful. They related to their black stockmen as to aristocrats of a separate and doomed order. No, it was the 'civilising' values of the middle class they despised along with weakness of any kind. They hoarded and squabbled over money, and were incapable of humility, introspection or self-pity.

But colonial circumstance made the idea of an upper class redundant in Australia. There weren't enough of them to go around, so interclass breeding was inevitable. In my own case, aristocratic genes were diluted by my father's choice of wife, who had, as a substitute for class, a carefully cultivated and precarious glamour, which was always on the lookout for 'commonness'. My father's family were beyond the possibility of the taint of commonness.

Now, perhaps, is the time to introduce my father's twin sister, Gilian, pronounced with a hard 'g'.

I see her in a smart felt hat and slacks. The skin of her cheeks is soft as chamois; her hair thick and white. She is tall and straight and has long legs like my father. She wears no jewellery or make-up, but she is a stunningly handsome woman. Her eyes are just like my father's, except his contain a residuum of the oceans he has traversed, whereas hers are hard as topaz. Before her knees were smashed by a horse, she was one of the finest riders in Australia. (Without ever saying so, she implies that her brother is an inferior rider, and everyone understands that it is not only riding she is alluding to. It was she who should have inherited Stanley Park. She who would have managed the property so much better than he.) She 'loathes' cooking and housework. In a photograph, she is shaking hands with a horse. I idolise her shyly.

'No wonder you're always sick,' she says to me, 'you're overprotected. When I was your age I was galloping horses bareback down the beach, and climbing trees up to the very top. I haven't been sick a day in my life! I don't suppose you've ever been allowed to climb a tree, have you?'

These words are the residue of the first of her two visits to Malabah. I was small and skinny then (before my tonsillectomy and consequent growth spurt), and drank iron compound in milk. As well, I vomited secretly at night, because I was the cause of my mother's imminent arrest by the police. I suppose that was why Gil insisted I was sickly.

At about this time my father had introduced a billy goat to our flock of sheep, in the hopes that its superior intelligence would dissuade them from stampeding into the creek and drowning every time a dog got inside the dog-proof netting. But 'Goatie' was far too clever to hang around with sheep, and continually arrived at our back door, having negotiated several dingo-proof fences and a flight of steps to get there.

It was on Goatie that Gil decided I should learn to ride. She produced, from under the house, a jockey saddle, and girthed it on to an already suspicious goat. Naturally I was dead against this. Goatie was a *friend*. But it was unthinkable to countermand Gil. Goatie made one loop of the grounds with me on his back, then fell on his side and played dead. Hoots of laughter from my heartless aunt.

Prince was next. I cantered around the paddock, thrilled at my astonishing ability to remain seated on the heaving lump of ungovernable flesh beneath, who pulled up unfailingly at the gate without my having to use the reins.

'Oh Mark, you are a *fool*,' Gil would say in that haughty way of hers. And my father would grin down at his hands and say, with patient fondness, 'Oh right you are [rye-choo-ah], old girl.'

I both knew and did not know that, in Gil's view, my father's most unforgivably foolish act was marrying Gwen. But I don't think I was conscious, at the time, of how my defection to my aunt must have galled my mother. I was too overcome with the pleasures of being noticed, and sprung from piano practice.

Gil's most voluble antipathy, however, was reserved for Great-aunt Gladys, that miser and hoarder who had somehow managed to lodge herself in the old family home, Haddington, in which Gil and my father (Boy) were raised, and which Gil believed belonged morally and legally to herself. The loathing was fully reciprocated by Great-aunt Gladys. Nevertheless, Gil 'parked herself' often at Haddington, in order to 'put the wind up' Gladys by threatening legal actions which all of us knew would never materialise, because Gil was as stingy as Great-aunt Gladys – which is to say, pathologically so – and wouldn't dream of parting with money for a lawyer. Instead she resorted to the pitiless stratagem of 'visiting' for weeks on end. It was here, when my father went to see Gil, or to do odd jobs for Great-aunt Gladys, that I was provided with clues to my father's background.

The air of Haddington ... how can I describe it? It was as if time had receded like a tide, but left a bouquet of itself, as the sea will leave its scent on a mudflat. As well, it had left behind clues in the form of objects. These objects, which Gladys had sequestered to herself by cunning and foul play, came from family members all over the country. The categories these objects fell into – furniture, letters, cabinets – were recognisable, but the objects themselves were uncanny. Furniture crouched in corners and along panelled walls like disfigured animals. There was a cock-fighting chair, which you sat in backwards, resting your arms along the curved, leather-bound back. It had come from Scotland, or England, or India, or Denmark, along the trade routes of ancestors. Silver gleamed through the half-light. There were cabinets with secret drawers. A musical box which you cranked with a handle, so that the prickly cylinder inside was struck by tiny metal prongs. There were letters, it was said, from Byron and Shelley, though I was never allowed to touch them. Once I sneaked a look in a drawer of an enormous dresser in Great-aunt Gladys's bedroom. It contained hundreds of pairs of gloves wrapped in tissue paper – satin gloves, kid gloves, gloves with real pearl buttons. From the other rooms I could hear shreds of grown-up talk – 'and after you've done that, Boy, the guttering needs fixing …' – while from far away, the racket of cockatoos, and the wailing of gulls down by the pier where Hal Boucher lost his leg.

There was an attic at the top of a flight of dark, almost vertical stairs. It took all my courage to ascend those stairs. Sometimes my sister helped by going ahead, then letting me grab her leg as I crawled up on hands and knees against the opposing force of vertigo. The attic's allure was irresistible. It was a storage house for time. Secret things under yellowing sheets. Flecks of dust in the brown light percolating through yellow blinds. Haddington still figures in my dreams, expanding, in them, to an endless surplus of rooms – a metaphor of mind.

Great-aunt Gladys was a 'physiotherapist' – which had something to do with a small room off the back veranda containing the sorts of contraptions you might find in dungeons. I don't think I ever spoke to Great-aunt Gladys, beyond the well-brought-up 'good morning' or 'good afternoon'. She was far too imposing, with her black dress, and black circles under her eyes, and silver cane. (Those black circles prefigured in a daguerreotype of a woman in crinolines.) It was said that she once had the Prince of

Wales to tea out on Gin Gin or Ban Ban station, and gave him a boiled egg, but I don't know if that's true. She was unmarried, like Gil, like many of the Wade-Broun women. 'Maiden aunts', they were called, the inference being that there was something unnatural, even pitiful about them. (There was a further or deeper inference: no man would have been able to tolerate them.) A subversive seed was sown in me, however, by Gil, by Gladys, and by all the spinsters of the line. They were terrible women, patrician and self-centred – but they were interesting, and they indicated another way of being female in the world.

It was at Haddington that I absorbed the universally held but tacit opinion that Boy had married beneath him and that his progeny were, consequently, tainted goods. I sometimes wonder if Grandy's Jewishness contributed to this judgement, or whether they simply believed Gwen the wrong class and temperament. Probably the latter. There were so few Jews in Brisbane that anti-Semitism would have had trouble reaching critical mass, and in any case, the great Australian schism of the time was between Protestants and Micks. Jews barely got a look-in. My mother's aspirations – her concern with clothes and accomplishments, her love of the arts, her ineradicable fear of the bush, and her clever mockery of country life – would only have compounded their disdain. All of which explains why it was that we so seldom shifted from the matriline across to the patriline.

We visited Nanna and Grandy instead, in their pigeon-box house just a few miles from Haddington, but infinitely far by every other measure.

Haddington was by the seaside on the outskirts of Brisbane. It was built in the colonial vernacular style, of cedar and other local woods. A confident and comfortable architecture, allowing for candelabra and formal dress inside, but acknowledging, with its generous verandas, the pleasures and freedoms of the New World. Along one veranda was a Brazilian cherry tree, rampantly overgrown, and dropping its red fruit on to the wooden boards. The fruit tasted like the word 'Brazil'. Parrots and magpies arrived on the back veranda, and were carelessly fed. There were squatter's chairs, on which you could lie back and raise your legs on the extended rests, enjoy an afternoon nap, or gaze out on to the bay and the jetty, where my father's friend Hal Boucher had his leg bitten off by a shark while they were all swimming together in 1912.

Nanna and Grandy's little house was in the post-Second World War suburbs, built on cleared swamp where, my father said, he used to shoot black duck when he was a boy. The windows were closed against Nanna's dread of 'draughts'. Green velvet curtains were drawn against the vulgarity of Australian sun. Instead of brash cockatoos and gaudy rosellas, there were pigeons cooing dismally their Sunday-afternoon tedium. But there were small sweetnesses, too, that you never would have found at Haddington. Violets under the front steps, and a trellis of small, perfect 'Cécile Brünner' roses. Nanna was proud of her cooking – strictly Victorian – and of the milkman's praise of the cleanliness of her milk bottles. She referred to Scotland as 'home', though she had never left Queensland.

Down the back of the plot was Grandy's vegetable garden, with a mulberry tree and grapevine. He was proud of his strawberries. I suspect that Grandy's garden was his small escape from small Protestantism. It was he who referred to the house as 'the pigeon box'.

And perhaps he escaped in other ways too. He helped to support a certain widow by the name of Mrs Green.

Grandy was bald, plump, fastidious, fond of well-cut suits, and grumpy with his wife. He had a delightful wheezy laugh. He sang bass in a choir, had an enormous nose, and was fussy about his food. Gout and bad digestion explained his occasional ill humour. The only thing I know about his family is that they changed their name from Weber to Harris when they arrived in Brisbane, sometime in the late nineteenth century. When Grandy won a scholarship to grammar school – requiring nevertheless a sizable financial investment by his parents – his mother and sisters sewed him 'seven new suits'. We never met anyone from his side of the family.

One of my jobs was to snip off, with a tiny pair of scissors, any tiny white hairs that had strayed on to his shiny scalp. And when we played 'Ride a Cock Horse', he insisted on singing the verses in his chocolatey deep voice.

'Don't *sing* it, Grandy, *say* it.' He was fond of me, but my sister was his favourite. Perhaps he discerned, where others did not, the nature of my sister's unhappiness. Perhaps he discerned a lot of things, but had the wisdom not to speak.

He and my father liked each other.

The only story I have of Mark's courtship of Gwen was of his first visit to her parents. He was not long back from Africa, unused, still, to the polite world. He had brought flowers, but what a laugh! They were gerberas! It was Nanna's favourite story, the gerberas. It contained resonances. Of Mark's lack of gentility, of his absurd and threatening masculinity. Of his stinginess. Whenever it was told, Mark would grin good-naturedly, and turn his hat around in his hands.

I see him coming up the road towards the pigeon box with his bunch of gerberas. His carriage — a slow lope, graceful, masculine. His gaze rests not at the ground but on the distance. The good shyness of him, yet he is bent on having what he wants. He is confident as a man, yet unsure of himself and clumsy in the aura of Gwen's loveliness. What a bundle of nerves and certainty, of push and pull.

He walks into her world from a place she has no experience of. She is slightly tardy for the marriage market of the time: twenty-six. Spinsterhood is close enough for her to feel the first lappings of panic touching her feet. He is promising her something unusual and grand, something romantic, a life of adventure. And then there's the war. It's as if all the people in the world have been stirred around like tea in a cup. All sorts of rules are being broken, and the young have to grow up quickly.

I see him coming along the street towards the pigeon box as clearly as any memory. But it did not occur in Sandgate. He would have walked down some other street, unknown to me, on the far side of the city, where once my grandparents had lived, where their daughter Gwen had her photo taken, dressed up and dancing like Isadora Duncan.

My grandmother receives him coldly. Her glance at the gerberas could turn them to dust. Mark is her first serious competitor.

Or perhaps it wasn't like that at all. Perhaps Nanna foresaw the troubles ahead. The isolation, the lack of doctors, the hard work (she works like a *navvy*), the snobbishness of the Davidsons. And her daughter would be hundreds of miles from her, unavailable except by post. And Mark so much older: forty-three to her twenty-six. Perhaps she regretted all the nice boys Gwen might have married, whom she had mocked and put off, who had steady jobs in the bank, or businesses of their own.

Gwen had received a secondary education at a boarding school in Stanthorpe. Only 7 per cent of girls in Queensland at that time were educated beyond primary school. She had been a prefect, the nuns had adored her. Afterwards she obtained a good position as a secretary. And her social life! Singing in operas, dancing, balls, going for picnics with all her friends, decorating the car with wild flowers, afternoon teas in a famous Brisbane café, wearing gloves and hats and the latest fashions sewed at home from pattern books. Then the WAAF and involvement in the war effort. All to be squandered in the outback with a tightwad old enough to be her father. Unsuitable in every way.

No doubt she and Grandy had troubled discussions about their only daughter. But Gwen resisted them for Mark. That cannot have been easy. Yes, I think my parents must have loved each other very much. A grand passion, with all the idealisation that implies.

Nanna. I cannot separate the person she might have been from the general consensus that she was a maker of mischief. And perhaps she *was* traumatised by sex, or rather its repercussions. One forgets how many women died in childbirth then – about one in four, they say. She had two sons, so perhaps thought of her daughter as an ally. A family friend told me that Nanna treated Gwen more as a sister, the inference being that the bond between them was not quite right. In modern parlance, she was a narcissistic mother. Which leads me to think (and there is further evidence for this) that Gwen chose my father as an escape from a stifling possessiveness.

But we never escape our mothers. Their habits of mind have life in us, either in the way we think, or in opposition to the way we wish to think.

My father was born in 1900. The structures underpinning his moral life were formed before the First World War; that is to say, by the nineteenth century. The whole of his life's journey was an extension, a playing-out of that epoch. It was a conservative century, of dominating classes who did not question established values. Manliness and patriotism underpinned Empire, faith in which he had learnt on his mother's knee, and had confirmed later by a boarding-school system inherited from England. During the war, and in Africa, he could live as the hero, close to his 'men', his 'boys'. But when all that was over and he married and settled, the heroism was reduced to fit the space Australia's post-war allotted him.

Freud and Einstein had no part to play in the making of his psyche. Modernity and its uncertainties would only reach him in old age, after he had lived cheek by jowl with his mistakes and sorrows which formed fractures in the assurance he had inherited.

One of the beliefs making up that assurance was that certain beliefs amount to natural laws because they are upheld by science, notably Darwinism. Men are superordinate to women because natural law made it thus, and whites are superordinate to blacks for the same reason.

These laws have predictable, though often regrettable – even tragic – consequences. For example, Aborigines were destined to die out in the face of invasion by a 'fitter' race. My father was neither aggressive nor cruel – he admired and respected Aboriginal culture and knew as much about it as most anthropologists of the time. But history had happened, for good or ill, and the consequences must play out. Admiration and respect, even friendship and love, were no match for natural law. Similarly, ambition and aspiration in women, beyond their biologically determined role as homemakers, was folly. Against nature.

One cannot leave out the females of his clan here, either – especially Gil, who pushed her way out of their shared womb a minute before him, and had dominated, loved and resented him ever since. Gwen was nothing like Gil. Gwen was biddable, feminine, comic, exquisite, moody, insecure, gifted and a hopeless rider.

I imagine he must have wanted a boy child very much. (Perhaps that was why I was called Robyn – a boy's name feminised by a 'y'.) It must have been difficult for him, the man's man, living forever amongst women, with their alien demands which he had no idea how to fulfil. He loved us, about that there is no question. But he loved us across an unbridgeable divide. Girl children belonged to mothers and should replicate mothers. That is, they should accommodate themselves to an eternally secondary, serving role. In his inadequacy, he fell back on the conventions of his time. His nature held no selfishness in it, but his ideology did.

The atmosphere inside my mother's time is early modern; her journey begins just after the First World

War and her gaze is fixed firmly towards the fresh new century. God most certainly did play dice in her century, and the human mind was open for inspection. She had the divided nature of the neurotic, striving to make herself worthy of herself. As well, the Second World War came along, complicating things, allowing women new ways of imagining themselves, offering new opportunities and roles which, however, had to be returned when it was all over, and the men came home.

My father was content with the explanatory science of his century. He did not worry about the Hegelian quest to search out the reason for things (until we've understood the reason behind things-as-they-are, we've understood them not at all). For my mother it was art, beauty and poetry – the needs of the soul – that revealed our essential nature. Of course, she had never heard of Hegel, yet her manifestation in time embodied those tensions, just as my father's embodied his.

Before they met, my parents were the representatives of two different centuries, classes, histories, moralities, expectations, cultures. But their shared time – the Second World War and its consequence, the fifties – defined the marriage. The war had unsettled things; after it, everything had to be put back in order. It was time to make families, replacing all those lives ruined or lost. Their individual distinctiveness was held in check by the clichés they abided by, and no one can live too far outside the clichés of their time.

My parents were an unusual couple. But not too unusual. Just unusual enough.

Ten

I was twenty-seven when I walked across Australia, with a dog for company, and camels to carry my gear. It was a deeply private act, which I assumed would hold no interest for others. I had no intention of writing about it afterwards, nor of recording the journey as it was happening. It was the doing of something just for itself.

Yet so personal a gesture – a wish to disappear beneath any radar – would beget its opposite. Before the journey was even over, I was front-page news, and later the story was repeated on the covers of hundreds of magazines around the world. Rick Smolan's gorgeous photographs lent a glamour to what I had done, to which I had been oblivious while doing it.

Of course that doing changed me. It gave me what I had known, inchoately, I needed – a kind of integration. Proof to myself that 'useless ugly stupid' was not *all* there was. But it did much more than that. It rerouted my fate and recast my prospects, an upheaval all the more disorienting for being unexpected. And it would affect others, intimates as well as strangers, in ways that were baffling to me at the time.

Here were different kinds of danger, requiring a different kind of prudence. Fame, that grand deluder, puts you at risk of ceasing to be yourself. It distorts not just how you appear to others, which doesn't matter much, but how you might appear to yourself, which does. I knew this instinctively, and my response was to retreat from it. I feared the loss of anonymity and privacy, and with it a particular kind of freedom: to observe rather than be observed. When retreat was not possible, I made a facsimile Robyn, a public identity to protect the private one.

All of which isn't to say that I eschewed the benefits suddenly bestowed – an enormous opening of opportunity. I had lost something but, at the same time, was being offered so very much. Negotiating those assets and liabilities, while protecting an internal space free from distorting influence – that was the task. I certainly had no sophistication to guide me, only an innate discernment that had directed my course so far.

The most important asset was that at last I had what I once feared would be for ever beyond my reach: money for plane fares out of Australia. (Can anyone today understand how urgent that desire was for my generation, and how difficult to assuage?) There were even possibilities waiting on the far side. Jonathan Cape Publishers in London had offered to pay me an advance to write a book.

But did I want to write a book? Who said I could write a book? I enjoyed writing for myself, and the article I had to produce for *National Geographic* was easy, because it was facile. I wrote a longer one for the *London Sunday Times*, and that had given me satisfaction. But a book? On the pro side, I reasoned that, if I did write it, the limelight would shift to the book, and I would be left alone. The way you might distract a pack of dogs with a thrown bone.

I was reading Doris Lessing at that time and, like so many others, had been bowled over by what she had attempted in her novels. Until then I had more or less avoided female authors. I already knew how women thought, how they saw and experienced the world. What I needed to know was how men thought. They were the inheritors of the enlightenment project to which I aspired. They ran everything, they were the powerful, and to understand them was to understand the world, the better to negotiate a place in it. Doris's writing spoke directly to the complexities of finding that place. Again it must be understood that at that time there were very few models for unconventional women to be inspired by. There was the sense that we had to make it up as we went along, out there on the front lines, without much to guide or encourage us.

I wrote to her, and said how 'useful' her work had been to me. She replied. We corresponded. In response to my hesitation in committing myself to Jonathan Cape, she said, 'If you can write a good letter you can write a good book. Why don't you come to England, since your publishers are here?'

So I did.

Via a stop-off in India, courtesy of dear Rick, who took me along as a sidekick on a photographic assignment.

There were many countries I wanted to explore, but India had never been one of them. The patchouli and incense; the hepatitis and credulous spiritualism coming back along the hippie trail only confirmed my bias against it. India was not for me.

Rick had to cover the Pushkar camel fair, in Rajasthan. The festival is now famous, and many Europeans go there.

But at that time, 1978 (or perhaps it was 1979), I think he and I were the only non-Indians present.

Another profound effect of the desert journey was that it informed a new way of looking at human history. Because I had begun to know a little about Australian Aboriginal culture, through an association with Eddie, an old Pitjantjatjara man who had decided to accompany me part of the way, I was able to compare hunter-gatherer ways of being with the cultural assumptions inherited from millennia of agriculture. I had been struck by how profoundly at home, existentially at home, he was. His ancestors had solved so many of the problems inherent in human existence. Goods were shared out pretty much equally, no one was left out. They were environmental scientists par excellence. And the philosophy of the Dreaming, in so far as I could penetrate it, seemed to me one of the greatest ever brought forth from human imagination: a theory of everything rendered into poetry.

Nomads, generally speaking, tread lightly upon the earth. Because they are constantly moving, they cannot accumulate a lot of *stuff*. They have to know their environments well, valuing and accumulating knowledge systems rather than goods. Agriculture, on the other hand, in its battle with nature, has created problems for us that have escalated until our species threatens its own existence.

These were nascent ideas at the time, and they were certainly not free of romanticism (the desire to escape reality rather than apprehend it better). Even so, they were working away at the back of my mind, and I knew I would need to explore other kinds of mobile cultures to see if my hunches had any value at all.

India was about the last place I imagined stumbling across that opportunity.

The Raika Rabaris were Rajasthani camel herders, and they had come to Pushkar to buy and sell their animals. Never could I have imagined, in my most starry-eyed fantasies, that nomads could look like this. The women wore bright pink chiffon veils bordered and embroidered with silver. Voluminously gathered skirts like mid-length tutus. Huge silver bangles on their ankles. Stack upon stack of bracelets up their muscular arms. The men were all in white, with huge scarlet turbans. In the dusk, they camped on the pink sandhills surrounding Pushkar, with their tethered camels, sitting around tiny fires, the women's silver reflecting spangles into the smoky air.

What if I could travel with *them*?

So it was that, after Rick had returned to the States, I found myself standing alone on an empty airport runway, in the middle, from my point of view, of nowhere, wondering how I might go about locating a gentleman called Gomal Khotari. Someone in Delhi had told me he knew all there was to know about the Rabari.

I seem to have had an unusually fateful life, not in the supernatural sense, but more mundanely, in this way: odd and unlikely events, coincidences, have produced enormous effects, fanning out into future time, and seemingly outside my control. Perhaps a strong fate is nothing more than a reckless disregard for consequences, which can look like courage, but is really something else — a curiosity greater, even, than fear. Or even more banal, a difficulty in saying no. In any case, this was one of those moments when I stepped into the unknown, unburdened by nous or knowledge, and stumbled across my future.

Young woman, recently left Australia for the first time, standing on the tarmac of Jodhpur airport, wearing (so I am told) a cowboy hat. For all she understands of where she is, she might as well be in a fairy tale. She has a chance to meet someone there who has information about a group of nomads she has seen, and been astonished by. (This makes it sound as if she knows what she is doing. She has no idea what she is doing.) She knows only that this folklorist will be busy entertaining a French journalist that week. On the small plane she has arrived in, she heard a passenger speaking French. Now she sees this woman greeting a man dressed in black jodhpurs, black kurta, black sunglasses, black moustache, and holding a black riding crop. She gathers every bit of courage to overcome her timorousness, and approaches the personification of elegance.

'Excuse me, are you Mr Gomal Khotari?'

He looks down at her. He pauses.

'No, but I know Khotari Sahib very well ...' He pauses again. 'Haven't we met somewhere before?''

She looks around at the extraterrestrial surroundings, and laughs in spite of herself. 'I seriously doubt that ...'

'But of course, you are the woman who walked across Australia ... I've just been reading about you in *National Geographic*. In fact I was thinking of inviting you to Rajasthan. I can take you to Khotari Sahib, but meanwhile you must come home and stay with my family. My father will be so interested to meet you ...'

I was led to an open Second World War jeep, which was instantly surrounded by children, so that my terrifying host lifted his riding crop which sent them flying and giggling. I was driven to a large red stone house, the front room of which contained nothing but a wall-to-wall mattress, coloured bolsters and cushions, and a black telephone on a very long wire. Tea was brought on squat tables by hurrying servants summoned by the clapped hands of the man in black.

The Narendra I eventually came to know would never clap his hands for a servant, so this must be another false memory. But I very clearly recall being driven to his farm on the outskirts of town – traditional round stone jhumpas with thatched roofs, joined by mud and dung platforms. Smooth limewashed walls inside. A breeze coming through the windows, cooled by grids of soaked reeds. I remained shy of him, and he too was taciturn. He led me through the rooms, and without looking at me, with a most graceful nonchalance, he picked up a solid-silver matchbox from a table (I was a heavy smoker then) and placed it in my hand. 'For your bravery,' he said.

I don't remember how many days I was there, nor whether I met the great Khotari Sahib. (I met him years later.) Everything was far too extraordinary to be counted out in real time. The colonel, for example, Narendra's father. Handsome, illiterate, rum-drinking, loyal to his brother-in-law, the Maharaja, feudal to the core, and famous throughout Rajasthan for his valour.

He would wake me at six in the morning, with tea.

'I will introduce you to someone who can train a camel to bring you your cup of tea.'

'Ah, er ...'

'But tea is unhealthy; you must drink hot ghee every morning, like me.'

'Colonel, I—'

'Here, drink it down.'

'Eeeuuusaaggghhh.'

'I am an old man, but look at my chest measurement! Seventy inches! My waist hasn't expanded in forty years! Hot ghee every morning. Today I am going to drive you to Jaisalmer. In the jeep.'

'Jaisalmer?'

'Yes, three days only. We'll leave after breakfast.'

Suddenly I remember the room I was in. And the bed. It was a four-poster. Mosquito nets. With a loo and bathroom attached, but no toilet paper. Instead, beside the loo, a brass pot with long spigot, containing water; beside it a piece of clean white cloth. Whom could I ask? Eventually I worked it out for myself.

So the Colonel and I bumped around the Thar Desert together, calling in to villages of every kind, where everyone knew and venerated him. He wasn't just famous throughout the state, his renown reached all the way to the capital. (Nehru had been his close friend.) There were all sorts of stories about him: for example, how he had shot a dacoit who had hidden in a herd of cows! No one else would risk killing a cow, but the Colonel didn't hesitate. He felled the dacoit with one bullet to the head!

'A dacoit?' I said.

'Yes, the most notorious of all. He would ride in to villages and hack off women's feet to steal the silver from their legs.'

In one village the men rushed out to give us opium; in another, bootleg liquor – a clear firewater with sediment in the bottom.

'What is the sediment, Colonel?' I asked when I could get my breath back.

'Crushed pearls.'

'Colonel, I don't really think I could eat anything …' (My stomach was in rebellion, requiring several stops to shit behind acra bushes.)

'You must eat. I am taking you to a place with a speciality.'

Somewhere hidden in the dunes of the Thar Desert, a minute village with a 'restaurant'; that is, a room in front of which there is an iron vat on a fire, and a man stirring the vat. No electricity. A table almost filling the room. Four chairs. Blackest night. Candles.

I am presented with a bowl and a spoon. I can see nothing, but the spoon clacks against something floating in the bowl. I pull over a candle and there, sticking up out of the fiery soup, are two unclipped goats' hooves.

But the next morning, there is Jaisalmer on the horizon, fuzzy pink in the dawn light, making my furious belly an insignificant price to pay for wonder. For an Australian girl of my background, this hilltop fort rising above desert dunes was hardly believable. It was something I might have imagined as a child in Malabah, after reading *Grimms' Fairy Tales*. Or *Aladdin's Lamp*.

As we drove through the dunes towards it, the Colonel informed me that Jaisalmer was the ancestral seat of his own clan, the Rajput Bhatis. This area had been their desert kingdom until it was integrated into the state of Rajasthan following independence.

Tourism had barely touched the place then, and it looked much as it must have done eight centuries before, when it made its wealth taxing the caravans bringing goods along a branch of the great Silk Road. (Opium was a legitimate trade item until fairly recently and, as my previous two days imbibing it attested, still used in most desert villages.) The entire citadel was made of yellow sandstone, the facades of its mansions carved into lace. Fabulously caparisoned camels swayed past us, arrogant Brahmin cattle pushed us out of the way in the narrow cobbled streets. Breezes funnelling down alleys were cooled by walls of filigreed stone. (I imagined the thousands of men, banging and grinding away with their chisels in the heat and the dust and the noise, labouring to lift the stone three, four storeys up. What mastery and confidence it took to create the coolness of a ravine in this scalding wasteland.)

In afternoon light the sandstone glowed like copper. As Uluru (Ayers Rock) will do, sometimes, after rain. I thought again of how antithetical the Indian aesthetic was to pre-European Australia's. The poetry of hunter-gatherers, in which landscape itself is foreground and animate, humans emerging from and disappearing into it along with all the other species. Versus the aesthetics of agriculture and 'civilisation', in which landscape has become backdrop to the drama of man. In Delhi, someone had said to me, 'I was amazed to hear how primitive your Aborigines must be: that they had owned Ayers Rock for thousands of years, but never thought to decorate it.'

The next day, far from Jaisalmer, we stopped at a cluster of tiny round huts in the desert. The Colonel had finally agreed that I had a fever, and therefore deserved to rest.

I was taken into a hut. The hut was made of clay, straw and dung. Around it, human feet, camel pads, goats' hooves, raised puffs of dust. Soft sounds, like soft low drums, or muffled thuds. Footfalls susurrating, scuffing. Far away, beneath a sandhill, men called at a well. A wheel creaked. Bells sounded through dampening dust. Through the door I saw women swaying away until dissolved in dust. Here, in the cooler dark, metal cooking pots, polished with mud, gleamed so strongly they hurt my eyes. Folded quilts, a few butter lamps, gods in a recess with incense sticks. Beside me, a baby slept in a cloth hammock.

Dust falls on the skin and on the things inside the hut. It lifts from the multitude of feet, wheels, hooves, ploughs and from hands working the ground. It shifts across the continent, settles and lifts. The dust here breathes a vital force, breathes feet, hands, hooves, ploughs, wheels. There is nothing virgin here. The child beside me has already seen millennia …

I was jolted out of my fever thoughts by the Colonel – time to return, to meet Minu, his daughter, Narendra's sister.

The woman who greeted me was cocooned in silk. From her nose, a ring of gold, like a nose peg on a camel. On her legs were weights of gold and silver. Her arms clinked with it, as she made the small movements necessary to adjust the chiffon across her head. When I walked with her, I was conscious of reining myself in. Her steps were the shuffles of legs chained by the softest most watery silk. She did not simply carry wealth, she *was* wealth. She could be, had been, used in exchange. When we walked outside, amidst strangers, she covered her head with chiffon, leaving a little gap for an eye to peer through.

Minu. An exquisite creature from an almost unimaginable world. Yet as often happens in India, she and I fell to talking as if we had known each other since birth.

We did not stop talking for two days. She was a great storyteller, able to do justice to a remarkable life. She was about a decade older than me. Raised in Jodhpur castle during the close of its glory days (pink Cadillacs, polo on elephants), she had been swept along in India's storm of change. Her and Narendra's childhood would have been astonishing enough, living in a labyrinthine palace that looked like a wedding cake. But the family drama was complicated by the fact that neither of them were the Maharajah's children; they were the children of his wife's sister. The Maharani, who had plenty of her own children, nevertheless wanted more, so took the children of her sister to live in the palace as her own.

'Robyn ji, I thought the Maharani was my mother. When we were first brought in I was just a little thing, running around barefoot in the zenana with nobody looking after me. I was ignored and left to myself to grow up. Then one day, the Maharajah who I thought was my father, and who was very frightening to me because I never saw him up close, passed by in his open Rolls-Royce. Well, he saw me and said, "Who's that dirty child dressed in rags?" Someone told him who I was, and he picked me up, and from that day forward I was his favourite. He gave me everything: the best clothes, the best jewels, the best horses, everything he showered on me. That made the others a little jealous, because I wasn't even his proper child, but how he loved me, Robyn ji.'

As for the handsome Colonel, also a favourite of the Maharajah, only later did Minu realise that he was her father. At some point, the children went to stay with their biological parents, though they continued going back and forth to the palace.

'Robyn ji, our father was crazy crazy,' Minu laughed. 'He couldn't bear that we were all short, so he would string us up each morning thinking we would stretch. He wanted us to grow an extra four inches. He refused to believe that girls were any different from boys, so he made us all wrestle with each other, go pig-sticking, play polo. Can you believe, after fathering six children, he still didn't know that women had periods, or if he knew they bled he certainly didn't know it caused discomfort. And all the women in his family, including our mother, were too shy to tell him.'

Minu found these tales of the Colonel's eccentricity hilarious, as did I. There was no hint of resentment or anger. Freud had no place here where the Bhagavadgita ruled. But years later, I would hear darker stories from Narendra, who did bear the scars of that domineering, charming and violent father. Father–son relationships are often fractious amongst the ruling Rajputs. Your oldest son is the one who will kill you in a palace overthrow, who will plot and intrigue against you to inherit your power and wealth. From Minu I learnt that the entire family was in a protracted war with itself even now – plots, threats, law suits, court cases. She was constantly trying to mediate between the warring camps, earning herself the title Little Loti (meaning she would tip one way, then another, like a round-bottomed drinking cup). Modernity might have arrived, but beneath the veneer of overseas educations and ideas of social justice, the old feudal structures were the same as when the courts flourished, the princes went to war over territory and the princesses performed suttee from the palace ramparts.

When the Maharajah died, Minu was married off to a prince in a remote area of Rajasthan. She had met him only for the briefest moment before the marriage, but they had exchanged letters, and of course had been thinking about and imagining each other for years. She was in love with him, she said, and happy to marry him.

But his was a provincial, old-fashioned family, who disapproved of the kind of freedoms a girl like Minu had enjoyed in Jodhpur palace. (Red-painted fingernails, for example.) When she arrived in her new home in Ghanerao, the gates closed behind her and she found herself in a prison whose function was to break her spirit.

Her marriage occurred several years before Indira Gandhi cut the Maharajas' privy purses, casting the former rulers back upon their own hapless incompetence. (Gandhi hated them because they had sided with the British before independence.)

'What could they do, Robyn ji? They were good at nothing but cutting heads, and plotting overthrows. Now they had to find ways of earning a living.'

Some became politicians, others tried to turn their palaces into hotels. A few were successful, others didn't know the first thing about management. Some had been educated in England, but that did not necessarily give them the skills or the desire to abandon feudalism for the experiment of democracy.

In Minu's case, sitting in her palace in a remote little village, there wasn't much hope of an easy transition. When the money strings were so unceremoniously severed, she remembered (shamefully) melting the gold and silver thread out of her sarees to sell.

But most of that turmoil was now behind her. The zenana had emptied; Minu's husband, the oldest son, inherited the property; his exquisite little castle was now a somewhat down-at-heel hotel; the elephant stalls were home to bats; most of the retainers had long gone; the hunting lodge was overgrown and occupied by monkeys; the Dalit, whose function it had been to go through the royal shit extracting the gold leaf ingested with food, had lost his job; modernity had arrived. Inside the castle, Minu and her husband could now live a much less restricted life, though she still had to pull the curtains of the car, or cover her head completely when she went outside the palace gates. She had been allowed out of purdah now to spend time with her birth family, in order to arrange her daughter's marriage to a Rajput boy living in London. Neither she nor her daughter would meet the boy before the marriage. It had been difficult to convince her husband that sending their daughter overseas was best, but she had persevered, wanting to save her daughter from a fate like her own – being locked in a compound at the mercy of harsh in-laws, every action examined, controlled, criticised, punished. Minu had told me curdling stories about the treatment of women in India. Burnt, sacrificed, tortured, sold. She was very concerned with women's rights, wanting to speak out, to make a difference.

One day we were all invited to lunch in Jodhpur palace; there must have been about twenty of the extended family and their spouses, around a table overwhelmed by silver tureens and Lalique crystal. At one point I was flattered by one of the men for being so brave as to travel alone. His wife immediately countered with, 'Well, perhaps as you are so admiring of her freedoms, you will agree to my getting a driving licence?' There were chuckles and then silence.

I myself did not know where I had got my so-called 'courage'. No doubt it had something to do with the games I played as a child – a female isolate in an imaginary and fantastical universe, battling the elements alone. Or perhaps it was because I had looked after myself since my mother's death, as there wasn't anyone else to do so. Self-reliance was a habit of being. But it was also to do with my time, my era. I took freedom as an essential right, accepting that there would be risks attached. I had been punished for that – contempt, threats of violence, violence itself. But there were assets too – as a female I had access to places and people forbidden to men. My particular era – the late sixties, early seventies – had inculcated the belief that there was no such thing as too much freedom, only too little courage. And no one can live too far outside the clichés of their time.

Had I tried to explain myself, at that long opulent table, I might have said that to travel is to leave possessions behind. You have to throw off the weight of things. Your safety rests in a lack of possessions, of having nothing worth stealing. But women carry in their physiognomy something which is coveted by men, capable of being stolen. Unable to divest themselves of this possession, women have found different ways of compensating. Eberhardt dressed as a man; others waited until old age made their sex less covetable. Still others took along a protector – a man, a gun. Travelling for women will always include this added element of self-consciousness. She will be alert to her surroundings in a singular way, unconsciously readying for flight. She will be skilled in camouflage. But the more she hides herself, the cleverer the hunter will be in pursuing her. Yet not to camouflage herself, while travelling in unknown territories, would be the height of recklessness, let alone disrespect. Perhaps more inhibiting than this are the internalised restrictions. Domesticity has been her métier. She is 'supposed' to be domestic. Never mind that she, too, might yearn for the wild places, for the pleasure of returning to our original purpose.

Travelling alone in Australia had been relatively easy. In India, everything worked against it. For one thing, I was immersed in 'servant culture'. I had to give up trying to prepare my own food, carry my own bag, drive a car. In the end I submitted to this lateral distribution of roles, and to a hierarchical structure as stable as a pyramid. This led to a feeling of being physically restrained and self-conscious, constantly watched. As well I had to be super-conscious of modesty. Shirts and trousers, long skirts. Must not be too friendly with men in case I was taken for a loose woman. (And all Western women were loose women, an assumption lent substance by the drug addicts coming into India along the hippie trail, fucking taxi wallas for fifty rupees, or by the beautiful naive Western girls who wandered around with barely any clothes on, or by the blue movies which were very popular even in the most destitute villages because even if there was no sewerage or healthcare or money to buy anything more than necessities, there would be a television set or a video somewhere everyone could watch. And on that television would be the most crass advertising imaginable – houses opulent beyond dreams, where bejewelled women in chiffon sarees floated around their mansions extolling the virtues of Harpic. And on the videos, Western porn. Lévi-Strauss nailed it when he said, 'The first thing we see as we travel round the world is our own filth, thrown into the face of mankind.')

I don't know how long that first period in India was. In memory it feels like weeks, but I know it can't have been more than a few days. At last, when it was time to leave, Minu and I were both close to tears. Such connections are rare in any circumstance, but across such divides, all the more precious. I gave her the book I had with me. *The Golden Notebook*.

Of course I would come back to India — I would stay with Minu in her remote castle, write about her brilliance and courage, preserving her marvellous stories. And I would travel with and write about the Rabari nomads, some of whom were often stationed in her village. The book would contrast the two fates: Minu, as socially elevated as one can be, yet a prisoner, her destiny shaped by sedentary cultures and their relationship to property. A Rabari woman, lowly, yet emblematic of freedom, and embodying the values inherent in nomadism. The project would be a natural segue from the ideas set in motion by contact with Aboriginal Australia. I could see it so clearly, it was practically already written in my mind.

In the meantime, I would have to produce the book about the journey across Australia for which I didn't even have a title. *Tracks* came only after handing in the manuscript. The *Sunday Times* piece had been very popular, so I was fairly confident about writing the book, and looking forward to its completion so I could bring that part of my life to a close, and move on.

Before I left India, a visiting astrologer assured me I would return in August. He was out by about fifteen years.

My new life in London swept India entirely away.

Eleven

Whenever she wasn't working, or making music, our mother worried about the well-being of her children: the one too plump, the other too skinny. Over-pro*tect*ive, as Gil would have said. She took us to a doctor in Nambour who prescribed iron compound for me and speed for my thirteen-year-old sister, who lay awake all night grinding her teeth, and couldn't keep her eyes open the next day. I've no idea how long this situation continued – probably not very long. My mother could have had no idea of the harmful effects of methedrine; it was a common medicine then, dispensed as routinely as aspirin. But again, the incident of the pills lives on as evidence of gross maternal failure.

Was our mother narcissistic enough to worry about her daughter's weight for reasons of her own vanity? Again, this is the inference taken but there are other possible interpretations. Neither my sister nor I were particularly beautiful children. But our mother loved us and was ambitious for us to the point of delusion. She was, as I look back now, a Jewish-ish mother.

My sister was teased at school by the Anderson boys. I wanted to defend her but cowardice made me mute, and

I walked home alone, taking refuge in the cubby house or under the mango tree or in the chook pen, to cry it out. There I would direct my compassion to the chickens or cats, whose sufferings could be alleviated relatively simply.

Of course she wasn't fat at all. She was pubescent plump, healthy and blooming. But wouldn't a mother hate to see her daughter made miserable? Might it not have been worth a visit to a Nambour quack?

We will never know. I do know that the real reason for my runtishness at that time had little to do with iron deficiency, and everything to do with the fact that Georgina Parker's mother murdered her husband.

One evening, I overheard my mother say to my father that Mrs Parker had murdered her husband. This was news to me, and the next day at school, I informed my best friend, Susan Stevens. But something didn't feel quite right about it. So the next day I quizzed my mother. 'Is it really true, what you said, about Mrs Parker murdering her husband?'

My mother's mouth opened and her eyes widened, and she laughed. 'Where on earth did you get that from? Do you want to get me thrown in jail? I hope you didn't say that to anyone. Did you?' She laughed again, and went back to her ironing.

The universe shrank to the size of a pinhead. My stomach rolled over as I saw my mother hauled off by the police.

'No,' I said, and slunk off to the toilet to vomit.

Thus did I vomit every evening, secretly, after dinner, for what seemed like many years. I lay awake at night, living, again and again, the day the police would come and throw my mother in jail, while next to me, my sister ground her teeth.

Eventually the horror passed, as all things do. And after that, I began to grow. I grew eight inches in a year. I grew past the possibility of leaping into my mother's arms, as I was now almost as big as she was. Everyone assumed that the growth spurt was the result of having my tonsils out. But in truth it was because the police continued to fail to turn up, thus gradually eroding the guilt of matricide.

Around that time my sister was sent to boarding school in Brisbane. She was fourteen. What a relief! No more bullying and the whole of Malabah to myself. But on the drive home, as we reached the outskirts of Mooloolah at night, I began to understand ... no more dramaturge for our Sunday-night plays. No more doubles on the back of Prince. No more *Marg*. I broke down and had to be brought into the front seat of the new Holden sedan with the glass gears, my newly enormous upper half cradled in my mother's arms, the suddenly extended lower half soothed by my father at the wheel, over the loss of the person I loved most in the world, and the void of loneliness ahead.

But I've gone ahead of myself again, and left out too much. I've left out the bushfires, when the whole of Mooloolah came together, the men blackened and bleeding from being at the fire front, belting the line with wet sacks, the women relaying water and food to them. I've left out the shearing shed where my father sheared our 240 sheep with electric clippers and my sister and I had to jump up and down in the wool press, while the big green carpet snake gazed benignly down at us from the rafters, and our mother brought lunch from the house – man-sized sandwiches and cordial drinks and tea in big Thermoses – and helped with the wool sorting on the long slatted table while the sheep milled about and panted in their pens, and the air was thick with the smell of lanolin and hessian. And somehow the shearing shed during shearing time, and the bushfires, are important, because at those times, my parents' segregated worlds came together.

It will be understood by now that Mark lived in the paddocks and Gwen lived in the house. I was becoming aware, not just of the rift between the two worlds, but of its implications.

In my mother's world my vocation was obvious – musician, singer, dancer, actress, bookworm (I had already written a little story with pencil in a small notebook, though, presciently, had trouble concluding it) – a product of cosmopolitan values. In my father's world it was equally obvious that I would solve the riddles of nature through scientific enquiry. By then I was beginning to show real musical aptitude, but I was also finding my mother's realm restrictive, and longing for the freedom of the paddocks.

And there was something more ominous in the air. It was as if an incoming tide of apartness was creeping between the two worlds. On some mornings my mother did not get up at 5 a.m. to set about her chores. And sometimes I would see her standing at the sink, just staring out the window with a strange look on her face. During one of the bushfires, a friend from my mother's past came to visit – Bobby Docker. He had a stutter. When he came back from the fire front with my dad, he was covered in soot and cuts. It was plain to see that he wasn't a hero like my father, who seemed to hold Bobby in friendly contempt, and wasn't at all concerned about his cuts. But my mother was concerned, and doctored him with cotton wool, Dettol and sympathy. Bobby Docker didn't stutter when he stood at the piano close to my mother, singing in a fine tenor.

And then there was Nanna. My mother seated at the kitchen table in Sandgate, her head cast down, her thin shoulders drooped; Nanna moving around the kitchen, quietly, as if listening, as if waiting.

I think, however, that I provided some solace for my mother at that time. I remember, quite vividly now that I attend to it, the afternoon that I presented her with a routine I had been working on. I dressed myself up in her old ball gowns, led her in from the kitchen and made her sit in my father's armchair. I put Gracie Fields on the wind-up gramophone, and mimed, 'I'm a char and I'm proud of it too and that's that, though charin's a thing that I 'ate …' There she is, a little, elegant, hollowed-out woman collapsed backwards in an armchair, a tea towel across her knees, laughing, as she might have said, 'to beat the band'. And I can feel the echo of what I felt then – the open, willing sympathy that is a child's love. I notice, too, that she is much younger than I am now.

My father lived in the paddocks and my mother lived in the house. When he entered my mother's territory he had the status of a special visitor. He would sometimes, of an evening, allow me on to his lap as he sat in his armchair, or come to read to me at night – Edward Lear verses, most of which we knew by heart, and would recite to each other, giggling, '"Ploffskin, Pluffskin, Pelican jee, there ain't no birds so happy as we,"' or essays from *Marvels of the Universe*, or *Black Beauty* when we felt strong enough to tolerate the tragic chapters. Yet there was always the sense that he was doing what was expected of him, what he had been instructed to do by his wife. That he, himself, wasn't fully there.

Looking back, I can see that the construction we forged – the family ship – sailed on a bias, its trajectory ever more skewed from true. And that was because my mother was the only one rowing.

To the outside world, my father was a Great Man. Kind, unassuming, heroic, capable, handsome, knowledgeable, ever popular, lovable. And he was, genuinely, all those things and more. But inside the family, the inadequacies showed through those worn places where inner worlds grate against each other.

Only once did I witness his anger. He was in the paddock behind the shearing shed. He thought he was alone. I peeked at him from around the corner. He had the reins of the horse in one hand, and with the other he was laying his stock whip, again and again, across the creature's back as if he would flay it alive. This disturbed me terribly, though I told no one.

And our mother? I know that, even before I came along, on Stanley Park, she was ground down by country life and yearned to return to the city and all that it represented – lively conversation, opera and friends, doctors who weren't a day's journey away, schools and opportunities for her daughters. Loneliness engulfed her; there was so little relief from it, except music and, I suppose, to some extent, her children. But now her children were growing up and away from her. And she was still a long, long way from the city. 'So near and yet so far,' she would say with that wry self-mocking smile of hers. The White Elephant was only sixty miles from Brisbane, but it might as well have been on Mars.

I go back to watching her in front of her mirror, angrily twisting her hair into an 'old maid's' roll, an incident that was probably triggered by my father refusing to give her money. Money for fabric, let's say, for a new dress. She had so very few. I can hear my father now, 'Aw, what do you want a new dress for, darling, you've got plenty,' and he would strike the item from my mother's Brisbane shopping list with his biro, just as he would strike necessities from my own lists when I went to boarding school, years later. He doles out money as if he were peeling off his own skin. It is not just a humiliation, it is a kind of annihilation. Here she is made to understand that she is not an equal companion through life's journey, not even a second-in-command. Everything she gives – her vivacity, her accomplishments, her charm, her grinding work and her mothering, even her body's love – comes already paid for, so to speak, in the marriage contract. It is at these moments my mother realises she is a semi-slave.

How did it get like this? Had she been ashamed for him, in the beginning, when he first displayed the Davidson stinginess? So ashamed she could not bear to 'make an issue of it'? Indeed, protected him from self-awareness by affecting not to notice it? People who want very much to be loved are shy of making demands. And perhaps, after standing up to her mother in marrying Mark, her pride found it hard to admit to his deficiencies. Nanna was always there in the background, waiting to be proved right, and to resume possession of her daughter.

The loneliness outside the marriage was hard to bear, but loneliness inside the marriage wounded and diminished her; her energies were failing, she was over forty and an early menopause was sending messengers ahead of its imminent arrival. Everyone and everything had stopped needing her.

Twelve

What can I say about that young woman who arrived in London at the age of twenty-eight? Was her arrogance in any way different from the generic arrogance of youth? Arrogance does not presuppose confidence. She seemed to have little confidence in her social self, yet obscurely, a deep confidence in her right to make her life. Arrogance of the quiet, watchful kind. Ignorant beyond measure, yet somehow rather enviable.

It shows itself in her quick dismissal of anyone who doesn't measure up to some kind of standard. It's hard to know now how astute she was in those assessments. The standard had nothing to do with accomplishment, social position, talent, status or celebrity. I think it was simply a quest for the genuine without which all accomplishment was mere gloss. Not greatness as measured by the outer world, but greatness within, a much rarer quality, and difficult to define.

Yes, that was what she was looking for. That was what she had always been looking for.

Naturally this judging faculty led to mistakes of omission as well as inclusion. I wonder if I, as I am now, would have made it through the narrow gate of her judgement. I think not. My devotion to doubt, my worn-down ego, like an old stump of tooth, my sympathy for everything that suffers – all this might have been contemptible to that younger self.

Enviably, she found it easy to write. Or if not easy, then at least not the torture it has become for me. The tooth of ego, upon which all desire for expression relies, was strong then and, she assumed, indestructible.

The ones who made it past the gate were afforded an open-heartedness that refused to see any smudge or blemish. These would be her mentors and family.

The first draft of *Tracks* was written in a horrible flat in a horrible part of London during a horrible 'winter of discontent'. There were bombs and strikes and rubbish piling up in the streets. As it happened, my article, which was the cover story of the London *Sunday Times*, was the last before a management lockout shut down the paper in an attempt to tame the print unions. London was in turmoil. The Labour Party was weakened, which would soon lead to Thatcher's election.

But all of that barely impinged on me. I painted the walls of the horrible flat what I thought was an ochre tone but turned out to be more like Ayers Rock at sunset – Central Australian vermilion. Nothing mattered but the writing and the torrent of memory. I remembered every single campsite of the whole eight-month journey. Memory so vivid and present it eclipsed, easily, the world outside the flat. I brought Steve, my new (my first) partner, over from Australia to live with me. He read each chapter as it emerged, and was a wonderful sounding board. Eventually he found work with a free legal and drugs advice service, so was able to bring news of street life inside the vermilion walls.

I noticed that, as I wrote, the memories were being subsumed into the book, such that I no longer had ready access to them. They seemed to blur and fade as the writing progressed, as if the book was cannibalising the reality it described. All that raw material chewed over by the novelising mind, and anything not useful to the purposes of the book, allowed to sink away.

I seem to have been unusually unsophisticated. But a compass needle had led me to Doris Lessing, to a generosity large enough to let a waif in. I met her the first week I arrived in London. She was living in a flat in Kilburn at that time, with her son Peter. It was a gathering, but she asked me to remain behind when everyone had gone home. I sat, literally if I remember, at her feet. Peter in another armchair, gnomically nodding. I gave an account of myself, knowing that only full frankness would win favour. There was courage in that encounter. Stating what I believed, what I was. Certainly it seemed to do the trick. We bonded, if that is the correct word for an affection between an older, much adored woman and a green young girl fresh from the colonies.

She came to visit the horrible flat one day and said, 'Robbie, you can't possibly stay here. You had better come to my place.' She had just bought a big house in Kilburn, with a little self-contained flat at the bottom. I had just finished the first draft of *Tracks* when Steve and I moved in.

I did not show her the manuscript until it was ready for publication. After she'd read it, she came down the stairs to see me, manuscript in hand.

'Well, Robbie,' she said, in a rather severe tone (my stomach fell to the floor), 'it seems you have written a classic.' That she liked it meant more to me than praise from any other quarter. She said, 'Don't bother reading reviews, they won't tell you anything useful about your work, only about current fashions.' I took her at her word, and read none of the reviews when they came in. I left that to Steve, and to my publishers, who nevertheless relayed the good news.

And it was all good news. Thus I became 'famous' all over again, this time as a 'born writer', which was at least a more palatable soubriquet than 'camel lady'. But in my own mind I was someone who had written one successful book, about one discrete part of my life that could not be reprised without descending into kitsch.

But if you write one book that sells mega copies, it is taken for granted that you will write another, whether or not you have anything to say. I had joined the writing factory, and writing factories produce books.

It was at the beginning of the era of writers having to publicise their work, by going on tours, speaking to the press, hawking their wares. Book as consumable. Author as performer. The limelight was unavoidable. I loathed it but over time became good at it. Or good enough. And I understood that it gave me a platform to say certain things. Things which my government (Conservative at that time) did not like. I understood that there was a responsibility attached to having a public voice.

Very quickly after publication, there were people who wanted to make a film of it, the most memorable of whom was Sydney Pollack. He took me to lunch and his opening gambit was, 'Honey, you're not gunna like what I'm gunna do to your book.' I liked him very much for that honesty, we had a jolly lunch, and he offered me a very large sum of money. To which I foolishly said no. I said no because I did not think the book should be sold to Hollywood. I owed it to Aboriginal people to keep some control over how they were portrayed. And as it was a quintessentially Australian story, I felt it should be made, if it were to be made at all, by Australians. Ah, the naivety.

★

I lived in Doris's flat for a couple of years, years spent absorbing absorbing, without being conscious of absorbing. I returned to Australia when crises demanded, or for birthdays, or Christmases or 'holidays'. It was assumed I would and should return. But it was an expensive way to live, and not just financially. I had money for the first time in my life, but did not know how to manage it. I supported people in various ways, but tended to nervous stinginess with myself, interspersed with reckless extravagance when I saw something that I could not possibly live without. That is to say, I was frugal in patches, and hopeless at keeping my money, much less making it grow. Such money was never likely to come again, yet how easily it slipped out of my account, dwindling and dwindling ... This anxiety and inadequacy regarding financial management has never left me, no doubt an inheritance of the Davidson fiscal neuroses, compounded by a feral youth. While it was true that I could be happy living in a humpy on the smell of an oily rag, alas I had a competing eye for quality, and a love of beautiful things.

Crises. A niece, Onnie, whom I loved deeply, perilously ill. My closest friend, Nancy, diagnosed with cancer. My

father's gathering frailness. Gil's gathering frailness. My
sister's grief and upheavals, struggling to raise four girls on
her own. My darling nieces whom I wished, somehow, to
protect from those griefs and upheavals. I wanted to make
my life in London, but the anxieties, responsibilities and
loves constantly pulled me back to Australia. We all wrote
letters to each other in those days. Weeks or sometimes
months spaced the letters. My dad sent me some stories he
had written about Africa (his careful pointy handwriting on
lined Croxley letter paper). They were *Boy's Own* yarns –
safaris, lions, amusing incidents – an Africa a world away
from, say, Doris's Africa which was a politicised Africa. My
father's disgust – yes, not too strong a word – when he read
some of Doris's short stories: sex, race, politics. He worried
for me, I think, in the clutches of such a dangerous woman.
I did not know what to do with his stories.

Smaller memories. The cockatiels I kept, fluttering
nervously around the ceiling of the flat. A jungle of pot
plants by the bay window, as if in defiance of English cold.
Hedgehogs coming into my kitchen to be fed. They were
persecuted by fleas. They allowed me to stroke their noses.
Doris's garden out my back door – Englishness penetrated
by a riotous Africa – pumpkin vines hoisting themselves up
through the roses. Her girlish fear of spiders, calling me to
trap one, or to kill it. Steve suggesting that Doris had blatantly
flirted with him during one of my Australian absences. My
odd pleasure in this. Inviting Bruce Chatwin for lunch
after a phone call. Talking until 6 p.m. A shared interest
in nomadism, but noticing that 'Bru' cared little about
contemporary Aboriginal experience – the aftershocks
of, and adaptations to, colonisation. We inhabited different

bandwidths, but became good friends. Years later I gave him the names of friends in Alice Springs, who became thinly veiled characters in his book, *Songlines*. In turn, he would introduce me to the 'catastrophe'.

Doris sewing African kaftans for me – three of them. My pleasure and embarrassment. I would never wear them, except when going upstairs to watch TV with her and Peter. Her kitchen, the slovenly colonial excess, like the garden. Her cats! Unspeakable feline familiars following her around the house.

Sitting with her in my flat, by the fire. Her anguish over Peter. (She had found a noose up the back yard.) Or enraged with herself because a new book just refused to be born. Why some should come so easily, and others with such difficulty? A mystery.

Realising that another of Doris's waifs was jealous of me. That her dislike wasn't necessarily personal, but rather a sibling rivalry.

Doris's generosity. Her perspicacity. The vast variety of people she would bring into her house, often giving them money. Her good and penetrating mind. Her moral courage.

And then, as time went on, Doris as queen, waifs maturing. The unenviable role of the mentor who becomes no less loveable, but is seen to be less infallible. The insurrection of daughters, then the tolerance of the daughters towards the mother, where before the roles were so clearly in the reverse.

Doris taking me to the opera. (English National Opera, never Covent Garden.) Peter settled into his chair upstairs, like an enormous and tragic toad prince. The three of us watching television together, while all around piles and piles of books, on the floor, spilling out of shelves and on to tables, cats and cat hair, the unEnglishness of all that casual largesse, the colonial largesse. Self-made, inquisitive, generous, singular, complicated, prickly, sexually competitive, brave. I understood all that in her. While from the tiny, rather squalid, primitive kitchen came food for fifty, of such divine wickedness – roasts, puddings, fat, cream, food to fell you into afternoon stupor – delicious, forbidden, old-fashioned food.

Realising all the different ecosystems of love – for the mentor, the father, the sister, the child, the lover, the friend. It seemed to me that I was constantly pulled this way and that to attend to all those loves.

Tracks had come out to clamorous acclaim. I had to do a publicity tour in the States, immediately after a tour in my home country. (Australia came at the bottom of the release list at that time if you were published in the UK.) I had not heard from my dad in a while. Was uncertain whether to send him a copy of the book, or wait until I was to go to Australia in a month's time, so I could take him a copy and be with him when he read it. In the end, I opted to post him a copy, assuming that someone else would do so anyway. I was nervous about him reading it, afraid it might inflame old wounds. There were one or two mild sentences about family suffering midway through the book.

I was taking a brief rest from the publicity demands before heading to Australia. The news came that my father was dead. A stroke. He had been reading *Tracks*, and it was the first sentence that upset him. 'I arrived in Alice with a dog, six dollars ...' He went to Mrs Wallace next door and said, weeping, 'Why didn't I ever give her any money?'

That was the first in a series of losses, each of which had their effect. My father's death, Gil's death, Nancy's death, Onnie's death, the loss of a friendship I thought unassailable, the catastrophic love affair and its aftermath, the death of confidence.

The feeling of having been knocked to my knees each time, and each time a little harder to get up. But keeping going.

And over time the travelling, the reasons for it, changed as well. Previously, living in other places meant an overhaul of comprehension itself, testing whether what had seemed self-evident was really only prejudice. (This kind of testing has dwindled in proportion to the homogenisation of cultures, such that contemporary travel – that is to say, tourism – is more the packaging of elsewhere to entertain an already formed self.) And being away from Australia, I could see it better, as a whole, the easier to write about it, to think about it. But the geographical displacements left me with no sense of ground. As if bits of myself were being flung all over the globe. The writing of books requires at least a modicum of stability. Then too, like anything, upheaval can become a habit. Leaving a place, you have the illusion that constraints are left behind. You feel lighter, fresher. But eventually the comet tail catches up with you, and the heaviness returns. You begin to miss, not so much the other places in themselves, but the self brought into being by those places. Time, too, becomes disordered, scattered, non-linear. You forget what happened where and when. Where you wrote things, or when, or where you left them. Losing things. Losing contexts. Losing the *through-line*.

So I lived in or visited many countries, returned to Australia, left again, returned to London, survived the catastrophe, lived in New York, returned to Australia and, finally, bought the long white room in the East End shoe factory with my friends, a purchase financed by the publication of a novel.

It was a bad novel, and there is nothing more demoralising than publishing a book you already know should be put away permanently in a drawer.

There I came to rest, in Blackbird Yard, surrounded by my possessions, sensing a reckoning was on its way, knowing I had come to the end of something but unable to think where next to go.

In the midst of the floundering, some acquaintances invited me to dinner.

The power of coincidence (synchronicity) on human imagination is irresistible, even when you know it is nothing other than number. But what ego can resist the idea that the universe gives a damn? The chances of Narendra being there were so vanishingly tiny that, in spite of myself, I experienced it as ordained. I had not thought of him for a dozen years.

He said, 'You don't look well. Come to India, stay with us. Do that project with the nomads you said you wanted to do.'

So that Christmas, having nothing to hold me in place, I went.

Thirteen

I was about eight when my mother first went away. By then I was taller than any of the girls my age at school, and an early pubescence was sending messengers ahead warning of its imminent arrival. I don't remember being conscious of where she had gone, or why. I felt no anxiety over the separation that I recall. Rather the opposite. Gil had come to stay, and that would mean freedom.

There was to be a fancy-dress ball. Dressing-up had always been a significant part of childhood life. Whether it was my mother's ball gowns, relegated, like the previous life they signified, to a wooden chest on the sleep-out, or whether it was the outfits she made for fancy-dress occasions, or whether it was the make-believe get-ups my sister and I wore in the 'blizzards' of tropical Queensland, the theatrical was always there, as natural to us as the prosaic reality it dramatised. I seemed, usually, to have been a fairy, and there is a photograph of me at Stanley Park, posed as such, under a gum tree. My sister has been Britannia, a Gypsy queen wearing bangles and reading palms, and, most stunning of all, she has been Night. That dress was long, flowing and made of layers of black tulle. I was allowed in for the fittings. A crescent moon and silver stars were stitched into the tulle, and she held a celestial wand. I can't remember what was in her hair – a crown, I suppose. She was simply the most magnificent being I had ever seen. When I requested to go as a bride, even my mother thought this a bit unimaginative, but conceded to my conventional vanities. So I went in white 'bridal gown' with a bouquet and veil and was very happy, both with myself and with my glamorous sister. Night and day.

But who was there now to dress me up? My sister in boarding school. My mother, somewhere, but not here. My father down the paddocks. And Gil in her slacks and manly felt hat.

Gil hauled out the 'Alice Blue' gown, made for me before my growth spurt. It was crushed, the hoops were bent, the forget-me-nots crumpled. The bodice was now so tight I couldn't do it up, and a big safety pin had to be used. The hem had risen to my calves. I stood in front of the long mirror, in tears, and said I didn't want to go.

'Oh, don't be so silly. You look perfectly fine.' My mother would have understood immediately the impossibility of showing up in an 'Alice Blue' gown that was humiliatingly wrong in every way and with which I had to wear lace-ups because I had grown out of my court shoes. But my mother had gone away, leaving a gap, and Gil, the substitute, only made the gap more deeply felt. It was only then it dawned on me that something had gone badly wrong.

My mother was in a psychiatric hospital in Brisbane, for the first in a series of electroshock treatments. My own memories here begin to fade out. Whether that is to do with my mother's illness, or because of the enormous changes occurring, or because my child's brain was pupating into an adolescent brain, I have no way of knowing. I remember crying under the mango tree after I'd been told that we were to leave Malabah. Otherwise, recollection enters a fogbank, and when it emerges on the other side, I am an entirely different person, and so is my mother, and my sister has grown up and wears Miss Balmain perfume, and there are no more paddocks for my father and me to roam in, and Malabah has vanished. We sold up just before the land boom, which would have made us rich. Mark's 'rotten damn luck' again.

What was Malabah? Something unaccountable. That I haven't even given a gist of it is to be expected. But the gulf between any gist I might give, and what Malabah really was, is so vast and enigmatic that it seems ludicrous to equate them.

It belonged to everyone, but was different for everyone. It is a dust of seeds containing pale, flickering images which bloom for an instant out of black space, then they are gone again. If I reignite one of them, I notice that it has changed. These motes of memory-matter, memory-light, are separated by distances of interstellar proportion, so that if I am to make any sense of it at all, I have to fill in those spaces with imagining.

And what about the characters left out or given bit parts? Mad Valerie, for example, who leant over the McPhersons' back fence whenever my father and I strolled through the paddocks, and yelled out, with a big friendly grin, 'Bbbb ... bbbb ... black snake,' the only words available to her, and which, once out of earshot, my father would mimic, always ending our laughter with, 'Poor old Val.' Or Harry Crack, who listened in to everyone's telephone conversations on the 'party line', and who saved petrol on the drive back from Nambour by cutting the corners, and cutting the engine on downhill slopes. And his shop, from which, after school, we bought, for a ha'penny, cubes of frozen cordial ice, wrapped in greaseproof paper. And what about the animals who shared our lives – those separate bandwidths of consciousness, whose strange Malabahs were contained between a wag and a growl, a miaow and a hiss, who nevertheless had their doggie or feline singularities? It makes me think of a Malabah without us, in the deep past as my father might have described it, as we strolled through the kikuyu grass together. A place contained by reptile minds; a place, perhaps, lacking the colour green. Or in the future, transformed in the perceptions of creatures with equipment different from our own.

My Malabah is a fresco of its time – post-war, unified in the objects we used, in our clothes, in the words we spoke or did not speak, in people's expectations and the way they behaved towards each other – that old ethical substratum communities used to have. How much of it is original, and how much is my own restoring work, I cannot say. Most of it is lost, and all of it is so full of mystery.

The gumboots under the house, my father showing me how to check them for centipedes. Do I remember turning them upside down and banging them on the ground, or am I imagining it? Then, *poof*, I am holding his hand down in the paddocks; it might be an hour later or years later … It might be in the close, narrow paddock which slopes down the hill below the cow-bails, or it might be in the far paddock by Mooloolah Creek, where whipbirds call a pure long note, then crack the air like gunshot, and I seem always to be chattering to him about science; subjects that make the chest swell to bursting with the wonder of it all, the uncontainable joy of it all ...

Then, too, my mother's death, still in the future here, still unimaginable, nevertheless has flowed back in time like bad blood, making a lucky childhood septic with what would one day happen. Beautiful Malabah, where it is always humming with sunshine, and each day is the beginning of creation and nothing is sullied, yet a shadow falls across it from that future event.

After Malabah, the foggy, purgatorial zone, then the underworld, which is so much harder to describe. Even to recall it involves a certain amount of shame.

Fourteen

Of all the houses I had lived in since childhood – over fifty before I gave up counting – Narendra's house in the Himalayas was the one that exerted the greatest pull on me.

But how to describe a house which, unlike a sentence, has a random (ungrammatical) structure producing all sorts of thoughts, like proliferating rooms, as in need of taxonomy as leaves? Well then: its first category, its kingdom if you like, was altitude.

At eight thousand feet the air had a sharp quality; nothing was out of focus. Sound, particularly thunder, rolled around the slopes unmuffled. Storms could be extreme – horizontal sleet blasting from the north-eastern side, from the line of shattered white peaks along the horizon. Usually, sunlight blazed down, so that you were pleasantly crisped when you stood in it, only to shiver in the shade. As well there were the transformations of monsoon, when oaks grew beards of lichen; fungi fruited from earth, trees, logs; dry gullies became waterfalls; leeches longed for you to pass by. Rain came down so heavily on the roof that you ducked instinctively. In between the downpours, there were mushrooms to gather; langurs and martens shaking their fur; pie dogs coming out from under some shelter, asserting themselves across the valley; wiry little women hurrying down the paths carrying great bundles of firewood on their heads.

The original bungalow was built of local stone at the turn of the twentieth century, by an English army engineer. He tucked the house into the nape of a mountain, protected from the force of those freezing storms.

The second taxon was its 'remoteness'. (Remote from the hubs of modernity.) There were no roads to the house. You had to climb through four thousand feet of oak jungle and terraced fields to reach it. (The Himalayas are young; time has not worn them down. Their slopes rise too confidently above you, making you dizzy even when you stand still.) Everything had to come up by pony, or carried on the backs of men. Phones and electricity only appeared in latter days and remained unreliable.

The third and most important quality, yet the most difficult to capture, was the aura of … I would like to say sanctuary, but it was more than that … it was a kind of force field Narendra generated, the sense that you (his partner, his guests, his dependants, his servants) were so protected that nothing would, or could, go wrong. He did not need to be physically present to create this atmosphere. His influence underpinned everything. With deceptive grace, he organised the complex, burdensome and interdependent systems that made such a life in the mountains (in India) possible. By extending a prodigal generosity that was as natural to him as breathing, by taking all difficulties on to himself and never revealing his own worries, you were made to feel that within his ambit, you could relinquish whatever troubled you, and simply be.

It was like a spell that enveloped the place, and even now, when I recall the house as it was then, I imagine it contained in a transparent sphere or bubble, something that would lift and float away without its Sahib to anchor it.

The first time he took me there, we drove up via a tiger reserve not far (as the crow flies, but far enough on treacherous mountain roads) from the house. On the way, we saw an elephant and her mahout by the side of the road. Narendra stopped and talked to the mahout. Rather than going into the reserve, he decided we would take this elephant through the jungle on our own, away from tourists. So I found myself on a square wooden board that was like an upturned bed, on top of an elephant, crossing a broad shallow river, then heading up a steep slope through dense jungle. The elephant was like a tank, forging its own path up the muddy inclines, using its trunk to rip branches away in front of us. After an hour or so, the mahout pointed excitedly at the ground.

'*Pag. Baag ka pag!*' Narendra and the mahout conferred.

'What is he saying?' I asked.

'Nothing … you don't worry …'

But then came a noise that went straight past the frontal cortex and into the amygdala, raising hair all the way down my back. The roar of a tiger, not forty feet away. We were at the top of an incline, still in dense forest; the tiger was at the top of a separate incline – a steep little valley between us. The elephant reared, trumpeted and waved its ears. We clung to the corners of the upturned bed. The mahout and his elephant got us out of there as quickly as they could.

Later the mahout told us that he was from Assam. Why had he moved from there?

'The stomach takes you to strange places,' he replied, accepting Narendra's generous payment.

Indeed the stomach does. In my own case, I had located the nomad project in Rajasthan, looking for a group of migrating herders who would take me with them. Foolishly perhaps, I had taken funding from a magazine, which meant I had to find a group to migrate with as quickly as possible, whereas it would have been more sensible to postpone everything, learn the language and do proper research. The Rabari were nervous of including a Westerner, saying, 'If something happened to you we would be held responsible and the government would punish us.' In one village the women had taken me in and made a great fuss of me. Success at last, I thought. A few days later word came from that village that although the women had liked me very much, and would enjoy nothing better than to take me with them on migration, alas, as I was obviously a man dressed as a woman, they might get pregnant, and so, regretfully, they had decided against it.

Almost a year had passed in this manner, scouting all over the Thar Desert with Koju Singh – a young Rajput driver provided for my services by Narendra, who was helping me in every way possible. I was still in contact with his sister Minu, but the family feuds, fed on jealousies, paranoia and resentment, were claiming her, and Narendra was, I believed, being scapegoated. I had not wanted to choose sides in the internecine war, but perhaps it was inevitable that I would have to choose his. It was also probably inevitable that we should eventually become lovers. He said he had fallen in love with me all those years ago, at Jodhpur airport. (The girl in the cowboy hat.)

He knew he was taking on a broken person, who would not necessarily be able to reciprocate his selflessness and care. I was not 'in love' with him. That capacity seemed to have been excised by the catastrophe. He understood that. Whether it hurt him I have no way of knowing. What did I provide for him in return? I think perhaps it was that the idea of me in his life gave him the imaginary possibility of escaping the tribulations of that life. And this, knowing that I was in some way useful to him, alleviated my guilt at my lack of reciprocity.

In Indian society, such an affair had to be carefully managed. Narendra slowly accustomed his staff to the idea that I was the Memsahib, whether we were married or no. They were already pretty inured to Sahib's unconventional love life. He had divorced his wife (an arranged marriage), which in Rajasthan at that time was outrageous. Not only that, he then conducted a very open affair with a wonderful dancer and artist, showing such flagrant contempt of conventional morality that it almost ended his political career.

So, under the protecting net of his social manipulations, and quite happy not to enter the fenced-off areas of his life which, at that time, included obligations to his immediate family, I was slowly absorbed into a structure different from anything I had previously known.

I retain an image of him from when we first met. He was dressed in white jodhpurs and kurta, seated in the middle of a vast green lawn. A local barber was shaving him, while peacocks as gaudily dressed as maharajahs posed on the stone fence and called like cats. I rather mistrusted him then, I think. Certainly I could not have imagined that in a decade, we would be a couple, sitting together by a bonfire on his Jodhpur farm, listening to the greatest musicians the Thar Desert has produced. The old leader, Rana Khan, singing some of his repertoire of 3,000 songs – oral histories of Hindus and Muslims, village people and courtiers, kings and heroes, goddesses and gods – his right arm gesturing emotional meaning. Mohan tending the bonfire, getting drunker and drunker on Sahib's rum. (Mohan was a Jogi, or Gypsy, descended from the first Gypsies who left India to find their way to Europe. These particular Jogis were itinerant hunters, but there was little left to hunt, and, as the lowest of the low, they were without access to resources. Narendra invited Mohan and his community to live on the farm. In return Mohan was to provide the table with a grouse or a pheasant occasionally, and tend the fire when the musicians arrived from Jaisalmer, to sing for their patron until three or four in the morning, when everyone at last, intoxicated by booze, music and the glittering desert night, staggered off to bed.)

All very wonderful, but as for the project … It was turning into a farce. The naive romanticism of the initial conception – those beautiful people camped in the dunes of Pushkar – had been well and truly scotched by reality. The difference was not of degree but of kind. The hardness of their lives, the fear they lived in, the constant anxiety because the end of their way of life was imminent. Governments always seek to settle nomads who are hard to control, hard to tax. And in Rajasthan, the traditional relationship between herders and farmers, a reciprocity beneficial to both, was being broken down by industrial farming practices, by government programmes penalising mobility, and by the sheer pressure of population on forests and grasslands. Migration, once a cause for pleasure and pride, had become a losing battle against the forces of settlement.

In the end I had to give up on Rajasthan, and crossed the border into Gujarat to find other groups of Rabaris who might not be under such pressure. Within a couple of weeks I had found a family happy to take me with them, part of an exodus of a million sheep and their herders, spilling out of Kutch, heading south and east to find grazing. There was no time to adequately prepare, but I grabbed the chance, reasoning that it might be unlikely to come again.

Travelling with them was the most gruelling and distressing thing I have ever done. I was ill and beyond exhaustion most of the time. So were they. My admiration of and affection for them was boundless. And though those terrible months tested me past endurance, they nevertheless confirmed my belief in the value of nomadic lifeways – the kinds of human qualities they foster.

Eventually I would write a book about the experience, which was like an evil twin to *Tracks*. *Desert Places* was about failure. It was an angry book, an anger not focused at the inequities of India so much, but beyond that, at the needless suffering inflicted on my species by my species.

The Himalayan house provided a reprieve from that anger. I could suck my lungs full of the crystalline air, grateful to be above the dust, disorder and frustration of the plains. And it was the one place where Narendra and I could forget our difficulties for a while, be together and relax.

After an overnight trip from Delhi, you'd arrive at the tiny train station where the plains ran slap bang into the hills. Here you could read the history of tectonic plates colliding, in the geological ripple of hills. One plate, broken away from Gondwana, carrying the Indian subcontinent on its back, had drifted north until it slammed into the Asian plate. Here was the visible line where that inconceivable force had crumpled the earth until it formed the highest mountains on the planet.

In the cool dawn light, you would load the jeeps, then begin the climb up the narrow road, winding up raw precipices of fractured rock, and as you climbed you could feel your previous life lifting from your back like drying mud. You would reach the little village at the end of the road, load the ponies, then begin the long walk up, Hanuman the manager ahead, carrying a rifle in case there were bears, over an hour climbing up the stony paths, lungs like bellows working the thin air, the little labouring ponies with legs of steel stumbling over the stones, over the trickling boundary creek where once a partly burnt body had left behind a hank of hair and flesh on its long journey down to the Ganges; and further up still, through the thickest part of the jungle where leopards left their pawprints and their scats, up past the pony shed until you could hear the barking of a dog way up above, and you'd call out, 'Maliki Maliki,' at the top of your voice, and five minutes later you'd hear him hurtling down towards you in a frenzy of joy because you have returned to him; and up further still until you'd arrive at the seat with a full view of the peaks, and you'd sit for a while, Maliki still twisting with delight beside you, then through the gate, to the house ... at which point you would notice that you had already penetrated the bubble or sphere or spell, where everything superficial and worrisome had sloughed away, and been left behind.

If Sahib was with you, the arrival would be a rather more tumultuous affair. Buckets of hot water would be brought, and when the hubbub of servants unloading the ponies and carrying in the far too many suitcases Sahib always travelled with because that's how he was, and the buckets filled with hundreds of roses picked that morning on the Delhi farm had been placed throughout the house, and the enormous quantities of food – meats and birds and fish from the markets, fruits and vegetables of every kind, sweets and chocolates and other surprises (and always, alcohol) – had been stored into cupboards, pantry and attic, then Sahib would say, 'Relax, Memsahib, you're home.'

We would sit on the veranda together, our feet in buckets of hot water, gazing out over the hills stacked behind each other like sheets of blue glass all the way down to the plains, while he poured his first Old Monk rum with Coke, and I would be brought an Indian champagne mixed with hand-squeezed pomegranate juice by Bishan or Chandrawallab or Bippin or Mahesh – local peasants whose fields scooped around the hills below us, who worked for Sahib, because Sahib provided security in the precariousness of their subsistence economy.

It took me a long time to accustom myself to the idea of 'servants' – so contrary to the Australian egalitarian grain. At first I tried to do things for myself – carry my own bags, dig in the garden, saddle the ponies – which behaviour was met with strained embarrassment on their part.

'No need to call me Memsahib,' I would say. 'Call me Robyn.'

'Yes, Memsahib.'

In a country with no government-provided safety net, an employer like Narendra was a source of protection that went beyond mere money. He was someone to petition when things went wrong. To act as a line of defence against corrupt police, corrupt bureaucrats, corrupt politicians; to furnish loans for marriages that did not accrue the crippling interest charged by local moneylenders; to provide access or bribes to obstructive or punitive agencies, to make generous donations to the temple, to be a bulwark against the whole rotten structure that people without influence in India are prey to. It was a paternalistic arrangement, but unlike the cold cash interchange of my own culture, it involved a complex human reciprocity that was so nuanced, I would never, in all the years I lived in India, get the hang of it. Yet when I bring to mind the people I love, certain of the staff and retainers, with whom I do not even share a language, are there at the forefront. Koju, my driver, who once said he would die for me if necessary. I did not doubt that the handsome young Rajput, whom I secretly christened Dreamboat, meant what he said. Bishan, a local Brahmin peasant who was head servant at the house. In another setting, with different opportunities, he could have been anything. Brilliant, refined, wise, beautiful. Chandrawallab the head gardener. An artist in spirit and a hopeless alcoholic whose flower arrangements were so exquisite that he was always forgiven for his binges. Mahesh, who cooked like a Chelsea chef. Hanuman, an extraordinarily gifted person. Dungar ji, Sahib's number one, a gentle giant of a man in whose presence you felt utterly safe. So many more, all of them so talented and able it was wrong that they should be so precariously employed, the only protection they had being the good conscience of their employer. But they did not see it that way, and nor did Sahib.

Narendra was progressive and maverick in his politics, 'modern' in his outlook, though he retained the authority and demeanour of a Rajput lord. But unlike many of the ruling caste I would meet, Narendra was also noble in character. That is, his instinct was to protect everyone in his domain, to take on responsibilities and burdens. But had he been cruel, stupid or mad, he would have received the same deference, if not respect and loyalty.

The world he inherited had ideals at odds with modern ideologies. In that world, deference to one's elders, to those of higher status, was automatic, and the idea of hierarchy entirely natural. If I ever teased him about this, he would say, 'I'm no ruler, I'm a kulak. And come the revolution you lot will have my head anyway.'

His mind contained many more layers than my own. By that I mean that the feudal structures of ancient India were still available to him. The 'modern' part of his mind was where it was easiest for us to meet. But the effort to understand the deeper layers was more compelling. In a sense Narendra WAS India to me, a portal through which to understand its fathomless complexity.

'Don't try to understand,' he would say, whenever I grabbed my head in bewilderment and frustration at some impenetrable or appalling new discovery, 'just absorb.'

The mountains were remote in another sense: we were immersed in a peasant reality as old as the dawn of agriculture – its dangers more primitive and acute than those of more pampered societies.

At first I had been cavalier about those dangers, and laughed when a well-meaning neighbour said, 'Madam, please do not go out unescorted. The bears will eat your face and other soft parts …'

The staff would urge me to take a couple of men with me if I wanted to go for a walk. But I found the protection restrictive, and longed to treat the jungle as I had treated the Australian bush, where I could venture anywhere I pleased, without even thinking about my place in the food chain. In the mountains, I came to understand viscerally what it is to be prey.

One day I took a group of staff and locals for a long walk down the slopes to a river gorge five thousand feet below. It was to be a holiday, a picnic. Along the way they told me stories (my Hindi was improving by then. Nobody spoke English). The story of the boy who had been stalked by a tiger only a few years before, along that very river. The tiger had leapt on to him from behind, clamping his neck – a quick kill. The story of a local woman who had fallen out of a tree while gathering wood, and broken her back. Her companions wedged her between two big rocks, and left her there for months until the spine healed, bringing her food, water and warmth every day, from the home village a few miles below. The story of the two boys who had climbed a tree to escape a bear. It had climbed up after them, disembowelled one and killed the other. The story of the woman gathering grass who was bitten by a cobra, and died while they carried her down to the village. The stories of the children taken by starving or wounded leopards at night. (One aspect of rural poverty is the lack of latrines. People are vulnerable at night when they go to the fields to shit.) They told me that in the tiny government schools, teachers often did not bother to show up. Doctors and vets in the government clinics often did not bother to show up. The government dispensary had no drugs: they had all been sold on the black market. My neighbours were amused by my outrage, my belief that this could be changed.

I was still a mountain novice when I made a ten-day pilgrimage to the peaks, walking and climbing all the way, accompanied by three of the staff. For them it was literally a visit to the gods. I took Maliki with me, and on the way back I finally learnt my lesson. I had convinced my companions to walk on ahead to pick up supplies, while I set up camp and built the fire, there in the deep jungle. They were extremely reluctant, warning me that the jungle was dangerous, that I should not be left alone, but eventually I persuaded them. This would be my first night in a tent, rather than in the bleak cement bunkers with bolted iron doors that were night accommodation provided to pilgrims. I gathered wood and got the fire going; night fell. All was as it should be – firelight, dark trees moving above me, a glittering sky showing between the branches. Suddenly, Maliki jumped into my lap, quivering. I shone my torch out into the leaves, to see the glowing eyes of a leopard circling around us. I strapped Maliki to me, while I sidled along the ground to gather wood to build up the fire – my only defence. But that wood would soon be used up, and I could not go further out from the fire without risking the leopard's pounce. Would the men return before the torch went out, or the fire burnt to nothing, or I had to sacrifice Maliki to my own safety? When they did return an hour or so later, they made Maliki and me sleep crammed between them in their tent. They took turns stoking the fire all through the night. They did not say, 'We told you so.'

As months, then years gathered, the mountain house became a home. By then I was commuting back and forth from London, visiting Australia, travelling in other countries, often to investigate nomadism, trying to keep the different segments of life bound in coherence. I had begun to make friends in Delhi, particularly with one family whose affections were then, and still are, of primary importance. And slowly I had become integrated into the structures of mountain life. Every few months, according to the Hindu calendar, I would attend the goat sacrifices at the little jungle temple not far from the house. People walked from their villages many miles away to attend, all of us bathed and in our best clothes. To me, this ritual addressed something as old as human consciousness itself – the guilt and necessity of life consuming life; the sacral nature of killing. And the sacrifice would also propitiate the forces to which human life was vulnerable. Would address the anguish of being able to imagine tomorrow, but unable to know what it will bring. Propitiation. Expiation. Guilt. Reverence. Anxiety. Bet hedging. All the flavours of disquiet in that bedlam inside our heads.

The deed would be performed by a Kshatriya or warrior caste. (A Rajput.) The trusting little goat, so used to humans, would be led to the temple, and offered to the deities. We would gather around, some of us a little apprehensive. (How the sacrifice unfolded would influence the future. And Bishan and I were always squeamish.) The sword would lift, and whoosh, in a nanosecond, what had been alive, had become ... what? The head (which always, to me, bore a puzzled expression) was placed at the temple entrance. The body was quickly hung in a tree to be butchered. The liver was seared immediately on waiting coals, then pieces handed out to everyone present as prasad. Inside of five minutes, we had ingested the essence of that goat-life. The rest of the meat was sent down to the house, to be curried in a huge metal vat over a fire, and distributed to all who would eat flesh. (And here in the impoverished hills, many Hindus pragmatically did; even Brahmins, if they got the chance.)

There could be bitter rivalries and jealousies in the villages, usually over land and inheritance. But when there was a death, all feuds were put aside. I was invited to come and pay my respects to a dying man in one of the farmhouses close by. There must have been forty people there, some having walked for many miles, up and down mountain pathways. Neighbours crammed themselves into the little room, to sit beside the bed, while others waited outside on the stone porch. People commiserated with the soon-to-be widow, with the sons and daughters, with the ill man himself, who despite his fragility managed to welcome people, acknowledging their effort. Due respect was paid, not just to the family, but to Death.

Ostensibly I went to the mountain house to write, but really I went there to reconnect to the wildness and silence of a deeper, older world.

I would arrive at the bench after the long climb, then amble along to the house, to greet and be greeted by the staff, everyone grinning and pleased that Memsahib was home, because Memsahib was not only soft-hearted, she provided a conduit to Sahib. And Memsahib was delighted to be with them, even though there was a chasm of separation, however sincere the affection. They welcomed me, they fed me, they looked after me, as I did my best to look after them. And understanding my temperament, they left me alone.

At first, the isolation would be deeply felt, and uncomfortable. I had to turn back into myself, dig into my own reserves. It was of a different kind to the loneliness of London. In solitude, in the wild places, something essential within begins to respond. The trivial struggles to get purchase. A different way of being comes foreground, while peripheral anxieties retreat. I had experienced something similar in the Australian desert, after months of walking in solitude, and I had been immersed in a similar state, as a child, in Malabah. It is a re-experiencing of the self as a node in a network – fundamentally connected to all that exists. It is, paradoxically, the opposite of loneliness. But you must be able to tolerate a lot of loneliness to get there.

In the mountains, what or how my peers thought was no longer of use to me. Their concerns existed within given structures which had fallen away. I had moved inside this other frame from which I looked out. And from inside this frame, I had to ask the question: What can be shed, what is worth holding on to? With what faculty does one make that choice? Can one ever be entirely inside another frame?

Whenever I returned to the London frame, everything seemed thin by comparison. People seemed hollow, and full of words. Just as, when I re-entered my own culture after the long journey across Australia, it appeared insane to me.

I went for long solitary walks through the jungle, was aware of sun and weather, immersed in a different kind of time. I studied the fungal life of the forest. In the evenings, with little to distract me, I taught myself to draw. I read deeply, in a way that had become almost impossible in London. Quiet, absorbed reading.

Once, I read all of Shakespeare's history plays, staging them in my mind, and for days afterwards, steeped in his language, stumbled through the jungle, talking to myself in iambic pentameter.

It struck me that the plays cast light on aspects of Narendra's experience. The collapse of feudalism and the rise of early capitalism. The old power networks based on favours, mutual obligations, under pressure from a different kind of exchange. Narendra was dedicated to the democratic process, had faith in the intelligence (and unpredictability) of the voting masses. Whereas democracy was something I either took for granted, or had lost faith in, I was never sure which.

In the early days of our acquaintance I could not have imagined that someone so remote from my experience would become so dear to me. And I had not seen, then, the selflessness of his nature: a kind of loving I had not experienced before.

On one occasion I had arrived in the mountains after weeks with the nomads, and was very ill. (I found out later it was hepatitis. There were no medicines or doctors.) I collapsed for three days, waking out of semi-delirium to find, without fail, Narendra seated beside the bed, reading, or snoozing, or drinking his rum. Always there.

Fifteen

In latter years I went to the house to write about my mother. I had reached the age at which she died, and it was as if she had been waiting beneath the cement, to crack it open. Memories emerged I had thought obliterated. Or perhaps they weren't true memories at all, I didn't know. I wrote bits and pieces, yet from the very beginning, organising it, making something of it, was difficult beyond measure. For whom was I doing this, and why? Above all, whom might I offend? The writing stalled and stalled. A hundred beginnings thrown away, pages and pages of notes stored in boxes, then forgotten. Nothing seemed quite right, or quite true, the memories too scattered, too untrustworthy. Everything I wrote was like debris in a centrifuge, at the core of which, exerting all the power, that purely mathematical point, my imaginary mother.

I sat at my desk, squeezing out a sentence here, a paragraph there, but soon enough my mind would leave the room and I would be gazing out over the jungle canopy, over the hills stacked behind each other like blue glass, down towards the plains. High up in the thin clean air, surrounded by forest protecting leopards and bears, I would think, how did I get here, so distant, in every way, from where I began? I could make out no direct line here, only a series of detours, shuntings, sidings, hold-ups, dead ends ... From up here, I thought, I should be able to make out some sort of trajectory. Something designed or imposed by will. A *narrative*.

I stared out, over the stone bird bath we had built years before, where Himalayan magpies, their long blue tails seeming to hamper their movement, came to drink. Or langurs sat, swinging their legs, or brown and yellow martens leapt and chased each other up and down the old walnut tree.

... stared out over the bird bath, over the forest, over oceans ...

★

I am observing Malabah from a position slightly to the left of the main gate and above the bougainvillea. The figure in the kitchen comes in and out of view, though the kitchen would not have been visible from this position. She is incorporated into this scene in the same way that a movie will change from a long shot to medium or portrait. She is concentrating on her tasks. Cooking, cleaning, ironing, sweeping, polishing, wiping the back of her hand across her hot forehead. She is working as a small creature will work to find food before a hard winter. A little person, neat and careful with her appearance, attractive. There are some things that I know about her. For example, she usually wears dresses rather than slacks. She listens to *Blue Hills* on the wireless, and Sunday-evening plays from the BBC. She plants flowers in the garden, in the 'rockery' she made. She is alone most of the day while her husband is down in the paddocks. There is a black telephone on the wall. The phone number is 81. She receives the *Women's Weekly* and books sent from the city. When she has read the magazine, she gives it to her children, to make paper dolls with. The dolls are kept in a shoebox under the settee. There seems to be nothing terribly wrong with this industrious, competent little woman, other than loneliness. She stops for a moment, the tea towel thrown over her shoulder, and stares through the kitchen window as if staring at a trackless desert in front of her.

Her youngest child has just come home from school, a welcome distraction from the desert. 'Give Mummy a hug, darling.' The child runs across the kitchen and bounds like a monkey on to her mother's body, legs around her waist, arms around her neck. The woman laughs and hugs the child, then lowers her to the ground. She spreads butter and Vegemite on bread. She puts the pieces on a plate which she hands to her child. The child takes a bite, then takes the mother's hand and leads her to the lounge room. The woman throws the tea towel over her shoulder again, and slumps backwards into the armchair. The child goes to the gramophone, stands on tiptoes, lowers the heavy round needle on to the record, and begins to mime for her mother, in a working-class English accent.

'"I'm a char and I'm proud of it too, and that's that, though charin's a thing that I 'ate."' Or perhaps it was '"Walter, Walter, lead me to the altar …"'

The woman throws back her head and laughs, showing the gold filling in her mouth.

The older child isn't home from school yet. Or perhaps she is unsaddling Prince, down by the shearing shed. In any case, she is not witness to this collusion.

My mother told me that when I was born …

'When you were born I wanted to stand on the roof of the hospital and shout for joy.' I have been told, by friends who are mothers, that sometimes a baby comes along with whom the mother falls in love. It's not that she doesn't love the other children, but this one, for reasons unfathomable – a kick of hormones? A surge of euphoria at the cessation of agony? Friends across eons meeting again? – is for her, in the moment of severance from her body, her beloved. The passion fades but what remains is a kind of complicity.

I've also been told that sometimes, after a birth, if a woman suffers depression, she will not find it easy to look into her baby's face. She will feel more comfortable if the baby faces away. Is this why Auntie Pol, the good stick, was invited out to Stanley Park to help Gwen? But that was later, wasn't it? When I was three? Was there perhaps some early break between my mother and my sister? Could that be an explanation for their difficulty? Or was our mother depressed after my birth, and could not cope with the demands of the older child?

After my birth, at Stanley Park, the nights spent pacing up and back along the battered linoleum of the corridor. Hot dry nights, the itching smell of dust, a kero lamp burning in the kitchen. The baby wheezing and struggling for air. Did Mark help carry the new baby up and down the corridor? Did he help with the older child, now so horribly replaced? I cannot see him.

This is woman's work. Enough to melt flesh off her bones. There is no electricity in the house yet. No telephone. A pedal wireless so that she can teach her oldest child 'correspondence lessons' for a couple of years before the school opens in Giligulgul. Still she finds time to play the piano and violin, to read the Penguin paperbacks sent by post from the city, to write letters once a week with a Parker fountain pen on blue Croxley paper, to grow vegetables and a few hardy flowers, to gather neighbours around 'once in a blue moon', for a 'sing-song round the piano'. And once in a blue moon, when Mark is still up in the top country ringbarking brigalow, and the older child is at school, or playing with pebbles and sticks in the sandy creek bed, she puts the baby into the reed washing basket on the back veranda, and bakes scones for a Devonshire tea with her friend Zoe. Tinned strawberry jam and whipped cream. She and Zoe together on the veranda of Stanley Park, laughing their heads off, or practising a performance together at the piano.

"'Funiculee, funiculaa, funiculee, funiculaaaaaa, echoes sound afar: funiculee, funiculaaaaaa ...'"

★

When *Desert Places* was published, I returned to Australia for the book tour. That gave me an opportunity, I thought, to gather information about my mother's history. But it was as if she had been erased. A serviette ring my father had made for her, an inscription in a Bible she gave me, a few notes scribbled in a little memo book regarding the Mooloolah School of Arts 'concert'. There were no letters. Her clothes and jewellery had been dispersed. Her old ball gowns, those treasures of my childhood, burnt. Most people who had been close to her were dead. Those who remained were too old to remember, or were wary of me, embarrassed to talk in anything but platitudes. The word 'suicide' was avoided.

I went to visit dear Ted and Bunty, now residing in a retirement home on Buderim Mountain where we had taken our Sunday drives all those decades ago. Nothing had changed between them. Ted spoke little English; Bunty hailed criticism upon his mulish head; Ted grinned. Bunty's take on my mother was that her depression had been a medical matter. My mother had been ill. She said, 'Once, in Mooloolah, she wouldna get out of bed. I said to her, "Pull yourself together, Gwen. Stop feeling sorry for yourself. You've got nothing to complain about." After you moved to Redcliffe, she was so sick then I didna want to visit. I couldna think of anything to say.'

My mother's heart had 'bled for Bunty'. There was to be no reciprocal bleeding from that stringent Scots soul.

One afternoon I gave a talk in Brisbane. At question time a blowsy woman stood up and said, 'You might be in a fancy suit now, but I've seen you in dirty nappies. Whaddya think about THAT?'

I went up to her afterwards and said, 'I am thinking of writing about my mother, could you tell me anything about her?'

'Your mother! What do you want to write about her for? Your father was the interesting one. He was the adventurer. Everyone loved your father. All she did was stay in the house.'

For the very first time in my life, I experienced a spasm of identification with that barely remembered mother. I saw the vista of her outback life open out in all its loneliness, felt the harsh judgements of the obtuse and the envious.

Only one old friend of Gwen's spoke lovingly of her. She, too, had been a neighbour at Stanley Park, a city girl like my mother, married into country life. I visited her in a suburb of Brisbane. Zoe had been Miss Post Office during the war, and was still beautiful, her hair piled up as it had been for the Miss Post Office photograph, placed on a table.

She said, 'Gwen was the funniest person I've ever met. She saved me out there. Kept me laughing. It was a hard life in many ways. Isolated. Sometimes when we took our children to school we'd have a half hour sitting out the front in the car. Gwen would take off the locals. We didn't talk about our marriages – personal things – the way you do today. Sometimes a comment about something or other and you'd share an understanding without having to spell it out. She was "under the thumb" with Mark. That's my opinion. I couldn't believe it when I ran into her in Brisbane. It was only seven or eight years later but I hardly recognised her. And I said, "Oh Gwen dear, whatever's the matter?" She looked so ill and broken-down. She wanted to talk, but her mother hurried her away. I wasn't invited to the funeral. None of us old friends were. We didn't know how she died. The family lied about it. Suicide was something to be ashamed of then. She loved you children, wanted the best for you both. She wanted opportunities for you that you'd never get out there. That's why she wanted to get back to the city. That and the loneliness.'

Before returning to London I had one small thing left to do. I had not attended either of my parents' funerals (had never attended a funeral at all), so it seemed fitting that I should liberate their ashes from the brick wall in which they were stowed, take them to where my sister was holidaying and together we would scatter them in the Pacific. Narendra was flying in from India, to be with me and, hopefully, meet my family.

The crematorium capped a hill on the outskirts of Brisbane. Surrounding it – wooden houses on stilts, brick houses like boxes, tree ferns and staghorns, jacaranda and coral trees, empty back yards, blind front windows. Nothing moved but air shimmering over the roofs of parked cars.

I was on sentimentality patrol, but in truth I did feel a disquiet, not because of any false emotion regarding my parents, but because collecting the ashes was a preliminary step in a ritual that would involve my sister. And the living are less predictable than the dead.

The man behind the desk was solemn and compassionate. There was organ music playing. The kitschness irritated me, the whole thing irritated me, I was doing something others had said I should do and I felt false to myself. I signed forms and waited. Two boxes and a plaque were placed in front of me.

In loving memory of my dear wife and our mother. I picked up the boxes. One, my father's, was heavier than the other ...

Something gave way in my body, somewhere behind the sternum. Narendra helped me to the car. He said, 'I'll go away for a while so you can be alone with them.' I sat behind the wheel with my parents in my lap, and sobbed, and could not stop.

I say I sobbed, but it was as if the tears wept me, so thoroughly beyond control was the outpouring. So this was normal grief. This eruption of some ethereal substance from the area of the heart.

When Narendra returned, he cleared the back seat of the car and laid his shawl along it. I placed the boxes on the shawl with the plaque. I picked some jacaranda blossom and surrounded them with it. I spoke to the dead.

I might have allowed self-consciousness to staunch the outpouring had it not been for Narendra, who neither extended sympathy nor attempted palliative. He was, simply, there.

He held my hand for a while, until I'd collected myself, then we set off for Bribie Island, two hours' drive away.

My sister and I had been estranged for a number of years, but as we had spent a tender if tentative afternoon together only the week before, I was not as apprehensive as I might have been about seeing her now. Her children would be there – my darling nieces. I wanted Narendra to meet them all, my family. I had lost them but this ritual would bring us together again, would absolve, finally, the legacy of the past. We stopped to buy sandcrabs on the way – our family's favourite food. I imagined embracing her. I imagined us laughing together as we so often used to do, when our father was alive. That familial laughter that reaches right down into the gut, that leaves you breathless and wiping away tears, that is like no other.

She was alone. The television was on, showing cartoons. I went to hug her but it was like approaching the same pole of a magnet – a repelling force that increases the closer you get. Everything about her said, 'You have done something unforgivable.' But what? Was she upset that I hadn't come earlier? Or later? Was she shy about meeting Narendra? Had she changed her mind about the ashes? Had I said something wrong to the nieces? What had I done?

She ignored Narendra, and began to talk about inconsequential things, which hid and at the same time accentuated what wasn't being said. She would not meet my eyes but bent to the dogs, crooning at them in a girlish voice. Narendra retreated into his own, watchful silence.

We sat at the table staring at the crabs. When she spoke her voice was cold, bitter – the tone of one who has been wronged. That voice vibrated with … What? Rage? It was more like loathing – the longing to crush something loathsome. I couldn't name it at the time, I never can. At the time I felt only a familiar, sick sense of responsibility – the need to atone for something, to apologise for a crime I hadn't known I'd committed.

Quite suddenly she said, 'Do you remember the dog that killed Auburn?'

Instantly I am on the back veranda at Stanley Park. I am very small. We have come home from somewhere to find that my sister's pet duckling has been mauled. I see it so clearly, the bundle of pale wet fluff, the eyes closed wrongly, from the bottom up. My parents try to resuscitate it. They drop water on to its beak. They give up on the duckling and turn their attention to my sister who is inconsolable. I see the duckling open its beak and I try to tell them all but they are oblivious. Sometime later I hear my father kicking the dog. He kicks it so hard it flies in an arc and hits the dust yelping. Or perhaps I have made up the dog.

'I remember very well. It was Wilga, wasn't it? The dog?'

'You were too young to know anything about it. Do you know that when Auburn was killed, I willed death to that dog? And the next day it took a poison bait and died.' She got up, smiled faintly, and her glance descended on me like a heavy cold paw.

'That's when I first knew my own psychic power.'

There was a silence which I broke by mentioning the ashes. Did she want to be alone with them? She didn't. Could she think of a good place to scatter them?

'I don't care where they go. Perhaps along Red Beach. You can see the old house from there. Dad would like that. She might not, of course. But perhaps she's learnt a thing or two since then.'

I was not in the habit of contradicting my sister but I felt that I would betray my mother utterly if I left her remains at Red Beach where she would have to face, for all eternity, the place where she had so violently ended her life. I gathered my courage and suggested that perhaps the surfside was better. A gateway to the Pacific and freedom. Wouldn't they both have liked that?

It was one of those post-sunset evenings that only Australia can produce. The light seems to penetrate matter and set it aglow. Luminous blue sea and sky, the sand a pearly pink. A couple of people strolled along the shore, otherwise the beach was empty for miles. Behind us, the melancholy scrubland of bottlebrush and paperbark.

We opened the boxes. The ashes weren't ashes at all, but fragments of bone and grit, the colour and texture of crushed shells. I watched my sister for clues. She cried a little. That brought tears to my eyes too, but they were hers not mine. We picked out slivers of bone to keep – a little from each box – and I ate a pinch of grit, then we waded deep into the waves and flung the stuff. Two porpoises appeared about twenty feet away, swam slowly towards us, then away out to sea.

My sister said, with that withering tone, 'Well, it seems our parents are happy. So here we are, pleasing our parents again.' I know that behind my sister's behaviour is pain. I have always known it, and always been incapable of assuaging it. Driving back in her car I touched her shoulder but she flinched away.

My sister and I are each other's bad luck.

★

I returned to the Himalayan house, Narendra returned to Rajasthan. I was on my own; there were no distractions, no excuses. The task: to write about my mother. A woman interred in other people's stories. A bad mother. A sick mother. A mad mother. A weak mother. A narcissistic mother. A mother who 'chose the easy way out'. (That was easy?) A mother who might have 'learnt a thing or two' since strangling herself with an electrical cord? It is a task like a task in a fairy tale. It is an impossible task that must nevertheless be completed.

Oddly, I was relieved that I had discovered so little about her. An imaginary mother somehow had more vitality than a historical one. Myth is fertile; fact is dry. As well, facts, like memories, are not always truthful.

My sister says I am like my mother, though in such a way as to make me think perhaps that is not an entirely good thing. When she says such things, I think of us as playing a game of Drop the Hanky. Which of us unknowingly has the hanky of doom behind us? Which of us is locked in a fatal symmetry with our mother? The inference is that it must be me. *The way my fingers twitch as I type the ends of sentences in my head, or play piano … thoughts that rise like deep-water fish … thoughts, perhaps, of suicide …*

So much time staring out over the bird bath, avoiding the task: and how could I be expected to write about that mother when I couldn't even make sense of my own life-without-narrative. I wasn't interested in the 'I' of self-reporting, I was interested in fate, in how things came into being, in the great indecipherable chains of causation that sweep us all through time.

Another war had kindled in the Middle East, the kind of war of which much would be written in history books. How dispassionately it would be viewed from the future, no doubt troubled by its own wars. This one would just be a story, lacking the lifeblood of the present. I sat by the radio, listening to pundits around the world expressing confident opinions as to the reasons for and outcomes of this war, opinions which would be rendered inaccurate by history. But that would not prevent the formation of new, equally certain opinions whose fallacy would, in their turn, be revealed in time. I had come to mistrust my own opinions; they had too often been proved wrong. But if doubt is all you have, how do you speak?

One evening, listening to the radio, I heard the voice of an Arab, beseeching British soldiers to let him collect the body of his brother from where it lay shattered and exposed after a bombing. His voice was hysterical, but what undid me was the stumbling, inadequate English, the powerlessness to communicate a need that was more important to him than his own survival: the need to collect his brother's body.

I began writing about my parents' ashes. About my sister. I had ended the passage with 'My sister and I are each other's bad luck.' But judging luck as good or bad is a matter of limited perspective. I wasn't happy with what I wrote and shoved it away in a drawer along with all the other scraps of paper holding rejected passages and incomplete thoughts – all of it tailings, all of it inadequate to the task.

And then ... at the time it seemed to happen all at once, but it was more an accumulation of half-acknowledged realisations breaking the banks of my incapacity, I came to terms with the fact that my mother could not, could never, be found, that the only wisps remaining of her tiny moment on earth were encoded in me – those tail ends of thoughts which rose in her mind like fish surfacing into the light, thoughts of which I am in some degree a continuation. We take our mothers into us; that is where they live. In order to write about her and her time, to honour that nanoscopic existence, I had to write about myself and my own time, even though 'I' would not be the same 'I' of my multitudinous past selves. Not a narrative, nor a reconstruction, but rather a searching through the mysterious residue left by time and events.

The way memory plays in the mind is not factual. It is sketchy, mythical, misremembered, contradictory. It is flickers of light on unfathomable darkness. We go back over and back over the past, watching it change with each take, not thinking of it as what happened so much as, what does it mean? What do we say about it, and what do we choose not to say? What we say is no more than a flicker of light on the surface of an ocean of the unsaid.

Sixteen

The actual business of leaving Malabah is nowhere registered in memory. The fogbank obscures everything from the moment of sitting under the mango tree weeping because I have been told we are to leave, until there we all are, staring out of various windows of the house in Clontarf, as if we have always been there, as if Mrs Wallace has always been our neighbour, and Ian, Ken and Donnie have always been the boys next door. The golf course bordering our yard has for ever been the place to wander alone in after school, and the canvas water-bag my father has set up for the golfers on our gatepost has been there from the beginning. There isn't anything before Clontarf. Malabah, even Stanley Park, exist simultaneously, but separately, on the other side of the fogbank, and a different version of the Davidsons live there.

On this Clontarf side of the fogbank, everything is crammed together and reduced. The Davidsons themselves are less significant. They speak and act, even dress differently. Their bodies have changed.

My father's daywear is loose Dacron shorts and sandals rather than long khaki trousers and boots. There are little traces of grey in his hair. My sister has left childhood far behind her. You can tell where she has been by the aroma of cigarettes and perfume. I, too, am someone else – as if, somewhere between Malabah and Clontarf, my softness has been exposed to the air to harden, like shellac. I do not talk in front of people. There are a couple of curling hairs growing down there, between my legs. I don't know what 'fuck' means, but I have heard kids at school say it, behind the toilet block.

My body is too big for me and I fold my arms in front of it to cover it.

My mother is someone else entirely. Someone who's been punctured and all the sap drained out of her. What had been contained in Malabah has broken loose in Clontarf. We could ignore it before, because we thought it was harmless. Now it eats my mother from the inside. At night it prowls through the house sniffing at us in our beds.

On this side of the fogbank, there are no Wilgas or Thumpers or Chittles or Yellow Eyes or Berthas or Goaties or Princes, or Black Cat or baby lambs butting at bottles of milk. Instead there is a budgie in a cage. It is officially mine, though I cannot get too worked up about the bird. I feel sorry for it, all alone in its little cage. One day I leave its cage outside, hanging in a tree, so the little thing can imagine it is free. A butcherbird somehow manages to kill it through the bars.

On the far, Malabah side of the fogbank, the Davidsons seem happy enough. At night in the kitchen, Mark and Gwen flick each other with wet tea towels and shriek with laughter and chase each other. The Mark and Gwen in Clontarf never do that. On the Malabah side, the family gathers around to listen to the Sunday-night play on the radio. Or invites neighbours over to watch *Pick a Box* or *Liberace* or *Hancock's Half Hour* on the new TV or to cluster around the piano for a sing-song, or to set off bottle rockets and pinwheels from the back stairs on the fifth of November. There are no Guy Fawkes Nights in Clontarf. No board games or dominoes on rainy days or building cubby houses behind the sofa. No 'Ploffskin, Pluffskin'. The piano sits in a recess but we do not gather around it. We watch television, lots of television – *I Love Lucy*. Nelson Eddy movies. Westerns. Nature shows. Or we stroll on the golf course of an evening, when all the golfers have gone home. My mother's and father's realms are mingled in the Clontarf house, though there is a miserly condensation of Mark's workspace set up for him in the 'garage': a bench where he can polish the agate and other stones he finds, or sand and paint the mangrove roots he makes into lamp stands, or gut and scale the flathead and mullet he catches in the bay. Although he is now a 'retired grazier', Mark keeps himself busy. He would like to go out opal or gold prospecting but he can't get away, because Little Mummy is ill.

Little Mummy has some new appliances in the kitchen. An electrical fridge rather than the old kero one that kept blowing out. A yellow electric kettle with a Bakelite lid like a bird's beak. An electric fry pan in which most of the cooking now takes place. But she doesn't cook as she did before. And we don't have a garden containing fresh corn and tomatoes and citrus fruits and loquats and mangos. Every night we eat the same things. Chops and three vegetables. Mince and three vegetables. On very special occasions, chicken and three vegetables. She seems not to be able to remember what to cook.

She wanders around the house as if underwater, and sometimes she just stands still. Sometimes she just stands still and tears leak out of her.

In the Clontarf house we all stare out of different windows, and inside each head a separate stream of thoughts rushes along and no one remembers the source.

We moved to this outer outer suburb of Brisbane, to be 'closer to doctors'. The move did not mark an end to Gwen's tantalisation, however. To reach Brisbane from Clontarf one had to drive across a two-mile-long bridge spanning the tidal bay, then through Sandgate to the train station. Who would drive my mother to the station? (My father would complain – about the petrol; the bridge toll – a shilling; the time.) And where would she go all on her own? Her previous life wasn't there any more. And she, herself, transformed.

'So near and yet so far.'

But at least the bay and the bridge provided some protection from Nanna, who lay in wait on the other side. We visited the pigeon box quite often now. For Gwen there were special treats. Grandy's strawberries dusted in icing sugar and served with cream. A bottle of shucked oysters, or a bottle of green cocktail olives. The sorts of extravagances my father might strike from a list.

For my father, there were ameliorations to leaving the country. He could go fishing. He could visit his dearest old friend, who also lived in Sandgate, by the sea. Decker, I think his name was. Something Decker. His wife's name was too strange and beautiful to forget – Mel. In the back yard of their house, there was a palm tree which grew like a fan. My interest in botany seems to have survived the fogbank.

So there we all are in the Clontarf house, a house almost as exotic as my Tyrolean musical box. It isn't at all like the other houses in Frost Street or Rogers Road. It is a two-storey house built by an Italian, on a narrow suburban block adjacent to an eighteen-hole golf course, at around the ninth tee. Because of the golf course (a couple of hundred acres of green turf and trees that undulate down to mangrove swamps), the Italian had built the house back to front. The 'back' of the house (vine-shrouded lavatory, garage) faced on to Frost Street, and the 'front' of the house (green cement patio, picket fence) faced towards the golf course. The house assumed the attitude of Cousin Barbara displaying her bottom.

The few fond memories I have of Clontarf are located principally with Mrs Wallace next door, or with her boys, or in our outside lav. It was there that my sister taught me to smoke before I was twelve. Rothmans cigarettes and, later, if I promised to scratch her back, a couple of puffs of a Russian Sobranie – a turquoise Sobranie, or a black Sobranie with gold filter tip. (When the dunny was pulled down, a new black-and-white flushing toilet squeezed itself into the upstairs bathroom.) It was my sister who brought back evidence of a new world coming into being, somewhere beyond the bay – Sobranie cigarettes, Porphyry Pearl sparkling wine, Miss Balmain perfume, white lipstick, transistor radios, black polo-necked skivvies, different kinds of songs with different beats.

My mother smoked Ardath or Craven A. Post-war cigarettes. Rothmans, Benson and Hedges, Kools: these marked a generational change. Ardaths on one side, Rothmans on the other; they were like the ensigns of opposing armies.

My sister had left boarding school by then, and was a 'cadet nurse'. No, I'm ahead of myself. There was the in-between period obscured by tendrils of fogbank. My sister in her school uniform, living with Nanna and Grandy, in a state of permanent fury and despair. She is a wild colourful bird sharing a cage with old pigeons. Why has she left boarding school, why is she living with Nanna and Grandy and not us? True, it would be very difficult to get all the way to her school from Clontarf every day. But why not let her remain a boarder? Was she pressured into leaving boarding school, to live with Nanna and Grandy, so she could step into the breach left by our collapsed and shrinking mother? According to family legend it was my sister who chose the house at Clontarf. (My mother hated the house.) But how is that possible? She could not have been more than fifteen. Why would adults have placed such responsibility on to a young girl? And why my sister? Why not some relative? One of my mother's brothers, perhaps? Or their wives? Or Nanna or Grandy? Or a family friend? (But apart from Mrs Wallace, we seem not to have 'family friends' and relatives do not visit.)

'Here we are pleasing our parents again ...'

Was she told to come home and 'look after Mummy'? Was this Nanna's doing? Our father's? The timing is difficult to work out. From our arrival in Clontarf, to the day my mother suicided, lay a period of about two years.

In that second year, my sister stays sometimes with us, and sometimes at the hospital where she is in training. She has a mustard-coloured pay packet. She buys a black-and-orange silk blouse that smells deliciously of underarms and Miss Balmain. She tells me that nursing is so hard that sometimes there is blood in her shoes. She and my mother have fights. One day, I see a tiny mother facing a larger daughter at the fridge. The mother shouts up at the daughter, and bangs her head once against the fridge. My sister's face is white and closed up. My father hovers around in the background saying, 'Aw, for gawd's sake.' His face is stricken, helpless, stupid.

Oh my darling sister, my darling mother, what is *wrong*? And when did it go wrong? I am stricken, helpless, stupid. I am too little. I am invisible, my claims feeble in comparison to the vehemence of their conflict. Theirs is the defining relationship here; it takes up all the oxygen.

There is another fight at Nanna's place. The most terrifying word imaginable, far more terrifying than death, is hovering in the air. 'Divorce'. Nanna is saying something to my father that I don't understand. My mother is quietly weeping. I have never seen my father respond in anger to anyone. He is angry now. He says, 'I haven't touched her for months.' I am by the dining table, unnoticed as usual because I am little. I have to stop this fight so I begin to cry loudly. I do not feel at all like crying, but it is the only tool at my disposal. They do notice me. Nanna says, 'Now look what you've done, you've upset the child.' My mother bends down and takes me in her arms. But I seem to have got this wrong, the incident surely occurred before we stepped into the fogbank, because I am quite small in this scene, and my sister isn't present.

One night in Clontarf (I have my own room in Clontarf), my father comes in and wakes me up. I can tell he is angry. He says, 'Go and sleep with your mother.' I refuse absolutely. 'Aw gawd,' he says, and sighs. And sighs again.

At night, in my room in Clontarf, sharp leaves scratch against the glass, and spur-winged plovers come right to my window to cry out. They are trying to get in. I do not like this room, however pretty it is. This house. The golf course. There are too many children at the school, hundreds of them. The clever boy with glasses follows me around. He has an unpronounceable second name and comes top in everything. The whole of Mooloolah school could fit into one of the classes at the Clontarf school. I don't necessarily come top any more. Sometimes I even come third. I have a crush on Greg Hamilton who lives across the road. He says our house is unlucky. I never bring friends home.

I am given my very own dog, Goldie. She is my first very own proper pet. That must have been for my eleventh birthday. It is around that time, too, that my mother tries to tell me about sex. She has been spending most of her time in bed. We are sitting on her bed together. She is yellowish and thin. She says, 'Now you know, don't you, that … man plus woman … equals child.' Of course I do, I say. I stand up abruptly and leave. I leave her in the same way that I leave her when she says that God came to her through the bedroom venetians, and held her hand.

Again, the timing is difficult here. My mother is very soon to kill herself. And yet, she is the one who insists that I am given a little dog for my birthday – a golden spaniel. When Goldie comes home, my father insists that the pup be kept in a box downstairs in the garage at night. The pup howls without cease. It is tearing my heart to bits. And my mother, resolute, no nonsense now, gets out of my parents' big double bed, comes to get me out of my bed, goes down to retrieve the pup, wraps the pup in a blanket, and together she and I, with the pup between us, sleep together in the big bed. I admire my mother very much, not just because she has dealt with the pup, but because she has stood up for herself. Eventually, the pup will learn to sleep downstairs, because I remember my father bringing her to me every morning at dawn. She, Goldie, skidding on the floor with glee as she races up the stairs, and in through my door to leap on the bed in joy and my dad grinning behind her, bearing the tea.

Another time, I must be ten or eleven. I am beside my mother on the wrought-iron stairs inside the house. She is slow, bewildered, underwater. She says, 'The doctor said I should be happy. I've got a loving husband, two beautiful children, I should be happy.' My mother says this in a puzzled kind of way. She agrees with the doctor, and cannot work out what her fault must be. Although I have only been on earth for ten years, I know, with my whole being, how unjust the doctor's words are. I know that the doctor is a stupid man, and that his stupidity makes him cruel.

His stupidity makes him dangerous.

I suppose this is the time when I stand up to my mother and wear what I choose to school. *Aren't you even going to kiss me goodbye?*

Another time, again, very close to the end. I have left my room in a mess. I cannot remember my mother ever shouting at me, but that morning she shouts – 'I am not your slave.' But I must think she is my slave, because I resent having to clean my room, and I think I talk back to her, if not out loud then at least in my mind.

I don't kiss her goodbye, and I am not taken to the funeral.

★

The next act opens on Tamborine Mountain, where Gil lives, and I am yet again a different person. Breasts have appeared. I have periods. (It was Mrs Wallace who explained, and showed me how to wear the ugly pad.) Goldie is gone. I am living with Gil in her house which is called Tulloch. The word 'Tulloch', on a bronze plate, hangs on the veranda beneath a set of antlers. One day my father visits and I hear them arguing about money; Gil says Mark isn't giving her enough to look after me.

'Oh Mark, you are a *fool*.'

'Gawd strewth, Gil …' He is turning his hat around in his hands. I feel bad that I am a burden to him. But later, when Gil tells me I use too much toilet paper and I should spend no more than two minutes in the shower, I rebel in my heart. Mrs Philps next door bakes a cake each week for us. Gil keeps it locked in the pantry, and gives me a piece each day when I come home from school.

Gil cooks abominable food. Unskinned brains leaking blood into lumpy white sauce. Huge fistfuls of boiled vegetables which, when she isn't looking, I stuff into my dressing-gown pockets. 'I loathe cooking and I abhor housework …' How she must have hated having to produce those meals.

I no longer idolise Gil. One day in the kitchen, I shout at her, 'I HATE you.' I am amazed at myself. I am not that sort of child. I am a good child. Mummy's pet. Teacher's pet. I am ashamed when I see the look on her face, and see that we are, all of us, out of our depth.

I ride a wild pony to Tamborine Mountain school and don't attend to what is said in the tiny classroom.

I don't care whether I come top or bottom. I throw Gil's horrible sandwiches away. Some days I skip school. There is rainforest to wander around in, get lost in. Waterfalls and rock pools. In one of these rock pools there is a 'vortex'. If you fall into it, it sucks you down down and you are never seen again, or your body turns up in another pool, way down on the other side of the rainforest. One day I see a brightly coloured crayfish coming towards me. It leans back and opens its pincers towards me, then creaks along its way.

I get lost in the rainforest one afternoon, and anxiously struggle through the wet growth to get home before nightfall, because I know Gil will be worried about me. I am not at all anxious for myself, I know exactly what I'm doing. Darkness falls before I reach home. I rush in saying, 'I'm all right, don't worry.' I am met with screeches. I look down to see I'm trickling gore from all the leeches stuck to me.

At some point I contract pneumonia. I have never been seriously ill before. I am allowed to convalesce under an eiderdown, out in the sunshine.

I know, more or less, what 'fuck' means and I seem to be in possession of a supply of 'dirty jokes'. I am popular at the little school because I know these jokes. I love the freedom of galloping around the mountain with my friend Margaret who owns the horses. They are skewbald ponies with mouths as hard as dingo traps. If they decide to bolt, there's no way you can rein them in. You just have to let go of fear, and fly.

The year I turn thirteen my father and sister come up the mountain to take me 'home' to prepare for boarding school.

It is only now that I become aware of the implications of my mother's death as far as my own future is concerned. It must be understood that I had not for a second missed my mother. I can't remember missing anything, not even Goldie the dog.

I had lived up on the mountain with Gil for two and a half years in a kind of bubble, developing breasts, tearing around on horses, listening to pop songs ... 'True love means planning a life for two / Being together the whole day through ...' I had experienced my first proper kiss. Gil and I and the Philpses next door had gone to St Bernard's Hotel for New Year's Eve. There was a band, and dancing, and pink crêpe streamers at midnight. I wore the white nylon frock with an orange silk flower at the waist that Mrs Wallace had made for me two years before. Mrs Philps let it out at the seams. At midnight everyone kissed everyone else. Shandies and sherry had made people happy. I was kissed by my dance partner. Lingeringly, on the lips. Long streamers were thrown across us all as we linked arms and sang 'Auld Lang Syne'. Outside, the rainforest closed around us, and the summer night sky blinked its lights through the dark. Inside, everyone was shining in a warm golden light. Gil smiled at me from across the dance floor and I smiled back. My mother was so completely forgotten it was as if she had never existed. She was far far away, in some other dark.

One month later, driving down the mountain, the new order of things was brought home to me. I was in the back seat; my father was at the wheel, as always, in his grazier's hat. But there was something different about him which made me love him even more than before, but in an achy sort of way. I knew with absolute certainty that I would give up my life for him if necessary, as if he were now younger than me. Next to him, wearing her black-and-orange silk top, was my sister, assured, fully fledged, and occupying my mother's place.

Seventeen

When, in my mind, I turn around to face the past, it often appears as a nightscape, illuminated here and there by spotlights, in which I can see enactments of 'something that happened'. There is truth in these enactments, yet each time I look at them they are altered, almost imperceptibly in some cases, grossly in others, and if in one a child plays her part, then moves out of her pool of light into the dark, she might reappear in the neighbouring one as an eighteen-year-old.

I was about eighteen when I hitched a ride on a truck going to Sydney. The truck left from a depot on the outskirts of Brisbane. I do not know who directed me to go to a depot. I would not have been able to work that out for myself at that time.

I turned up at the depot at night. A man said I could sleep in the bunkroom until the Sydney trucks left, in a few hours. I did not want to sleep, but I also did not want to disobey the man. A little while later, he came into the bunkroom expecting sex. I fobbed him off and sensed that he was, if not relieved, then at least phlegmatic. The attempt was routine, as expected as roast on Sundays with the wife.

Or perhaps when innocence is as palpable as mine must have been, it acts as a shield. I was frightened, but not primarily of the man. I was frightened of my own inadequacy in the face of the rules of the world, of which I knew nothing.

I had a sleeping bag, sixty dollars and a packet of Drum tobacco. That much is clear. As well, alert, animal fear – that terror of living which, nevertheless, does not negate faith in one's personal indestructibility. I suppose I assumed that if I just went forth; if, in every moment, I stayed open to whatever the moment delivered …

But before I climb into that Sydney-bound truck, and by way of explanation for the abandonment of my home state, I must return to the map of Australia, and to my father.

Australia is pink because it is a part of the Commonwealth. We are an independent, self-governing country, but we still love our Queen who is our Head of State. The Queen, in turn, loves us, and sends her male progeny to school here – the sort of elite school my father attended before the First World War.

My father is an exemplar of Australia's conservative values. Pride in our efforts during both world wars, the manly qualities of short back and sides, emotional reticence, bravery in battle, adventure and daring-do, a profound regard for and identification with the British Empire, a sense of natural (that is to say ordained by nature) subordination of women to men and of inferior (less fit) cultures to superior ones, which is to say our own. It is an ideology tempered by the egalitarian values that characterise our national spirit (giving someone a fair go), made possible by everyone tacitly knowing their place.

Of all the states, Queensland upholds these values best, and is most disparaging of dissenting values. Queensland is referred to by the rest of Australia as the Deep North. Many Queenslanders are proud of their deep northness, and turn the derision on its head. My father votes for Bjelke-Petersen, he of the right-wing country party – a peanut farmer, sly, outrageous and corrupt, known for the kind of one-liners that made southerners laugh with scorn. For example, in regard to the sale of condoms, 'We don't want any of that sort of thing up here.'

Up here was the antithesis to Down There, meaning the libertarian cesspits of Sydney and Melbourne.

As I said before, I did not know my father very well at that time. I had lived with Gil, away from him, and then in a boarding school whose extortionate bills flayed him mercilessly, causing him to cross almost everything off the lists of necessities I took to him. 'Aw gawd, what do you want shampoo for, darling?' Scratch. 'Aw gawd, Rob, you don't need a bra, do you?' Scratch. These events were as shaming to me as they had been to my mother, so going to him with a list was an absolute last-ditch option. On the rare occasions that I was at home in Clontarf with him, the days were a fugue of emptiness. I cooked the same meal every night for him, in the electric fry pan. Mince with onion and tomato. Boiled potatoes. He would sit in his chair in front of the TV and say, every time, 'Oh thanks, darling, by jove eh?' and eat the grim mess with apparent pleasure. And in the mornings, always, there he would be at my door, grinning, with a big cup of tea. But no Goldie bounding on to the bed, and no reason to get up that I could think of.

Boarding school took four years of my life, but I don't know where I was at the time. Or perhaps that period was a variation of the dissociative state which by then seemed to me the natural one. I stared out of classroom windows, my mind wandering and proliferating. Often I was literally elsewhere, skipping classes and hiding down in the music rooms playing the opening bars of Rachmaninov concertos, or pounding the life out of polonaises. Mozart was boring, though to be fair to that young self, I never found Bach boring, only achingly difficult to play in any way that did not make him sound that way. I had never been to a concert (what was a concert?), but I had seen a movie on TV about Chopin, in which he dripped blood on to the keys. On the rare occasions I went home for holidays, I would pick my way through my mother's sheet music on the old German upright which, as the years passed, went more and more out of tune while here and there ivories lifted off the keys and were lost. When I left that dear piano, it smiled goodbye like a toothless old streetwalker.

I liked the English and French teachers, so was good at English and French. I wrote poetry which pleased them. I found maths fascinating but could not be bothered to learn the equations. Physics and chemistry were interesting at a global level, but tedious in the classroom. As for the study of life, to which I had once wished to dedicate myself, I now found that it was, amazingly, the study of death. Pickled animals, moribund teacher, leaden books, the stench of formaldehyde. Miraculously I seemed to do well enough in exams, so something must have penetrated the trance-state. Not that it was expected that I should excel academically. In 1964, a school like St Margaret's was principally to train young ladies in how to snag a 'man of the land', or, if your aim did not quite reach that high, or your parents were city-dwellers, then at least to marry a lawyer, doctor or accountant.

How this was to be accomplished was something of a mystery. Boys were an exotic species sometimes spied at a distance when we attended church services outside the school grounds. The only boys I had ever seen up close were the Wallace boys next door in Clontarf. I liked them, though was shy with them. Believing myself to be either invisible or ugly, I maintained a haughty aloofness in the presence of people I wanted to know.

My sister worried about my retardation in the seductive arts. 'You have to talk,' she said. 'It doesn't matter what about, just say anything. Just be animated.' This seemed unprincipled to me. If it didn't matter what you said, what was the point of speaking? I tried it out on the Wallace boys and was amazed that it worked. But I couldn't keep it up. Were boys so gullible as to be fooled by such falsity? How could you respect them if they were so easily duped? And once you had run out of pointless things to say in an animated way, what then?

There being no boys within cooee of boarding school, it was fertile ground for the cultivation of 'thrills'. I, too, was caught up in these hormonal undertows. As the one suffering the thrill (unrequited love for an older girl), I had to be the one she chose above all others, for her fleeting, ambiguous attentions, which could be kind, seductive, mocking or all three. Her best friend detested me, and inflicted pinches so extreme as to leave bloody bruises, to be withstood without a flinch. It did not enter my head that the thrill phenomenon was associated with sex. We were merely practising strategies in that age-old power game between lover and beloved – a game I would prove singularly unsuited to win.

Besides thrills there were Georgette Heyer romances in the library, in which females swooned masochistically after powerful wrong-headed males. And there was *Hamlet* – the abridged version, lacking an enseamed bed – with whom I felt erotic identification. If I had been there in Elsinore rather than that drippy Ophelia, things would have gone very differently. Phantom marriage proposals while sitting on the lavatory were still prevalent, but none of these urges was grounded in a clear idea of the act of sex.

If you went to a posh school like St Margaret's, it was assumed you would want to go all the way with LBJ. Certainly our principal, Sister Jean-Marie, did, because when that Great Leader arrived in Brisbane, a contingent of St Margaret's girls was sent to wave at him, as once we had waved at the Queen of England. We were not informed in any coherent way about the war to our north, where Australian boys were being sent to help the Yanks protect the world from Communism. Or perhaps we were told, and it was one of those facts that turned to fundamental particles when it hit the vacuum inside my head.

Sister Jean-Marie was nevertheless something of a progressive, and her leadership marked a turning in the school's ethos. It was she who brought in a handsome Franciscan friar to play guitar in our chapel. (He wore a cassock just like the outfit I once imagined for myself in childhood, when I dreamt of being a Wandering Dew setting forth into the unknown, beyond the gates of Malabah.) She who hired a male physics teacher — a gawky, large-eared man with whom the zoology teacher was not so secretly in love. She who instigated 'talks' in the assembly hall, about such things as 'necking' and 'petting'. She knew that our future lay in a modern world run by Americans, and that the old ties to England belonged more naturally to the era of her predecessor, Sister Mary. She allowed Saturday-night 'jives' in the new function room. Girls could bring their LPs and dance with each other while the teachers and nuns sat around the walls, tapping their sensibly shod feet to a music that intended to obliterate them.

Suddenly I see myself in the Mary Quant dress. A halter-neck dress, linen, with big black-and-yellow daisy print on it. A 'keyhole' at the back. I must have designed the dress for Mrs Wallace to sew. I wore white pointy-toed shoes — slingbacks. Who bought them for me? My dad? Surely not. Did my sister talk him into it? Did my sister buy them for me? With her nurse's pay? Most probably.

I am wearing the faux Mary Quant shift. White slingbacks. I am with my sister in the Brisbane Botanic Gardens. I have set my hair with bobby pins and sprayed it stiff with Alberto VO5. Who has helped me with this? My sister is taking me out for the day. We laugh together as we parade through the gardens. There is nothing for us to do in the gardens, and we do not expect to have anything to do or to meet anyone. Yet we parade, showing ourselves off. She is in love with a doctor. They will get married. Underneath the halter-neck shift I am wearing stockings with suspenders and a cross-over bra. They are uncomfortable, the shoes are uncomfortable, the stockings ladder. Being a woman seems inevitably to involve physical constraint of some kind. I adore my sister and she is 'proud' of me. I think she feels relieved at not having to be responsible for a child any longer. (The Mary Quant dress is not a child's dress.) And my sister is, after all, only recently out of childhood herself. Twenty, perhaps.

Perhaps that is the day she takes me to one of her parties, where I meet her fiancé and other medical students. I drink rum and Coke, and suddenly the glass coffin of shyness is shattered and I find myself sitting on men's laps, talking in funny voices, making them laugh. Totally but totally ANIMATED. Then, just as suddenly, I crash out in the bedroom, weeping and inconsolable at the futility of existence.

And yet, a miracle. I left St Margaret's school with two scholarships. One of which was to the Queensland Conservatorium of Music.

My dad and I stand facing each other inside the school gates on the last day. He has come to collect me. Everyone else seems to have gone home. He is wearing his grazier's hat. The blue Toyota truck is parked outside. I have been waiting, nervously, to tell him about the music scholarship, which was the one I wanted to take.

'Dad, I got a scholarship to do piano studies. Only it's eight dollars a week and I'd need ... probably another ... two or three ...'

'Aw gawd.' I had wounded him, right in the wallet where I knew he suffered.

'But I can get a part-time job and—'

He is uncharacteristically cross now; or rather not cross – he never got cross – but stubborn, like a backed-up mule. He had seen the end of his torment of school fees, and now this ...

'Gawd strewth, what do you want to go and waste your time with all that for? No. No, you get yourself a secretarial job or something, until you get married.'

My dad and I would eventually become the dearest of friends, but at this moment we are strangers to each other, and our walks together in the paddocks of Malabah belong not just to another time, but to entirely different people.

During those walks he had led me to believe that the Great World would welcome me when I grew up. That HE would welcome me. The betrayal was something he inherited with his ideology – a natural thing, beneath the radar of self-awareness. The Great World was not for girls.

I see him standing there, hurting, resistant, the girl in front of him feeling the old shame and anxiety whenever she has to ask him for anything, these two introverts wishing they did not have to deal with each other. And I have to wonder who I would have become had the conversation gone a different way. Would I have overcome my paralysing performance anxiety, and excelled at the piano? Would I have remained mediocre? Would I have taken up a different instrument, joined an orchestra overseas? Become an academic rather than a performer? What people would I have met, loved, befriended? What music would I have heard, what composers would I have fathomed? What books would I have read? What would I have understood about my life? Would my mother have returned eventually in the way she did? Or would that never have become necessary?

People given to regret tend to forget that the road not taken might have turned into a dead end round the first bend. Had I set out on that musician's journey, I might have failed my fate in any number of ways. And would I have been able to sustain the level of commitment, the hours of practice? What I do know is that a road forks right there, at the moment a daughter loses the last vestiges of confidence in a father's regard for her.

It might seem odd that I did not fight for the scholarship. But I lacked conviction. What happened in a conservatorium anyway, other than more piano practice? My knowledge extended no further than the school gates. Outside those gates were unknown roads, one as good or bad as another. There was nothing in my existence so far that could help me choose.

Thus, when those gates closed behind me, I entered the portals of adulthood with a woman's body, the face — so said one of the teachers — of a Leonardo angel, a shyness so profound that it amounted almost to aphasia, and the mental development of an eleven-year-old.

And where was my mother during this time? I thought no more about her during school years than I had on Tamborine Mountain, but her death had proved useful once, in a moment of extremity.

I was in trouble for something with a teacher, and without really thinking about it, I began to cry, saying, 'I don't have a mother.' It was spontaneous and at the same time calculated. I was surprised at it myself, and surprised that the ruse worked. Apparently other people could feel sorry for me when I felt no such sorrow myself. It is easy to say now that my mother must have been quite close to the surface of the cement, even then. But after that one manifestation, and pretty much until her re-emergence thirty-odd years later, she now disappears beneath consciousness altogether.

Eighteen

Illuminated beneath another spotlight: a white-brick-veneer flat with aluminium sliding windows. A friend from school has invited me to rent a room with her there. Her mother must have furnished the place. It is a modern flat, but not modernist. Modern in this sense means the kind of cheap development built in collusion with corrupt governance, which uprooted the lovely old wooden houses characteristic of a more graceful century.

There is music on the record player – Sérgio Mendes. It is, I think, 1966. Or 1967, perhaps.

I am smoking heavily by now. Everyone smokes. Every house and every office in the Western world has little burn marks on the edges of tables and desks, where fags have been left and forgotten. My sister shares her Rothmans with me when I visit her. We spend our entire time together cleaning the house, washing nappies and smoking. We don't have money for clothes but there is always money for fags, which are, like food, automatically shared. She, like me, has only one dress. The mother of a schoolfriend has made mine for me. (I remember the first dress I bought with my own money – plain black crêpe fitted at the waist.) My sister is overwhelmed with babies; her marriage has its difficulties. She has so little time or money for herself. I fall in love with each of the children as they arrive, but the grand passion is with the first one, Onnie.

Perhaps because of the children, or because I myself am no longer a child, the old tensions between us have dissolved. And there is always the familial laughter that reaches right down to the gut. Even so, dominance and submission are so deeply encoded in our kinship, they are unassailable.

In the little white-brick flat, I am a country cousin. The others have clothes, parents, certain shared ambitions, and are so much more knowing. They can see their way ahead, or rather they do not have to see ahead because their futures already have a shape; their futures will follow along preordained routes, like water along stream beds. There will be marriage. (To a lawyer, or some other professional.) There will be children. A house. Then a better house. My flatmates exist within a continuum. But I have to make my own stream bed as I go. Having no idea how I might do so, I attempt to join their stream and eventually find a boyfriend – a sweet man, handsome, good-natured, not part of the law-student gang. He is an engineer, and therefore not as eligible as a lawyer. He is something of an outsider in the law-students' milieu, perhaps in any milieu. He attends the same parties, but inhabits the outer rim, which I share with him. The lawyers seem not to like girls much. They talk about 'tits' in such a way as to make you feel ashamed, and then foolish if your shame shows. Yet they, too, are on the lookout for the right one to marry. My flatmates know how to behave with them and what to do, know how to hold out on full sex until you are pretty sure a proposal will eventuate. Or how to have full sex without damaging your chances. Rum and Coke is a popular drink. Whisky and ginger ale. Vodka and syrupy orange. Often a mix of all three followed by an evening spent wrapped around a porcelain toilet bowl. Other drugs have not arrived on the scene just yet, at least not in the little flat.

The *raison d'être* of the flat is as a safe courting ground before the mature part of life begins.

The engineer is kind and funny and he never uses the word 'tits'. He asks me to marry him.

It is all I can do not to leap out of the chair I'm in, and run for the horizon, so deep and certain is the refusal. It is an instantaneous and categorical rejection of entrapment.

Another four significant events, then we'll get out of that white-brick flat. One: I wish to lose weight so I take 'diet pills' – speed. The same amphetamine pills, no doubt, that my sister was given when she was a child. Like her, I grind my teeth all night and fall asleep during the day.

Two: I search the papers for jobs. I have frail qualifications for any kind of employment, but have taught myself touch typing from a Pitman's book. I find a job shifting papers around on a desk in a warehouse. There doesn't seem to be much to do there, certainly nothing to which I could contribute opinion or skill. On my second day, the owner of the warehouse strokes me up and down with a 'vibrator' – a just-new thing he has imported and wants to 'try out'. This makes me feel queasy, but pushing him away would somehow be worse. (I sit very still, like prey in the cross-hairs.) He lets me go. I do not return. For a while I sell tickets in a casket agency. Then I see a job as a library assistant at the university. It is a menial job, pushing books around on a trolley. Thanks to the pills, I nod off a great deal in the stacks. I am too shy to go to the refectory for lunch, so stretch out in the Dewey 900s to sleep.

Three: one day I pick up a book. It has new binding, which is perhaps why I choose it above others. It's called *Catch-22*. I take the book home and read it all night and, calling in sick, all the next day. When it is finished, I call in sick again, and read the book a second time. I hardly recognise the war the characters are in, it is so unlike my father's war. Nor could I say that I 'understand' Yossarian or Milo Minderbinder or Major Major Major Major. Simply, something in me vibrates at the same frequency they do. This was the first indication that there was something Beyond. A place, an idea, something outside the boundaries of the place I was in and the expectations of that place. And it provided the hope, or intuition, that I was not so freakish after all, that my inexperience and ignorance would somewhere be forgiven and I'd be taken in.

Joseph Heller, speed and a library: such combinations of blind luck can turn an existence around. I began to read, naively of course, identifying with characters to whom I devoted more love, generosity and compassion than I knew how to show real people. The novels were teaching me what all good novels can: that it is better to understand than to judge.

I am not sure that there is a direct causal link between *Catch-22* and the first small, but significant risks. But certainly the devouring of books was coeval with newfound courage. Not only could I now face buying and eating my lunch in a public place, I also responded to a message I saw tacked to a university noticeboard. A room for rent in a shared house. I rang the number. I reached the zoology department.

Four: I have dressed myself up in my cream crêpe dress. I have set and curled my hair and applied full make-up. (Brown then blue then white eyeshadow, eyeliner, pencilled eyebrows, thick pancake then beauty spot.) I wear cream stockings and cream shoes. My heart is beating so hard I fear that it might show its pulsing through the crêpe. I am mortified by sweat under my arms. When I meet Carden, I see immediately that I am all wrong. She wears sandals made out of old car tyres, and no make-up. I am younger than she, by half a dozen years. She is doing her PhD in zoology. She is kind. (Immeasurably, unaccountably kind.) I am invited to move in.

Thus I find my first exogenous family in a many-roomed old colonial house in Indooroopilly, near the university. It has vast upper and lower verandas, cedar doors. There are blue-tongue lizards downstairs, outside my room. (I feed them with banana. I feed myself with tins of mushrooms.) Before too long, I begin to join in the life of the household. In the evenings we gather on the upstairs verandas to drink wine from casks, share cigarettes (I now smoke Drum tobacco — rollies), and watch fruit bats flying over a mango-coloured sky — thousands of them, then thousands again — while listening to music from Nashville, New York, London — places infinitely far away, infinitely longed for.

One day, at the university refec, there's a trio performing something classical. No one is listening to them. They play above the noise of plates clashing and students arguing. I see that the music is an irrelevance. It belongs in another century. A little last door closes behind me.

I am the youngest member of the household (the mascot), which hovers around the half-dozen mark, depending on who is travelling, whose friends are crashing there, who enjoys semi-permanent residency because he or she is fucking someone with permanent residency.

At Hillsdon Road, no one loves the Queen and there are no short back and sides. War is a source of shame, not of pride. The war in Vietnam is particularly shameful. There are piles of dirty washing-up all over the kitchen. One of the men, lazing about on the veranda, has an Afro. And under the house, living in the dirt there, is an itinerant 'poet' with a sleeping bag.

What is my poor dad to make of all this? He comes to visit me once, wearing his grazier's hat, and none of the 'long-haired louts' stand up to shake his hand. Perhaps he went home and confided in Mrs Wallace next door. Or perhaps he kept his worries to himself.

I felt his vulnerability acutely, however, and it filled me with guilt. My duty was to protect him from anything upsetting, including myself. Especially myself.

I must have visited him at least once, because I recall an argument in his kitchen, about independence in Rhodesia. 'Aw gawd,' he says, exasperated at last. 'You don't know what the hell you're talking about.'

He was right about that at least.

Having an idea of what one talked about required a basic grasp of first principles. But how does one acquire first principles when everyone else takes them for granted and has long since moved on to middle and final principles? How was I to catch up and, at the same time, not let the unknowing show? Most of my opinions were received opinions, suspended in a void of ignorance.

But I was watchful, I listened and mimicked, and then tested the mimicry against ...

Against what? That is the mystery. Some sort of innate discernment. Something intrinsic to the individual, which the individual had no hand in creating. A tendency, the origin of which is hidden from us, yet it rules our fate. We think we own it, but we own nothing, not even our thoughts which rise to the surface like deep-water fish.

In my own case I did not inherit a noble, charismatic or morally courageous character; I was given a restless, questing character. The sort of character that wants to get behind the act, to the truth of things. (The quest involves a rebegetting of the self: being one's own mother.) Such a character can display reckless disregard for consequences, often misread as bravery.

It seemed remarkable to me that most people took their existence for granted. They had no idea that they were lodged in a sliver of light hurtling through infinite dark. They did not consider that all their actions, large and small, would have infinite ramifications. They moved through their time like billiard balls, knocked into life by the first hit, then shot around until pocketed. When the commonplace of death presented itself, they would be aghast, as if they had never believed that it might come to them really. There would be no time to ponder what importance darkness might have shed on light.

Death and I were already well acquainted at that time. I smoked very little dope and not often because when I did

Death came in through the French doors of my bedroom to terrorise me.

I seldom contributed to conversations about worldly matters. Yet I remember quite vividly having a disagreement with a university radical in Hillsdon Road. He led demonstrations and had Bob Dylan hair. I proved to him (he was surprised and unconvinced), one afternoon, that there was no such thing as free will. We lived with the illusion of it, had to live with it, but every instant was determined by the incalculable instants before; it could not be otherwise. This was not an idea I had absorbed from other people or from books; this was something I *knew*.

Just as I knew that the only sensible form of social organisation was anarchism, though I would have known nothing about the political movement, nor been able to use the word in a sentence. But it seemed self-evident that if there were no constraining forces whatsoever, no one would have anything to gain or lose. Humans would behave well for the simple reason that there was no reason not to. They would gain nothing from being bad, because everything would already be available to them. Everyone would be totally free, and with such freedom there would be no one either to clamber above or sink beneath.

The social structure of Hillsdon Road encouraged this view. We cooperated with and cared for each other without compulsion or rules.

Sometimes we drove, in the evenings, to a waterhole in the bush, to swim naked, or walk through the scrub, learning the plants and the birds. My mentors took me seriously enough to educate and include. They lent me their books, and they consoled me when, in orphan mascot style, I wept at the unbearableness of existence.

Such people are the heroes. The ones who help others come into being.

I worshipped them, but at some point I must have felt I had absorbed all I could from them. I don't know what prompted me to choose Sydney. In any case, a pattern now began to express itself. Throw bombs over your shoulder, throw seeds into the future, so that by the time you get there, something will be growing.

★

It is about nine o'clock in the evening. I am at a truck depot on the outskirts of Brisbane. It is 1968 and I am almost eighteen years old. There are road trains parked around. Possibly there are petrol and diesel pumps. I ask a man about a lift to Sydney. Yes, he says, but not for several hours. He takes me to a bunkroom where I can sleep until the trucks are ready to leave. I lie on the top bunk though I am not at all sleepy.

Only one or two glimpses of the journey down remain. The driver took pills, and drank coffee and alcohol. I don't remember the arrival at all, or rather there are various arrivals in Sydney. The first that comes to mind, I seem to be getting off a train, not a truck. Certainly I have never been here before. I have nowhere to go, no one to meet. I begin to walk through the streets. Perhaps it's a Sunday, because there is hardly anyone in the streets. Brisbane is the only town I know anything of – a viscid, dawdling sort of place – and I had assumed this would be different, more tightly wound and dense. It is different in other ways. The kinds of buildings never seen before, it is thrilling to see them, shoving up against each other, leaning into the street, brick not wood, two storeys not one, no yards separating them. Some seem to be empty.

Newspaper blows about and I think of a poem I'd liked at school … 'like rats' feet over broken glass'. Indeed there is broken glass here and there. A man in a greatcoat walks towards me up the other side of the pavement. He lurches over and grabs me between the legs. My elbow strikes him in the chest – a completely automatic response. He sniggers and stumbles away.

A year later I would know this area quite well. Ultimo. The only human corpse I had ever seen would be discovered there. A car parked in an empty street. An old man asleep along the back seat; though he wasn't asleep, he was dead. A wino, probably. Perhaps even the man who had accosted me. And perhaps he was not all that old after all. Certainly everything about him was grey. His face, his ankles, his clothes, his open mouth. I don't remember informing the police, though I assume I must have told someone. Then again, I would be just as likely to have left the responsibility to others, at that time.

I know that I walked a lot that first day. A muscle memory of achy feet. And I know that I found a park to sleep in. I am pretty sure it was Centennial Park. In my memory the policeman is on a horse. (Were there park rangers then on horses?) He moved me on, so perhaps I kept walking, found another park. Or perhaps I moved to a denser grove of trees.

I don't know how many nights I slept in Sydney's parks. Or in the laneways behind rows of houses. Generally

I preferred the parks, of which Sydney had many, each more ravishing and extraterrestrial than the last. New trees, new leaves! Humboldt on the Orinoco could not have been more thrilled by the exotic forms he found.

I drank at public fountains, cleaned my teeth and washed in public lavatories, or sometimes, timorously, in hotel 'rest rooms'. By day I walked. The cardinal points were so deeply engraved in my awareness that I found urban patterns confusing. I was attuned to the sun and slant of shadows, to horizons, to on- and off-shore breezes, to landmark hills, so that even when I lost my way in the maze of obstructing streets, my body knew where it was. One day I walked all the way to the headland where the ocean entered the harbour. This was the kind of coast I had not seen before. An uncanny sea, pulsing into small beaches held between cliffs. The water not Queensland blue but glassy green and cold. Southern.

Wherever I walked, I was aware of roots protruding from asphalt, of plants pushing through cement cracks, of figs clinging to roofs and walls, of oysters clustered on pylons. The city was a crust over what was fundamental, and the crust could be kicked away as easily as moss from a rock.

The city's rules could not apply to me because I did not, as yet, know what they were. I was following more elemental rules. I was here as an explorer, arrived from a separate kingdom. Not for a moment did I feel myself to be deprived or pitiable. I lived as an aristocrat, rich in my poverty, in perfect liberty, answerable to no one, expecting nothing and asking for nothing other than to be left to myself.

Everything was new and potent. I was absorbing, occupied with absorbing, knowledge. How to avoid danger, how to be invisible, how to discern the overall shape, the geometry of the city, the kinds of people in it, the low and the high, their houses, the different densities, different costumes, even the different dogs. I don't remember what I wore, what I ate, to what extent I was hungry or lonely or frightened. I think fear was so constant and well integrated that I did not pay it much attention. What memory brings me now are flickers of elation and moments of amazement, on a ground of mundane dread.

On one of my walks, I came across an abandoned cottage in the inner suburb of Erskineville. It was near a railway line. The garden was a rank tangle, there was a lopsided FOR SALE notice in the front yard. I saw a cat slip out from underneath the house and disappear around the back. Perhaps I crawled through a front window, or perhaps I came in through the back. What I remember is the idea: 'This is where I will stay, in solitude, for as long as it takes. This is where I will find out what is within me.'

Nineteen

The cottage was divided equally into four rooms, with a porch at the front. Out the back was a lean-to kitchen and cement bathroom. Beside the bathroom, a barren old plum tree.

One room contained a treadle sewing machine like the one my mother had used on Stanley Park; in another, a gas heater and an upright piano, walnut veneer peeling from it like sunburnt skin; in a third, a double bed with springs but no mattress; nothing at all in the fourth. There was some sort of cooker in the kitchen, and perhaps a cupboard. I can't make out much more through the obscuring distance. Gas and electricity must have been available, though I remember lighting candles.

If houses can be said to be metaphors of mind, then this poorly constructed, neglected little cottage, isolated and unkempt, hiding from sight its few useless pieces of furniture, fairly represented mine at the time.

My first days there are obliterated, but I would have been out on the streets, hunting for what I needed. On rubbish collection days you could find everything necessary to furnish a mansion. It was astounding what people threw away. It was on the city's superfluity that I would now learn to live, as monks used to do, though without needing to beg.

I soon discovered the profligacy of markets. I took home boxes of vegetables and fruits that the market sellers discarded. I boiled the produce and mashed it into goo.

Sometimes I went around to the side doors of restaurants just before closing, to ask for food the workers were throwing away. I was invariably met with a civility that would be illegal now, I am sure. Today it would be necessary to go to a designated place of charity, where those who have little and those who have much must behave like separate castes.

I walked everywhere, though occasionally asked bus drivers for free lifts. I don't recall ever being turned down. Had I been, it would not have troubled me. I don't recall being treated with contempt. I remember amiable indifference.

In the daytime, I studied people. Young people, grouped together, tribal. A beautiful girl with black hair wearing a white Victorian nightdress with red patent-leather, lace-up boots. There were various other 'looks' available – headbands, à la American Indian, worn with cotton kaftans recently imported along the Asia trail, and reeking of patchouli. But the style I could afford could be purchased in junk shops for almost nothing: 1920s satin and silk nighties, long and loose. A Grecian-goddess look, with sandals. No bras, no knickers, tassels of armpit hair.

During my night prowls around the Cross and in the parks, I saw things that would become visual mementos of the time. A young soldier back from Vietnam on R and R, fucking a prostitute in the doorway of a block of flats. Both fully dressed, both standing up, she leaning up against an art deco column, eating a meat pie.

A woman wearing a sailor's hat, douching herself over a drinking fountain in Rushcutters Bay Park.

I did steal from time to time – milk from front porches in the early mornings before occupants awoke; flowers from gardens that no one wanted, no one admired. I took them back to the cottage to fill bottles on windowsills. These criminal activities were last-resort strategies which twinged my conscience. But what I shamelessly stole was books.

In the compost of my mind were all the books I had digested so far. *Catch-22, Down and Out in Paris and London, Voss, The Vivisector, Nausea, Siddhartha.* Vonnegut, Dostoyevsky, Balzac, Kafka, Baldwin, Camus, KAFKA … so many, and so passionately if naively consumed. I did not have a system of reading: that is, books that began at one level of understanding, then progressed to the next. I read so haphazardly that one sort of information did not connect logically with other sorts of information, thereby forming a kind of grid. Inevitably I would sink in a welter of half-grasped facts, or fall straight through huge holes in the grid. If this were true with novels, it was infinitely worse with newspapers. Had I stolen a paper along with the milk, there was nothing within me with which to decipher the information there.

To understand a newspaper you must have a grasp of systems, institutions, the social structures we all live within. You must have at least a rudimentary knowledge of geography and history. You have to have some inkling of what came before, in order to understand what exists now, and how it might lead into the next thing. Too many key concepts were missing to make deductions. I did not know how a bank functioned (I had never been inside a bank), what a bureaucracy was, what a political party was, how a company was formed or what it did, what constituted a nation or how those nations came to be. How and why had governments and their rules arisen? How had police formed to enforce those rules? Who had agreed to this? In short, by what process did emergent social structures happen and how could one begin to figure out their operation?

I understood power relations only as they existed between individuals. Now I needed to extend that understanding to systems of power. Until I did so, I would lie low, beneath any radar, my existence unrecorded anywhere.

Again this makes it sound as if I'd reasoned things out. Not at all. The desire to stay beneath scrutiny was blind instinct – a feral urge towards liberty, fertilised by the zeitgeist.

The inner directive was to isolate myself so I could begin to piece together something acceptable using whatever I could glean from my investigations, from my reading, and from the residue of Hillsdon Road. These I would use to build a functional individual over whatever footings remained after my mother's death, when everything had come undone. Once I found out what was normal, I would be able to orient myself in relation to that norm, and eventually pass as normal myself.

The cottage would provide temporary shelter in which this work of transformation could take place – the first phase of the autodidactical or, rather, autogenic project. Then would come the second phase, in which the construction would be tested beyond the safety of the cottage, out there in the Great World.

The scrawny unloving cats, living their lives in the low dark beneath the house, emerged at night as long flat shadows, to drink the milk I gave them, looking back over their shoulders with implacable mistrust. Thus we shared the cottage, anonymous and ignored, controlled by no one.

I don't think I was aware of the unusualness of this project of mine. If there are no conventions available to you, you are unorthodox by default.

Certainly the spiritual adventure of solitude was no guarantor of happiness. There were days when it was impossible to get out of bed. I would see, with relief, the beast of melancholy disappearing over the horizon, only to find, a little later, that it had circled around behind and was at work again, dismantling, destroying – a periodic annihilation of everything I had achieved. But I had never expected freedom to come without cost and I understood early that it is not knowledge that makes one happy. Delusion and forgetting make for happiness. Happy people did not know that the partition between everyday consciousness and the stranger places is tissue thin. They did not enter the abysses there, or understand that staying out of them, being 'normal', requires effort, will and vigilance. They thought reality was what it looked like.

I wish I could write about that ancestral self as if there were clear continuity between us, but I can hardly believe we are the same person. I cannot enter her mind as it was, but as I imagine it now, from this far-distant perspective. From what source has she mustered the courage to do what she is doing? She is so unformed, so utterly devoid of nous.

But inside the timidity and ineptitude, what extraordinary drive. Where did it come from, that drive?

I am not helped by a lack of evidence. She must have sent letters home, innocuous and full of lies. But there are none extant that I know of. She seems to have had no interest in documentation, as if it might stem the flow of experience.

Valéry said that one's ignorance is a treasure, not to be casually spent. Certainly my ignorance (my awareness of it) was (and continues to be) incalculably valuable to me. Usually the human ego cannot withstand insult and struggles to hide its deficits, not just from the outside world, which doesn't matter, but from itself, which does. Lucky for me a sense of shame outweighed egotism. My ignorance being unfathomable, learning must therefore be immeasurable. A life of exploration and investigation lay ahead, an endless evolution towards humanity, and that was reason enough to drag myself out of bed, to force the gaze outward, reason enough to stay alive. It is very good indeed continually to plumb the depths of one's own ignorance. There is no better goad.

In the immediate, it was the city I had to come to grips with. It took a very long time, decades, before I would feel entirely at home in a city, to see it as something unto itself, and not as something obscuring nature. Perhaps, even now, I am temperamentally feral in a city. In any case, by the end of that period of solitude (my guess is that it lasted about three months), even though Sydney's codes remained abstruse, I knew I could survive in it.

I was unhappy and lost a lot of that time, but what adolescent isn't unhappy and lost? I remember the grimness of it. Fear and friendlessness. Darkness falling without warmth or company. Candles in bottles and execrable food. Yet not for a second would I have considered myself hard done by or unlucky. I was making my own line, as orphans are required to do.

Besides, I had my inner world to retreat into (though the inner is not necessarily safer than the outer) – a tremendous universe only intermittently inhabited, as far as I could tell, by a reliable overseer, and often populated by people who thought things quite independently of me. I had never spoken to anyone about the bedlam sealed in my insignificant skull. Nor had anyone spoken to me about theirs.

I don't know what induced me to decide that I was ready for phase two. There were odd jobs at first: washing dishes, waitressing. Eventually I found work as an artist's model. How did I find out about art schools? I think it must have been when I approached some young people in a park – long hair, guitars, the smell of dope. Sick with shyness, but trusting them. Perhaps it was via them, or people I met through them, that I found places to crash for the night, then spare rooms in shared houses – huge old houses, run-down, but elegant and cheap to rent. In Paddington, Redfern, Centennial Park. In Edgecliff, in Bondi by the sea ...

So it was that I often found myself in strange circumstances, with strange people who behaved in strange ways. I cannot remember his name: a very white-skinned, blonde man. His head was all skull and very little flesh. He took massive amounts of drugs in a phlegmatic way, without self-drama. When high he would pick up willing disabled people and invite them to bed. He liked the way a hand might fall in the wrong place, he said. The unexpected, tender nature of it. He enjoyed giving himself and his pick-ups drug pessaries, he said. I do not remember any kind of discomfort or embarrassment when he confessed these things to me. In any case, they were not confessions because they contained no guilt. He simply described his proclivities and desires. There was no sense of shock or distaste on my side. When you are a stranger in a strange land, the ordinary is no less strange than the bizarre.

There was another artist's model at the college I found interesting. I think her name was Gretel, or Gretchen. She began to earn money as a stripper in the Cross. I went to some of her shows. From there she discovered her calling as a dominatrix, abandoning her doctoral dissertation for a no doubt more lucrative future.

A painter, giving me Mandrax and red wine in the toilets of the art college. His waist-reaching mane of black ringlets which he lifted from his pouting face with freckled fingers. Later, in a room with him, listening to an LP … 'he not busy being born is busy dying …'

A man at the door of the Erskineville cottage. I don't know who he is. I invite him in. He is conservatively dressed, attractive, not at all unsympathetic. I am curious about him. For some reason, he undoes his flies, takes out his penis and places it on the keys of the piano. There is nothing threatening about this. His penis is flaccid: the action matter-of-fact. Then he goes away.

Two students, a girl and a boy, are visiting from the art college. They smoke dope and ask me to get into bed with them. But this is precisely the border at which my open-mindedness closes, at least in regard to myself. I had not read Aristophanes' description of the sundered soul searching for its other half, but I certainly would have been in agreement. In spite of everything I had experienced so far – the predictable, unerotic encounters; the crude phallic ethos of the sixties; the forced sex and semi-rapes – somehow the idealisation of sex as a sacred revelation, private and precious, had survived the violations. Physical love was the place where one might taste transcendence. But that could only be shared with The Other. Not two or three of them.

This business of sex, at that time: I slept with men because everyone did. It was simply expected, like shaking hands. There was little pleasure in it, at least for me, and I suspect, often for the men, beyond the release of jizzom and the collection of scalps. That said, I was not as promiscuous as most. I was too shy and odd for flirtation, and usually silent in any gathering larger than two. Silence is enigmatic. It generates anxiety. Thus I was not a genuine success in the sexual arena, lacking both arts of seduction and sisterly ease. As for women, I would certainly have slept with them but for a suspicion that in doing so I would risk disappearance altogether. Sex with men was like water meeting rock. Each retained its identity. Sex with women would be like water meeting water. But I liked women and found them beautiful, arresting and desirable.

The poet must also be mentioned here. Again I have no inkling of how we met. But his car, a blue Holden, is parked outside the Erskineville cottage.

He is inside reading aloud to me. From 'The Crow' and then 'The Blue Guitar'. Followed by Sylvia Plath. 'You do not dooo, you do not do / any more, black shooo / in which I have lived like a foot / for thirty years, poor and white, / barely daring to breathe or achooooo ...' I could recite several poems by heart by the time he left a couple of weeks later. We slept together but I don't remember sex. I vaguely understood he was a junkie, though he had been careful not to let me see him shooting up. I knew people shot up heroin, but they belonged to a different class. They were drug extremophiles, and regarded as braver, cooler and scarier. One night he was very ill. I wanted to get a doctor but he was adamant that I must not. If I did they would haul him back into prison. One evening we drove up to Palm Beach, past the bourgeois houses fronting a lagoon. My friend got out, and from the boot of the Holden pulled a fishing net. This he cast into the lagoon. We stripped off our clothes and waded out, catching fish, shrieking with delight. The lights in the houses went on. We were 'busy being born'.

Drugs were used casually and without questioning, which is to say they were part of the culture. There was marijuana and hashish, magic mushrooms, LSD and any other hallucinogen going the rounds. An afternoon comes back to me. A room I had helped paint white, in some old collapsed mansion I was staying in. A beautiful girl with dark hair. Coloured cushions and a mattress on the floor. Chewing the seeds of a baby woodrose, a dried flower one could purchase in florist's. Spending the next several hours holding our tongues between index finger and thumb, because of a fear they would slip down our throats and suffocate us. Another room, in Balmain. A sexual encounter and LSD. His room full of plants, which begin to take over the walls, the ceiling, the bed. I am Titania and he is Oberon. We dance naked in the infinite woods of his bedroom. Bad trips too, longing only that the hell would be over before madness engulfed completely.

And splendour. The muddy shrouds of ordinary perception peeled away to reveal ineffable splendour.

Most of my modelling work was at the East Sydney Technical College – a handsome sandstone compound made by convicts to house themselves a century before. I got plenty of work because I knew intuitively how to put my body into shapes that were interesting to draw. I had still not seen a living painting, but took in what the teachers said to their students. One day I visited the Sydney Art Gallery. I did not know how to behave there, but very quickly anxiety was dispelled by a painful wonder and longing. The pictures were not of anything; they were unlike anything I had seen before, abstract and unintelligible in any ordinary sense. Yet their makers had projected into form the uniqueness of one human mind, in a way that spoke for and to another (to me) in a profoundly evocative language. That day is so branded on my memory that I can relive it even now, feel again the mysterious excitement those paintings caused.

It was not possible for me, at that time, as I was, to imagine myself equal in spirit to the people who produced such things. I had to become a solid something before it would be possible to know what the something could wish for. It is hard to explain this awareness of incompleteness. I knew only what was not right for me.

Nursing (my sister's wish, to toughen me up), university studies (universities taught nothing about life), marriage (a life of servitude), the conservatorium (five hours' practice a day to perfect an anachronistic and irrelevant art). I could turn from them all, but towards what? I had sensed that what most students learnt at their tertiary institutions was not supposed to stay with them. It would provide a temporary gloss to be abraded later by the demands of the world of marriages, children and production lines. An education was not meant to establish a foundation for the infinite enquiry ahead, nor to provide a ballast to stabilise the soul as it explored vast oceans of ignorance. It was not meant to change anyone, but rather to be a temporary diversion from the necessity that everything remain the same.

I wonder what direction my life might have taken had I been capable of assuming the right to the category 'artist'. The very word reeked of pretension, or was an order of being so vastly far off that I could not even imagine aspiring to it.

And yet I believed there was something in me that must be brought forth. What could it have been that I thought I had within me? Only an impulse forward into the stream of life, a primitive belief that if I watched and listened, if I explored that stream without defending myself against whatever came my way, that unnamed something within would respond with something true.

Just as *Catch-22* had blown on some feeble ember within, so those paintings teased into life a longing for expression that music had not been able to do. It was, therefore, through the making of marks that I determined to locate 'the source'.

I bought half a dozen pots of cheap poster paint. A brush. Thus equipped I sat in front of the white wall of the empty room in the Erskineville cottage. I would go down to the root of myself and, from that place, would produce something entirely my own. How long I sat there I don't recall. I don't think I even made a mark. What I remember is devastation. 'If you bring forth what is within you, what you bring forth will save you. If you do not bring forth what is within you, what you do not bring forth will destroy you.'

The destruction in this case was positively Dostoyevskian. The bareness of my existence was an anguish I had never felt so acutely. To have all that cruel, bottled-up longing, without a drop of capacity, knowledge or wisdom with which to express it. To be unable to find anything to fling against the hurricane of meaninglessness that lies at the root of reality. To be torn always between desire and fear, wanting so much to belong in the Great World, yet lacking an essential self-worth. To find out what a life like mine might want, what it might need, what it might be able to give that was of any value. That might make it anything but 'useless ugly stupid'.

I returned to the schoolgirl habit of writing bad poetry. Occasionally I thought I could glimpse a glint of gold down there amongst the tailings, but just as I struggled for the words to express what I had seen, the glimmer was covered again, and I could not bring it up into thought.

Yet amidst all that mess and striving, the failure and poverty and despair, I began to throw threads across the holes in the net, to make connections, to build. Eventually I formed a queer facsimile of an adult, a freakish development full of mistakes, but if you didn't look too closely at it (and who would care enough to do so?) could pass. My construction stood. I had climbed through the cottage window psychologically an eleven-year-old, and emerged from it months later at the age of nineteen.

That period set a pattern that would recur for decades. Restlessness, interspersed with long periods of living where I did not belong, accepting my own strangeness in the midst of strangers, at the same time trying to empty myself of whatever habits I had brought with me, habits of being and believing. To doubt everything gained so far: to put it to the test of new perspectives, of difference. You have to begin anew in each locale, learning references, finding a place inside a different frame, building new grids in which to catch new information. I would not remain in any of those worlds: that is, make them my home. Homes were things it was necessary to escape from. If you did not leave them, what happened to future selves? If you did not leave them, you were stuck with remaining who you were. Being a stranger is partly exile and partly the attempt to be at home everywhere.

Loneliness is unavoidable, of course. But it is not the worst thing. Indeed it can be a useful thing. A fertile thing. It is, after all, the deepest part of us, however much we are meshed into the lives of others.

Twenty

Narendra Singh Bhati. Sahib. My 'companion of first resort' for over twenty years. In all those years, I don't think we ever spent more than two consecutive weeks together. But wherever we were, in London, or Australia, or India, we would ring every day if possible, our conversation as basic as bird calls, letting each know they were being held in another's mind and heart.

He was taciturn by nature, and he kept me outside certain parts of his life. But that wasn't what made him, sometimes, illegible to me. There were depths in that psyche (you could drop a pebble into it and never hear a splash) I had no way of reaching. For one thing, he was religious. And out of that religiosity came magical thinking, superstition – states of mind conceptually and emotionally unavailable to me.

I was (and remain) a materialist. An atheist. I don't deny that I have wished for faith (it must make existence so much easier), nor that there have been anomalies shaking at the struts of my beliefs. (I don't know what to do with those anomalies so I simply let them exist without explanation.) I have been convinced and hugely enriched by certain Buddhist teachings and practices, particularly in their dialogue with Western cognitive science. In any case, when I read my first Buddhist text at the age of nineteen, it struck me as simply true, as if it were describing something I already understood to be the case. Buddhism did not require a belief in God or the supernatural, nor did it provide an end to questioning. But Narendra's religiosity was as much a part of his make-up as his skeleton. It wasn't something subject to doubt.

Several years before his death he had 'converted' from being a Hindu believer to being a Muslim believer. People of Muslim background form 10 per cent of the Indian population. The Hindu majority has increasingly become antagonistic towards that minority. This antagonism has been fed by Hindu fundamentalists via their grass-roots organisations and by their political-front party, the BJP. As a Congress politician, Narendra had begun to spend a lot of time with Muslim communities, publicly taking up their causes. He had been visiting the old Sufi imams in their various mosques and darbars around Rajasthan, and they had begun to teach him their versions of Sufism. Converting to Islam put Narendra once again at odds with the prevailing sentiment. To me it seemed just a change of brand. Slightly different outward forms but the content more or less the same. But looking back I can see that there was an inner transformation going on, and I cannot tell if it was to do with his being ill, or with the appalling tension he was under, or with the formation of a new layer of identity as a follower of Allah.

We did not share the same intellectual background either, our education and reading wildly disparate. But when I gave him books to read he immersed himself in them and it seemed to me that he took them in better than any other reader I knew. Montaigne's *Essays* became his particular favourite. He would return to them, again and again, quote bits to me, chuckling. And I saw that Montaigne's mental processes were accessible to him on more levels than they were to me. Narendra's mind still contained a sixteenth-century stratum. He could understand and recognise Montaigne as a kind of contemporary.

He was, I think, a born politician, his skills honed in the murderous power struggles of the feudal courts. He was the shrewdest judge of character I've ever known – his insight into people's deepest natures, and hidden motives, infallible. I often relied on his acuity in that area. His insight into people I knew, people important to me, was truly astonishing. He saw humans as they were; not constraining them between 'good' and 'evil', but seeing through their deceit and self-deceit and, without rancour, acting accordingly. His organisational abilities were prodigious, and his public and personal courage made him a very visible target. I did not have to see the no doubt unpleasant aspects of his political life – the deals and compromises he had to make – but I was aware of the pressure he was constantly under. I admired his courage, but understood also that the favour-trading must involve moral contradictions I was grateful not to have to think about.

The enormity of the political struggles, the cross-fertilisation of old and new, the stymying complexity, the fallouts and catastrophes that were always imminent, the moral ambiguities with which you were daily confronted, the impossibility of controlling anything, the sense of helplessness in the face of so much need, the sheer magnificent endurance of people, the generosity and sweetness of people, the way that sweetness could turn to its opposite in a second – all this made India a most difficult place to live and totally captivating.

Like most couples, we found ways of accommodating each other's secrets and foibles and incompatibilities. But there was one habit of his that put tremendous strain on the partnership right from the beginning. Knowing the stress he had to endure, I tried to be tolerant of it.

He was addicted to rum. Alarming quantities of it, and taken daily. The word 'alcoholic', a Western concept, held no meaning for him. He simply 'loved his drink'. When he drank and became sentimental or silly or boisterous, I saw him within a context – the Rajput lord in a Mughal court, doing what Rajput lords had always done. Besides, when he was not drinking, he recovered his grace completely. In India I could avoid the bingeing hours by disappearing, and letting him get on with it. But in England his drunkenness was conspicuous and embarrassing. There he was judged by the standards available, which were rather righteous compared to Indian tolerance.

I had struggled to make Narendra's world (my world in India) translatable to my world in the West but his world was inevitably judged by the other world's standards, their unconscious assumptions that their own values were universal values, their own way of being the correct way of being. You cannot square such widely separated realities. You can only live between the two, never integrating them.

Nor could my non-Indian friends easily imagine the kinds of politics Narendra was immersed in, the everyday reality of threat. It took me a long time to understand it myself. The different forms it took. What it required of him.

I had inklings of it, early on. We had planned to drive up to the mountains from Delhi, but a curfew had been imposed. Sikh separatists, agitating for independence from India, had staged attacks in Uttar Pradesh, our home state in the Himalayas. Bombs had exploded in a nearby town killing scores of people. It was known that secret bases had been set up in the Terai, at the base of the mountains, through which we had to drive to reach our home.

Narendra suggested we should drive up in any case, as he did not believe the threat level was high. By then I knew him well enough to trust his acumen and instincts.

Normally the drive was a ten-hour nightmare of destroyed roads, mile-long lines of trucks stalled in front of railway crossings, accident pile-ups, traffic jams ... But this time the road was empty. By the time we reached the edge of the Terai, evening was falling. There was an army checkpoint. Narendra opened the glovebox to retrieve his identity cards. Inside it was a pistol. We drove fast through the forest. There was not a light, not a sound.

That period also saw the beginnings of the rise of the BJP, the political face of a Hindu fundamentalist fascist organisation, now led by Prime Minister Modi. Narendra detested them, and everything they stood for. But that outspoken and very visible opposition made for dangerous enemies, putting him at odds not just with political rivals and their thugs, but with members of his own family, and their thugs.

Ours was a complex and fragmented kind of life, conducted in at least three countries and several homes. Immensely privileged in one sense, yet characterised by instability, disquiet and jeopardy in another. Often, for me, there was a feeling of unreality, as if I had taken a wrong turning somewhere, and couldn't get back to where I was supposed to be. I could not fit Narendra into my other lives. Even inside my Indian circle of friends he was somewhat anomalous. He was simply untranslatable to the other territories I inhabited. So our 'marriage', and the Indian reality it made possible, could not really be shared. I could not firmly lodge myself there: a fundamental commitment was lacking. And he could not lodge himself in my other lives; that possibility was pure fantasy.

The two decades of our marriage fall roughly into two halves. The first, through the nineties, while my work and his kept us both in constant movement; still there was an underpinning assumption that the plate-spinning would eventually calm down and our lives become more 'normal'. The second was characterised by the gathering realisation that the plates were crashing no matter how frantically we ran between them. That phase was about decline, and it involved a huge psychic cost.

In the first phase I could accommodate the exhausting, unsettling travel, not just between different homes in different continents but a shuffling of different versions of myself. The self brought into being inside one frame was often at odds with the self brought into being in another, so that the mind had to be compartmentalised, each compartment shifting from foreground to background depending on where I was.

Attempting to amalgamate these incompatibilities required heroic energies, and in the second phase I had discovered that my energies were not, as I had once assumed, limitless. Pressures were mounting on us both, and the structures which held our lives in some sort of equilibrium were breaking down. Part of me longed to escape, to flee down any avenue that might take me back to where I was supposed to be, whatever that might mean. But I lacked the courage to make a clean break. In the dark time Narendra was all I had. And I was all he had.

Twenty-One

The club was a large room on the second floor of a nineteenth-century building. A wide staircase led up to it, via a reinforced door containing a little shuttered window. The room had recently been done out in red-and-gold flock wallpaper, red carpet, fake chandeliers. There was a bar along one side, a small commercial kitchen and bathrooms at the back. All the windows along the western and northern sides of the room were blacked out. You might think this would attract attention to the nefarious practices going on behind such dark oblongs, but the police received their cut from the proprietors of all the gambling establishments, including, recently, this one. They would raid sometimes, but always with forewarning, so that the respected and/or rich and/or dangerous clientele could leave in time, or be escorted into the back rooms, leaving only the naive and unimportant to display at the courthouse.

Inside the room, police were referred to as 'dogs' or 'pups', depending on their seniority.

The roulette table was by the windows along the western side. A blackjack table was in the north-west corner. And at the front of the room – that is, the northern end – in a position from which, had the windows not been occluded, you could look out over the square and straight into the courthouse, was the poker table.

My table.

I had a friend at that time, Jay, who was a little older than me and vastly more sophisticated. She wore her hair up, always, and her eyes were dramatised by dark eyeliner à la Cleopatra. She was studying medieval literature. I think it was through her that I was drawn in by the tentacles of what was known as the Sydney Push – a loose alliance of members of the bohemian intellectual life of the city: radical, outrageous, risk-taking. I shared a house in Paddington with some of them. As at Hillsdon Road, I was the youngest.

Perhaps it was Jay who told me that this new club, the Regency, required staff. Girls, of course, to serve drinks and deal at the tables. We went together to meet 'the boss'.

I had never seen anything like him. He wore a bottle-green double-breasted suit with a black lace shirt and canary yellow tie. His hair was black and shoulder length, the back of his head somewhat flat. His skin was white. He wore rings. One big silver ring was set with onyx and an eagle. There were two gold tie clips. His ethnic origins were Greek; his accent working Australian. He wore a daring amount of aftershave, so that the smell of fags and Brut trailed him like a spirit bodyguard. Two of his fingers were missing.

I sat with him at the poker table. It was immediately apparent that I had a knack with the cards – perhaps all those years at the piano. Lovely, slippery Kem number-one cards imported from England. Blackjack did not interest me, and somehow Jay looked better at that table anyway.

But ah, the green semicircle with me at its hub, fanning out a short pack, stacking chips with the left hand while calling the bets, flicking Kems across the baize, taking 2 per cent of the pot at each concluding hand. My addiction to the Transcendent Game was immediate.

To my right each night was a little table with coffee, whisky and, when the length of the game required it, Ritalin tabs. (Sometimes a game could go on for thirty hours with nothing but toilet breaks and plates of sandwiches.) The boss played for the house and, as my competence grew, let me take his place when he had to go off somewhere. I was bedazzled. By the boss and his cohorts, by their language (a rich slang which regretfully I did not record), their outlaw humour, and by five-card stud.

Poker is not just a numbers game. Of course, registering what cards are out on the table, and therefore what the probabilities are for being dealt the card you need, and what the other players are likely to have in the hole, is important. But arithmetic is the least of it. To be a really good player, you must be able to read human vanity, greed, fear, cowardice, recklessness, desperation, pleasure and self-deceit. More importantly, you must be able to control the manifestations of those qualities in yourself. You must display fearlessness and unpredictability by admitting to a bluff while, at other times, bluffing but letting on nothing. If you play for the house, you must also know how to keep one kind of player at the table while quickly emptying the pockets and getting rid of another kind of player, whom you know is an inexperienced one-off (a mug punter). There will be occasions when you do not wish to win, even if you are pretty certain you have the best cards. You may wish simply to stay in the game, so the serious punters, who you want to come again and again, don't leave. The longer they remain, and the higher the stakes, the more the house can skim off the pot, but more importantly, they will enjoy the game and return, or bring in their high-rolling mates. You want very good players to come to your table, as much as you want bad ones, even though you might lose large numbers of chips to them. And if they are on a winning streak, you want to keep them at the table until their luck turns and you can recoup some of your losses.

To run a club successfully requires a king's ransom of finance behind you: to continue paying the police; to shore up undermining from long-standing clubs who have bought fidelity from police and clients and do not want upstart competition; and to ride out losses on the tables. As well, it is useful to have a more indefinable kind of credibility, backed by money, but ultimately to do with class. And Lenny, the boss, did not belong to that class.

The last of the players had gone home, 8 a.m. had come and gone; we were still sitting around, shoes off, feet up on chairs, Lenny lamenting another loss at the roulette table. He had even been talking about going back to 'work' to keep the club open. I did not enquire, but was pretty sure this would involve balaclavas and monkey wrenches. He also thought he might open another, smaller club to serve the criminal hoi polloi. The easier money (no overheads like flock wallpaper) would subsidise the Regency – his dream of becoming a guv'nor; that is to say, to move up the social pyramid.

'Live by violence, die by violence,' he said, for the thousandth time. It was a mantra his cadre used, preparing them for the kinds of deaths they might have to face. And though I did not understand this until later, it also recommitted them to the laws of the underworld – a moral code of a kind.

The doorman. I've forgotten his name. Big and burly, likeable, funny – an old mate of Lenny's, and therefore a mate of mine. For the first time in my life I was earning a reasonable wage and had saved enough to think about what should be done with it. Jay suggested enrolling at university. The Sydney Conservatorium of Music was another possibility. In truth I wasn't galvanised by either, and vacillated. Lenny said I was 'bein' a fuckin' mug'. Procrastination won in the end; applications for university enrolments closed. I could defer any decision for another year. I mentioned this as we tossed back our whiskies, swallowed more Ritalin, and spread out the morning papers bought from the Oxford Street corner.

'Whaddya mean, the registrar has closed the applications?'

'Well … just that … the date for lodgement has passed.'

'What's 'is name … this registrar? Where does he live? Does he have kids?'

I would like to say that a pit of anxiety opened in my belly. But no, my response to the offer was hilarity at the idea of the blameless registrar being visited by the doorman, and the pleasure of being thought worthy of such consideration by the soldiers of the underworld.

The bedazzled cannot see darkness.

Besides, I was in love. The boss was somewhere in his forties, and married. I was nineteen. I was his lover inside a circumscribed world, and was therefore no threat to what lay outside it. Whether his wife agreed with this is a question I never thought to ask her, or myself. On the couple of occasions I'd met her, I liked her very much, and had no desire to trespass upon her realm.

I had long since moved out of Erskineville and begun to meet people who took an interest in me, appeared to find something in me worth cultivating. Perhaps it was only their own goodness they saw. Perhaps all *tabulae rasae* are irresistible. Perhaps it was the simple currency of youth and good looks. My face has always seemed unmemorable to me. Just as, when a child, I studied it in a mirror, it was as if I might forget it myself if I didn't keep checking. Jay and I must have been gorgeous, but only she derived a kind of confidence from it.

With my newfound wealth, I had bought a turntable and classical music records to which, when I wasn't playing poker or reading, I listened, educating my ear. Lenny usually requested Beethoven. One evening, as he was undressing, he took a pistol out of somewhere and laid it on a chair.

'What the hell is that for?'

'Whaddya think it's for? So they won't have much luck.'

'They?'

Lenny looked at me long and hard.

'Never mind,' he said. 'Nothin' to do with you.' I did not see the pistol again, but each time we got into the car, he made me stand back while he opened and closed all the doors, and turned the ignition key.

When I say I was bedazzled, I do not mean that Lenny's was a world I considered remaining in. I may not have thought coherently about it, but the instinct to absorb and move on was an irresistible undercurrent that carried my life along. Jay would also never have thought the club milieu worthy of commitment, but that had to do with something more subtle, some expectation of life different from my own. I never thought of myself as slumming, merely as passing through, and that would be true of any world I entered. I took it on its own terms and lived inside its coordinates. All niches were equally interesting, equally worthy of attention and participation. Being able to move, as a denizen, rather than a tourist, through all layers of society, was essential to me. Not simply to experience otherness, or even to be a participant observer, but to become other myself. In that sense, I had no single peer group in whose identity I could fully immerse my own. Most people I knew might have arguments about all kinds of things, but always within the same frame of reference. An unconscious frame, a given.

Newspapers were no longer the entirely arcane documents they had once been. I was never without a book in my hand. (The crims in the club were oddly impressed by this. Lenny and his kind had made their pacts with the devil, seeing no realistic alternative, but it did not mean they thought it the best kind of life.)

And outside the club, in the air one breathed, was revolution.

Having perceived the fields of power, seen how the interests vested there controlled us all, having understood the structural underpinnings of injustice, how language could be twisted to legitimise any lie, to be not only horrified at systemic inequality, but believing it could be dismantled, having named these forces … we, the generation of the sixties, could take them on and change everything.

We were part of something large and important that was coming into being all over the world. We were shaking things up, turning everything over, in order to design something better for everyone, not just the few. The imagined future was a place where all humankind might flourish (might have the opportunity to bring forth what was within them). To bring about such change would require bravery, even recklessness, because new ground was being broken and there could be no protection other than the protection we afforded each other. There was solidarity across so many different groups then, which might have different interests, but shared the same faith in change. 'Personal identities' were not set in stone but fluid and multifarious.

Sixties idealism is easily mocked a half-century on. But what I remember was the goodness of heart, the way individuals recognised and looked after each other. The seriousness of intent under all that chaos. And the courage.

I was still frustratingly behind in my comprehension of such noble sciences as economics, forever saw myself as nibbling at the outer edges of understanding, yet the principles of the revolution were easy to grasp, and accorded with what I already knew. The society we had constructed was absurd, and so one must dissent from it, and live one's life differently, as a kind of experiment. 'Freedom' was the foundation, but it must be available to everyone, to all the groups left out of the Enlightenment project, anyone excluded on the basis of race or sex or class.

But even though I was part of the great turbulence, I seemed to lack some ingredient necessary for proper ideological belief. Total conviction made me uneasy, as if

I were being asked to join a religion. It wasn't the ideas themselves I had trouble with. It was more that such ideas had to be lived out in the messy real world in which no one could predict outcomes. Good and bad, right and wrong tended to bleed into each other. Life was so infinitely complex, it contained so many contradictory strands, surely there could be no total system for understanding it. Everything human was fallible, incomplete and steeped in ambiguity. So whatever grand schemas my species came up with were bound to be inadequate, must always be provisional and constantly tested.

Thus I lacked the basic components of ideological faith — Manichaean temperament and a blindness to contingency.

I was too uncertain to defend this uncertainty. Besides, how does one articulate a point of view that holds contradictory points of view? There seemed to be no language for doubt, so I kept mine to myself, hoping that, as I learned more, I would be able to join in the collective dogma with more assuredness.

It did not strike me then that there was a paradox in the politics of that time. The big questions we struggled with were existentialist in nature. The search for personal authenticity, for 'truth'. Yet our ideals were collectivist. Marxism and individualism were an interesting but fractious couple. To keep the balance between them required nuance, openness, the willingness to listen to other points of view, to people who thought differently, lived differently, behaved differently.

As it turned out, the tumult and soul-searching wouldn't matter too much. Our hearing was not acute enough to catch the whirring of the great engines of consumerism which would pluck the sting of politics from the tail of the sixties, and turn the rest into product.

Being female at that time was painful and exhilarating. Becoming aware of the history and weight of one's oppression, of the semi-slavery one had been born into, was a hard awakening. At the same time, there was the possibility of grasping freedom from those constrictions, of being part of some new way of being. To be a person, rather than 'just' a woman, whose worth had been measured in relation to men, or to her biology.

But what an ancient burden had to be dismantled. How many archetypes had to be reconfigured. And how would men – who, after all, we loved – be induced to relinquish their dominance. The powerful do not return power without a struggle. To complicate matters, men who called themselves feminists at that time were often a bit, well, drippy. And, you got the feeling, full of covert rage.

The best thing about our new consciousness was not what it revealed about structures of oppression, or the burden of history, but what it fostered between women. Women learnt to value each other in a different kind of way at that time. That is to say, to love and admire each other, to give the same value to each other as unconsciously we had hitherto given to men. Those friendships (sexual or not) tended to withstand the complexities of the age, and long weathering. At least in Australia.

While I found it very easy to love other women (I had always found that easy), I was not interested in their literature. I already knew how women thought and what concerned them. I had to learn how men thought and what concerned them. They, after all, ran the joint. And they did the sorts of things that I wanted to do. They were the beneficiaries of the Enlightenment project to which I aspired. Why waste time on the literature of second-class citizens who had received only offcuts from that project? Women had to educate themselves (pull themselves up by their own bootstraps), to fully participate in the uplands of culture. Ditto all the people who had been left off the list. Blacks, the disadvantaged, the poor, the variously colonised. Everyone deserved a place at that high table, where the greatest productions of human thought and imagination were served.

It was tough that we women were out there on the front lines without benefactors or mentors, but we had each other, and the obvious justice of the cause would guarantee progress. All that was required was courage. 'No such thing as too much freedom,' we said, 'only too little courage.'

There was an added ingredient to the complex mix constituting my feminism at that time. I had seen my mother murdered, so to speak, by the ideology of male supremacy. Not that I blamed my darling father for this murder; he was merely a pawn in the game, a victim to that ideology no less than my mother. But it is hard to trust men when you think of them as players of a game not only skewed in their favour but potentially lethal.

So many women had been erased, it had been accepted as the natural order of things, just as my dad had seen his inherited beliefs as ordained by nature.

All the habits that had regulated relations between the sexes (as between races and classes) were being challenged. Yet there was great camaraderie too. One should not forget that camaraderie, and the struggle to find common ground across the front lines of the sex wars. But behind those front lines, it was women who sustained women and, in my own case, they still do.

Though still unworldly and ignorant, I understood myself to be older, in some ways, than many of the people I knew. I was the only one, for example, who knew how to talk to Lena. Poor Lena, who arrived outside the shared house in Paddington. It was night-time. She was naked. She needed my help because there was a war going on between extraterrestrials and … I can't remember the other side. She possessed vital information and both sides were trying to get hold of her to extract that information. I wrapped her in a blanket and tried to soothe her. We were on the street. The ambulance arrived. The ambulance men were part of the conspiracy, she said. Perhaps I was too?

'No, I'm not a spy. I won't let them hurt you.'

I travelled with her to the hospital and made her drink the pink fluid in the tiny paper cup. She remained in a psych ward for a while. Years later, I heard that she swam into the sea and didn't swim back.

There were many casualties of that wild anarchic era. I am grateful to have been swept up in it, grateful to have kept myself a little in reserve from it, grateful to have survived it.

Eventually I did enrol at the conservatorium and was taught by a very fine pianist. There was tremendous work to be done, correcting faulty technique. A concentrated, boring practice. As well, the study of theory, demanding a concentration made difficult by nights at the poker table without sleep.

At some point I had to play a Brahms rhapsody in front of an audience – a dramatic, unforgiving piece. I managed to get through it, but walked offstage to throw up. As I retched into the lavatory, I knew the life of a performer would never be for me.

I decided to leave the con, and somewhere within, I knew I had done with Sydney. As if a wheel had made a complete turn. I hesitated, not knowing where to go next, but certainly I had come to the end of something.

Lenny had opened the second club, where I sometimes worked. A basement in the city. Men never came in to play before two in the morning. They played with real money, never with chips. A different kind of poker, less elegant. The Regency was going down the toilet. Jay had long since left.

It had been a long night. Lenny and the doorman took me home at about ten in the morning. I seemed to be staying at another flat. Had I left Paddington?

The two men were high, and wanted to come in for one last drink. All I wanted to do was crawl into bed and sleep forever. There was no one in the flat. I allowed them in.

An hour or so later, I asked them to leave. But they didn't leave. I felt tears rise to the bottom of my eyes. Unthinkable to cry in front of them. There was a knock on the door. A young hippie kid, as gormless as a chick just out of its shell. He saw me weeping and tried to be a 'hero'. He was bumrushed out of the flat, then Lenny and his doorman turned on me. I had broken an underworld rule. And it did not matter that I was unaware of it.

A knife appeared from somewhere. Held at my throat. Lenny kept the doorman under control, but did not stop him. What was happening could not be stopped. It was a manifestation of the law. The doorman's talent for violence had been unleashed. It must play its course. I suppose it went on for an hour, the punishment. Making me understand the rules. Who and what I belonged to. I stood up to them and showed no fear whatsoever. I even taunted them. Eventually the doorman left. Lenny stayed. I hit him. He hit me back.

I'd like to imagine I left Lenny's world immediately, but maybe not. And how long did I stay at the conservatorium? No idea. Eventually I told Lenny I was leaving. He pretended to coerce me, but I knew it was not serious. Perhaps he was relieved. He gave me his onyx ring, with the silver eagle.

Nor do I remember why I did something completely out of character. I rang my dad, and asked him to come and get me.

My dear long-suffering dad, the love of my life but someone I barely knew. I don't remember my reasoning, or my state of mind, but contacting him would not have been done lightly.

I had to act against the force of habit. Not asking him for anything was right at the core of my love for him – a mix of not wishing to be disappointed, not wishing to be humiliated and, above all, not wishing to be the cause of his distress.

Yet this time I did not doubt that he would come, and did not doubt that he would want to come. Perhaps because this was the first time I had been honest with him.

So began the period of getting to know my father.

Twenty-Two

My dad and I stood side by side, in an amphitheatre of orange sandstone. The walls were scored white by the trunks of ghost gums, and furred at the top with spinifex. In front of us, a rock-hole, dense swarms of green budgerigars skimming its surface.

Tiny fish rose in glittering billows when we tossed crumbs on the skin of the water which was cold and deep. We would not swim in it; it was our drinking supply. Kangaroos, wallabies and dingos shared it at night; emus visited in the afternoon.

Up on a nearby escarpment, on a flat sandstone surface, was an acre of bora ground – spherical stones laid out in circular patterns. We had spent the morning there, putting the stones back the way we imagined they ought to be. My father was upset that cattle had disturbed the stones. It was an entirely futile gesture; the cattle would come again. He grumbled that the area should be fenced and protected, but we did not mention the people to whom this ceremonial ground belonged. It was only a matter of decades since they were here, dancing their country, keeping it healthy.

A couple of miles away in the other direction were the opal mine shafts, as abandoned as the bora ground. We were the only people inside the horizon.

My dad had set up our camp a mile or so from the waterhole. From the back of his Toyota he unloaded two camp cots, a fold-up chair, swags, billies, a camp oven for damper. We had gathered gidgee wood on our way there for our fires. It makes the hottest coals. This dwelling without walls was as comfortable and safe as any house, grander than a cathedral. At night, before the moon had risen, the sky above us was so packed with glitter it cast shadows.

Looking back at the two of us there, I understand that time has passed differently for my father. For him, the eight years since his wife's death is nothing at all. They may have been hellish years for him but it was a hell that scudded by ever more rapidly. For me, at that time (I was not yet twenty), her disappearance had occurred in another epoch, an ice age before. You have to grow towards old age to feel time's acceleration. Then, too, from my dad's point of view, in that remarkably short period between his wife's death and now, his child had transformed into an adult, whereas he had not changed at all.

In those eight years he had managed to conceal his sadness, or revealed it in ways that only close people could discern. (His eyes misted up too easily. Certain songs made him turn away so you couldn't see his face.) In those eight years he had known little comfort, I suspect, but he had kept himself busy. He had bought a fish tank which he decorated, and knew the fish as individuals, with their own personalities. He kept his house, cooked his simple meals, rose early, visited the Wallaces next door, and his friend Ted

Decker in Sandgate. He made friends with a young girl who lived down the street and who was, I suspect, a better comfort to him than his biological daughters. He built a tall feeding stand for wild birds. Hundreds came at a time. Each morning he put out fresh water in a canvas water-bag for the golfers who teed off a few yards from the front fence. He went fishing, prospecting, on his own or with a mate. He made fanciful objects – lamp stands or sculptures made with mangrove root. He polished agates, faceted gems he had found. He carved into soft stone. I am astonished now at the fineness of the things he made, whereas then, I did not see that they were remarkable. I did not associate him with artistic endeavour. That was my mother's realm.

We never talked about her, of course, but she must have been very much with him. She was not with me at all. But without my knowing so, she was within.

My father was an explorer and adventurer, who had been made redundant from those larger purposes by the demands of post-war domesticity. During the years of marriage and parenthood, his horizon had shifted closer, as if a wall had spread itself along it. But out here in the bush, in his true habitat, he could expand into his most natural self. I didn't falter when I followed him down the mine shafts. I had complete faith in him.

The shafts were twenty to thirty feet down, dug from the rock by men who had come out there fifty years before. They had walked from the nearest town, a hundred miles away, in pairs, with a wheelbarrow between them for carting picks, shovels and water. One would dig at the site while the other would take the wheelbarrow to the waterhole, to fetch a drum of water. A day's walk each way. Then they would swap. Whether any fortunes were made out of these opal fields, I very much doubt. They never became famous, like Coober Pedy or Lightning Ridge. Here, it was mostly boulder opal that was mined, not the high-quality pinfire that might have warranted so much hardship.

My dad made a ladder with green sticks and rope. He went down first, checked for snakes, made sure the struts were stable, then called me after him. From the bottom of the shaft, a thirty-foot tunnel followed a seam of ironstone where silica gel had been trapped in tiny bands, and turned to milky glass. We crawled along on our bellies, brushing away the redbacks, until we reached the end. There, by candlelight, we scraped and clicked at the rock with our picks, watching for a glint of colour.

Back in Malabah days, as we strolled the paddocks together, he would talk of 'the Cretaceous', a word as powerful as a spell, evoking all that time before our time, when the world was contained in minds alien to us, seen by eyes different from ours, perhaps a world without colour at all. A time before wonder and science and speech.

A hundred million years ago, this place, where we were, was a vast shallow sea. Though 'where we were' was much further south then, closer to the ice.

The area was warm and wet. Streams and rivers fed forests and floodplains where sauropods roamed. They left footprints in the mud which in time turned to rock – signatures for primate minds to ponder, a million centuries after the creatures had vanished from the earth.

The sea had been rich with plesiosaurs, pliosaurs, ichthyosaurs. In the air were flying reptiles, terrible to see. Evolutionary currents surged back and forth, leaving myriad extinctions in their wake, raising new variations on themes. Corpses sank into silt: shells, fish, dragonflies, dinosaurs, whole skeletons or single bones or ferns like pressed leaves in a child's botany book. They rotted, or fossilised, or left their mark between layers of mud.

Slowly the sea began to dry out, becoming so acidic that it leached silica from the sandstone. Grain by grain, the rock above us had been worn and weathered, the silicious water seeping down, down, feeling its way into gaps and seams, nodules and hollows, filling the bones of buried beasts. There it waited until time transformed it into glassy potch or, if chance lined up the silica spheres in a particular way, a substance able to diffract light waves, spangling them into rainbows. The opal waited in utter darkness until some agency brought it to birth in light, until some eye and mind evolved to see those rainbow rocks and be amazed.

All of this unimaginable slowness, unimaginable force, creating the stage for a father and daughter, chipping away underground.

I think there was a tiny spark, or perhaps it was a sound. My father's pick had hit a small, partially opalised dinosaur skull. We spent the day trying to extract it whole. Brushes and tiny implements and infinite patience. But it was no good. Part of it crumbled, leaving us with two perfect opal fangs. The rest we left *in situ*.

I wonder what we talked about. I wish I could remember. I am sure we laughed a lot. We would not have broached anything personal. He would not admit to his sorrows. I would not trouble him with my life in Sydney.

We would not have talked much in any case, both of us quite inward people. We pointed things out to each other – the tiny marsupial mice with bottlebrushes on their tails, who raided our tucker. The birds. Perhaps we talked about the people who had moved through this country before us. Or the geological time that had formed the features around us. We would have shared chores – filling the billy. Making the fire. I would have been clumsy and self-conscious, attempting to emulate his skills.

Above ground, on one of our walks around the spoil dumps of old workings, we found porcelainite. If you touched your tongue to it, it stuck. He carved a rhinoceros into the porcelainite, an exquisite thing, one of my most precious possessions. We found opalised sandstone. Insignificant-looking rock you imagine on the surface of Mars, until you run water over it. Then it's as if a light has gone on inside it, and its old oxidised skin flashes every colour of the spectrum.

We drove back to Brisbane. I moved into a shared house with friends. I studied Japanese at the university, and worked at various jobs, one of which was as a research assistant at a medical institute. My job was to look after the animals used in experiments. I lasted about two weeks at the end of which I euthanised one of the dogs, let all the others go and stole a pup, whom I called Diggity. She would accompany me on my walk across Australia.

I formed the deepest, most important friendship of my life during that time, with an American woman, Nancy, a zoologist. Though 'friendship' doesn't do justice to the intensity and depth of that attachment. When we conversed (and our conversations could go on for many hours, many days) it felt as if something greater than the sum of our individual thoughts had been expressed. A sympathy in which nothing needed to remain mute. I visited my dad from time to time. Sometimes we drove out to where my sister lived with her husband and four daughters.

One day I received a telegram. COME TO ARMIDALE IMMEDIATELY. LOVE JAY.

Jay had been teaching at Armidale university. She was living on a farm outside the town. Cold, treeless high country. Big galvanised-iron wool sheds, empty green paddocks framed in barbed wire. I was to meet her in her rooms at the university. I still did not know why she had summoned me. She wasn't in her rooms. In her stead, a large man with a Rasputin beard, charisma around him like static.

Igor was French. He had been involved with the Polish experimental theatre maker Grotowski. There was to be a 'workshop' based on Grotowski's method, in the corrugated-iron wool shed on Jay's farm. Igor swept me into his bearish arms. I think he was wearing a fur coat. Jay was in love with him. My mistrust was instant and deep.

There was a fashion at that time – the 'workshop', in which egos were stripped down past delusion so that the work of reconstruction could begin from a ground of authenticity. This particular version was designed originally for actors, and when you witnessed the bravery of the theatrical work that arose from the process, you had to be impressed.

All very well, but participants in such workshops must have faith in the integrity of the facilitator. There was no denying Igor's power. He was a magnetic, generous and talented man. And a Svengali egomaniac.

I don't remember how long we were at it. Maybe it was only five days. I know we slept very little, ate very little. The intensity generated by the circle of people baring their souls did not let up for a moment. What I remember very clearly was one of the final questions Igor asked each of us. 'What is the substance of the world in which you live?' Some took a minute to answer; others took half an hour. When it came to me, the unconscious spoke for itself, and was truly surprising to me.

'Fire, sun, hot wind, purity, bright burning air, desert desert desert.'

This was the ignition of the decision to go to Central Australia, to leave everything behind me, and walk into the desert, shedding burdens as I went, burning away the false and irrelevant until I reached ... I had no idea what I might reach, though it seemed I had approached it often.

I must add here the tone of the times. By 1972 the sense of purpose and possibility engendered by the late sixties was dissipating. There were still specific issues around which groups coalesced – feminism, Aboriginal land rights – but the idea that the whole world might fundamentally change had pretty much gone in the garbage bin of romantic delusions.

A strand of the counterculture had branched off into the medievalism and banality of New Age. Others had gone back to doing what they always would have done had the late sixties not intervened: joining the great drive to reproduce, make money and buy stuff. Mass distraction was the new form of control, filling in cracks where the subversive could take root.

I feel myself hurrying towards the end, wanting to leap over decades, race towards release from this fairy-tale task. It is exhausting to sift through the sediment, exhausting

to keep repeating 'I, I, I'. It's like running past wait-a–
while vines.

Nancy was to die far too soon. She would die the same
year my father died, and Gil, his twin, who took me in after
my mother's death. The siblings died within a fortnight of
each other; it was the same year my oldest niece Onnie
came close to death, and my first book came out. I was
living in London that year, but came back to Australia
twice, once when I learnt Nancy was ill, once for my niece
and family. But I missed the deaths, the funerals.

By the time we went prospecting together, my dad had
lived cheek by jowl with his mistakes. When, eventually,
I made the journey across the desert, it must have seemed
like a vindication, like he hadn't done such a bad job
after all.

He died reading *Tracks*. I was not with him. He did not
complete the book. That I was not with him is a sorrow
too deep to be eased.

My mother's death is relevant here, shadowed in my
incapacity and frozenness. I had not attended her funeral.
I did not attend my father's funeral. I left everything to my
sister to organise, to cope with. It was physically impossible
to have been present at his death, but I could have made it
to the funeral. But it was as if, in not ritualising his death,
I could keep him alive somewhere, a phone call or a letter
away. 'I am travelling, and unable to be with you, but you
are still there. You are all still there.'

Burial of the dead is one of the markers of our humanity,
they say. It separates us from other animals. But it is too late,
then, to weep and grieve. We should have been weeping
for their lives. Death should be a simple putting away.

A cardboard box, a fire or burial; it hardly matters. And no gravestone – no mad postponement of the inevitable – our ineffably vast irrelevance, our erasure. I believed this then and still believe it, and yet, when I held my parents' ashes in my lap, years later, that frozen heart of mine was scalded and boiled by grief and love.

Twenty-Three

Dark times. Gathering density through the second decade of life with Narendra.

I was still based in London, in the long white room, commuting to India to stay with him occasionally, or up in the Himalayan house on my own. Sometimes, when he could get away, he would come to London for a few days. But there was a cost involved in the separation of worlds. The sense of there being a centre with which to compare elsewhere was constantly dissolving.

There had been too many losses in too short a time, with no assimilation of one shock before the next came along. I would get up to my knees, only to receive another blow.

The past had come back full force, with all its inhabiting ghosts. And I was far far away from anywhere I was supposed to be.

I did not confide in people about this fragility. It was a source of shame, and some bewilderment. Wasn't I the strong one? The indestructible one? Hiding my true state, I felt myself to be more and more isolated. When I looked up I could see nothing but rubble to the horizon. So I didn't look up. I kept going.

Narendra was struggling in his own blasted landscape. The structures he had put in place to hold up his life, and to protect that life, were failing. The BJP was in power in Rajasthan, and they could now act to destroy their old enemy. There were court cases, threats, financial betrayals, audits, land disputes – the sense of predators closing in, vindictive and merciless. I had invested in an agricultural company Narendra had floated. The company failed. I knew of these problems but only in outline; he wouldn't furnish me with details. Whenever I pressed him his response was, always, 'You don't worry about it, yaar.' But I did worry about it. My security was enmeshed with his but I could neither understand his arcane money dealings, nor could I get him to finally sort them out. There are no tastes so expensive as a Rajput gentleman's. The show of wealth continued but the wealth bucket had drained.

Most of the time my connection to him felt very safe. But there were other times, particularly when he was drunk (and as the pressures increased so did the alcohol), when I was distressed by the chasm that lay between us, because I could not leap over that chasm, or pretend it wasn't there. As well, his religiosity was becoming increasingly dogmatic and vocal. While I knew it was his way of finding safe ground, that didn't make it less alienating. At such times, intimacy was replaced by radical loneliness.

At around that time, perhaps a year or so before, Narendra had undergone heart surgery in Bombay. They had 'lost him' on the operating table. When he came out of that hospital he was a different man. A couple of the closer servants confided their beliefs to me. When Sahib hovered between life and death, they said, another, more malignant soul had partially entered his body. Sometimes the old Narendra was there, sweet and kind. Then, without warning, a harshness would appear – angry, unpleasant, righteous. Certainly he had plenty to be angry about. My inability to help him or soothe him, for one. Often my presence irritated him. So I would back away.

A sense of myself at that time is of someone running to escape her life: what her life had become. Escape Narendra, escape India; above all, escape grief. I careened down various avenues in this attempt, including a stupid affair – the classic route of the coward. Narendra was kind about it as always, even parental. But it wounded him.

Still, the bond of friendship remained strong. We still spoke on the phone almost every morning. Those bird-call reassurances: I am here, are you there? Yes. Are you there? Yes. Being held in someone else's mind and heart. But increasingly, these calls were evasions, as each tried to protect the other from anxiety and worry. In truth, our lives were unravelling, and the partnership was too burdened to sustain added loads.

One morning, I was about to catch a flight to France. I was waiting on a taxi to take me to the airport, and I was waiting for Narendra's call.

The call came.

He said, 'Don't you worry about anything. You just go.'

'But are you all right, tell me what's happening over there?'

'Nothing, yaar. You don't worry. Everything's fine.' He was calm and warm. His calmness was soothing, as it always was.

Weeks later, when I finally flew into Delhi to meet him, I found out what had been happening on the other side of that phone call. While I had been waiting for the taxi, he was sitting outside the jhumpa, blood gushing out of his head, falling all over him like a cape. His skull had been opened by a hatchet. The police were at his farmhouse. The exquisite farmhouse with the thatched roof and jali windows. An ambulance had already left with two of his men who had also been seriously wounded. A second ambulance was waiting to take Narendra to hospital. But he would not get into that ambulance until he had made the phone call to me.

Perhaps he would never have mentioned it, but at the airport, when he came inside as always to usher me through, he looked gaunt and grey. I said, 'Serge, whatever's the matter? You don't look right.'

'Nothing, yaar ... we'll talk about it later ...' Then I saw the six-inch line of metal stitches down the back of his skull.

It was an attack from a consortium of enemies – political and familial.

It is difficult to work out precisely when our difficulties began seriously to tip the balance, which of the many straws did the deed. Perhaps it was on our last holiday together, in Venice. Again, sequential time eludes me. It must have been before 2000, before the Twin Towers came down, before Onnie's death.

It was winter, I remember that. On our last night in Venice, eating in a restaurant, he collapsed. I shouldered him back to the hotel. He refused to let me call an ambulance, saying that if he was to die, he would die there with me, and not in some hospital where he couldn't speak the language. If

I argued with him his distress increased. I sat up with him throughout the night. I did not call an ambulance.

The foundations of his psyche were feudal, though most of the time those pylons were obscured by a more recently formed scaffolding. But the threat of death revealed the deeper structures starkly. At that depth I was of no use to him. He rang some old godman in India, who chanted through the telephone which Narendra pressed to his chest. All night the chanting came down the phone line into Narendra's heart, while I kept close to the hotel phone, ready to pounce on it if necessary.

He survived what presumably was a heart attack, and a week later he had returned to his problems in India, and I to mine in London.

But the first night back home, I woke suddenly, transfixed with fear, my heart pounding at a terrifying rate. I tried to move but it was as if my body was cemented to the bed. I couldn't move a limb, and was utterly unable to comprehend what was happening to me. The only way I could regain some sense of control was to compose a conversation, an argument, in my mind, between the devil, St Michael and a girl. (God knows where St Michael came from. I had no conscious memory of who he was or what he represented.) My mind flew to keep ahead of the storm – verse after verse in iambic pentameter, hour after hour, until the first sheen of light at the windows, at which point the storm subsided and I could move, and then I could sleep.

It was as if something had been waiting until I had no resistance left.

I refused to acknowledge I was ill. 'Breakdowns' happened to other people. I was too strong to be broken.

Doctors cannot cure a mind of itself. Only a mind can cure itself of itself. (How shameful, what weakness, that my mind was doing such a lousy job.)

Besides, it felt to me, even during the worst of it, that what I was experiencing in some sense did not fully belong to me. Had I lived in another century I would have believed I was haunted. But then what is a ghost? Someone who is powerfully present but cannot be seen. From some separate, safer place within, I observed everything. Suicidal thoughts were constant, yet somehow, because of that detached, watching self, I believed that I would not kill myself.

One night I was jolted awake by the smell of my mother.

What we know about these extraordinary states depends on what lens we use to view them – scientific or religious, Darwinian or Freudian, medical or spiritual, observer or subject.

The subjective, in my own case, went like this.

I am in intolerable pain. It is a pain that no drug can get at because it is lodged somewhere between the physical and the mental. It is as if an immaterial body occupies, in exactly the same space, my material body. And the immaterial body is being disembowelled.

I wake, after one or two hours of sleep, and the evisceration has already begun. I am open from throat to pelvis and the organs are exposed and tumbling from the body. I lie on my side and hold the gash together and pull myself around it. I think, I can bear this much but if it gets one degree stronger I will not be able to bear it.

I wake straight into it; there is no liminal moment in which to prepare or adjust, or pick up some sort of mental weapon to fend off terror. The terror is so great that it overwhelms any other possibility of thought. This is what I will feel at the moment of my death. This is how it is when the torturers come, when the hangman comes to take you to the gallows. The stomach roils, the limbs are numb, the mind cowers, but there is nowhere to hide, no plea to be made, no one to help you or be with you as you face the unfaceable. What monstrous sadism could think up such cruelty: to place self-consciousness inside a mortal, animal body?

Or ...

I lie in bed, thirsty. My mouth is dry, my lips cracked. It is somewhere in the middle of the day. Night and day mean very little because I don't sleep for more than an hour at a time. I cannot make myself reach for the glass of water beside my bed. It is not that I have no will, but the will is detached from the body. My mind is a heavy grey weight. 'Just get up. Just get up.' But I don't get up. I don't reach for the water beside the bed, which might as well be light years away. It is easier to be thirsty.

Or ...

I get up at night, throw on a coat and go to the local shop to get wine and cigarettes, chocolate. These are the things I live on. I don't bathe. In the street I am frightened that someone will see me, talk to me. Back in the flat, I don't answer the phone or the door. I sleep in snatches, seldom more than an hour. I long to disappear in sleep. But pain jolts me awake and there is no escape from it. I sleep like a cat. On a chair, on the floor, in my grimy bed.

My bed is a raised platform at one end of the room. There is a big industrial window beside my bed. I can look down to the courtyard three storeys below. I could roll off the bed and fall down to the courtyard and it gives me comfort to imagine this. Just as it is comforting to imagine using Narendra's pistol to blow my head to bits. *Bang* to the side of that offending brain. And then again, *bang*. And again and again. There is relief in it, something like getting to the source of an itch. There is similar relief in imagining someone or something filleting the muscles in my back. Slicing muscle from the bone, as if I were a fish on a slab.

I dream often that I am a fish being cut up, filleted, fried. I see that there are other fish. They have human faces. They cry out in agony but the cooks are oblivious. They fillet, cut up, fry and do not notice.

Suffering is undignified. It is not how one wishes to be seen, to be thought of. Then, too, one does not want to burden anyone. Or to see impatience or withdrawal in their eyes. One never knows who will be frightened by distress, who will feel inadequate in the face of it, and turn away. So it is better to keep your injuries hidden, to avoid the added insult. You begin to quarantine yourself. As for 'society' – that outer ring of acquaintances and colleagues amongst whom you must build your life? I had already seen, close-up, what *Schadenfreude* could do. People think of what will be useful to them, who will be useful to them. Those in spiritual crisis are not useful to anyone, except perhaps as currency for gossip. Old saying: crows feed on the backs of wounded buffaloes.

Thus loneliness begets loneliness.

Was this what my mother experienced? What she suffered? What many suffer? If so, why aren't there more suicides? Two per cent of people suicide, and that is already more deaths than are caused by all the wars. The human condition is beyond bearing. Is that the truth we unlucky ones know? Are we less deluded than the happy ones, the ones who know how to forget? Is it cowardly to kill yourself, or is it cowardly not to? Who will judge this?

I tried to write from inside that place, but it was hopeless, distorted by the frenzy, exhaustion and tedium of pain. Memories came. I tried to make something of them, a sentence here, a page there, typed or scrawled, haphazardly stashed in boxes or files, left in addresses in different countries, then forgotten. And when, years later, I came across them, I often could not credit that I had written them.

I had been given an impossible task, a fairy-tale task. I was to write about my mother, not because I wanted to (I very much did not want to), but because she wanted me to.

One morning I said to Narendra on the phone that I didn't think I could make it. That no one should live like this. If I saw a dog suffering like this, I would put it down. Two nights later he was in London, in my bed, holding me. 'The demons will have to get through me first,' he said.

There were periods of relative sanity, but inevitably, in such a way that I could never figure out what the cause might be, the grip would begin to tighten again. Then, two or three or four weeks later, when for reasons unfathomable, the grip loosened, I could go about the routine of my life again, not with alacrity or pleasure, but with an acceptable facade in place. My concentration was shot; I could no longer remember names, titles, dates. When I tried to write, there was sludge in my head and certain words, quite ordinary words, refused to be called up. I couldn't remember whom I met last week, what I did yesterday. Sometimes I would stand in the middle of the room trying to remember what I had to do, where I had left something important. Ten minutes would pass and I would remain stranded in the fog, furious with myself, ready to weep with frustration. Sometimes, like an ambush, I would be out in public and find myself unable to speak. The conversation taking place around me was beyond me, as if I were watching a movie, or aliens. I longed to be back in my bed where nothing was required of me. Though that bed was also the place of torment.

And then …

I had returned to Australia and was on my way back to London. I received the news that Onnie had died. Why hadn't I picked her up and brought her with me? Why hadn't I rescued her, protected her, *saved* her?

And finally …

Weeks had passed with no word from Narendra. I was beside myself with anxiety. He had disappeared and there was no way of finding out what had happened. No one would return calls. The servants, when I got hold of them, were evasive. Should I fly there? No, they said, do not come, Sahib says do not come. But where is he. What is happening? They would not say. There was no one I could talk to. No one I believed.

I knew that if I went to India he would avoid me, find a thousand ways to fob me off. So instead, I drove to Ireland, to a Buddhist retreat on the coast where I could pull myself together and decide what to do. I was physically exhausted by the drive, by chronic sleeplessness. Close to the retreat, I got out of the car to settle myself before facing strangers. When I got back in I found that my whole body was shuddering uncontrollably. Tears were gushing out of me, unstoppable. I could no more drive the car than fly. A car stopped. A young couple got out, also heading for the retreat. They smiled, friendly and open. Need any help? Then they saw what they were dealing with. Their smiles changed, became starchy, embarrassed. I saw how quickly you can move from being a fellow human to being a problem, and that dehumanising glance frightened me more than anything. But it was beyond me to stop shaking. I seemed to have no control over my body at all. I said, 'I don't feel well, could one of you drive the car into the retreat.' When we got there, they melted away. I got myself to my room, but now the physical agony was overwhelming. What would happen to me? Who would help me? Was I to die here? I ran a hot bath and sat in it. I lay down on a bed. I got back in the bath. I lay down. I got back in the bath. Nothing brought relief. I was in hell. I was in hell. There was no one left in my life to ring, no one to turn to, I was utterly on my own, all the threads connecting me to the world were severed. I made myself go outside to sit on the grass, in the sunshine. But when I looked into the grass, at the small insects there, I saw reality as it is: every entity eating or being eaten, hunting or being hunted, the universe one vast grinding stomach gorging, digesting, shitting itself out and gorging itself again; there was nothing else.

This state lasted for two days. Eventually I asked someone at the retreat to drive me to a local doctor. The doctor gave me sleeping pills but even on triple the dose, sleep only came for an hour or two, before the frenzy began again.

Shame. To be seen to be in some animal state, beyond culture. Shame. I was taken to the doctor again.

He gave me antidepressants. I had no faith in the pills but, having no will outside suffering, I agreed to anything. I accepted the pills as a dog or a cat would accept them.

Six days later, the shaking had stopped, the terror had abated enough for me to feel that I could drive the car, though I still didn't get more than two hours' sleep at a stretch. I drove back to London, but instead of retreating into my flat to convalesce, instead of seeing another doctor, getting help, instead of putting myself into a hospital or a madhouse, I travelled to Paris for a friend's birthday. I must not let anyone down. I must not let anyone know my state. I must not burden anyone. I must get through this on my own.

What you are best at is also how you fail. One of my strengths is a high tolerance of discomfort – physical and mental. My independence, my reluctance to ask for help, my pride, my assumption, developed in childhood, that I must look after myself because there was no one else to do so; those habits of being now worked against me.

The doctors called this 'depression'. Was there ever a word more inadequate to its manifestation?

When I think back to that time now, it astonishes me that I functioned at all. Yet in the years of welter, I continued fitfully to write, I kept up some sort of social life, and when I couldn't get up, I read my way through a library.

I would not wish what I suffered on anyone, and pills eased the tightest grip of its manifestation. And yet ...

There was something deeper in this matter of my 'illness', deeper than all the things that can go wrong in a life, deeper than cocked-up chemistry, deeper than my mother's suicide, and I still believe that in the right environment, under proper care, a tormented mind can be restored to health without the necessity of drugs. But where one might have found that 'right environment', I don't know. It was not available to me. And it was certainly not available to my mother.

Would she have survived had she lived in this decade rather than in the fifties? Why did she suicide and I did not? Was she stronger or weaker than me? Or is that an irrelevant question to ask? Did I experience a 'breakdown' because of her suicide? Would I have experienced something similar anyway, because of my own fragilities and experiences? What is the relationship between my mother's despair, and my own?

What I do know is that the breakdown was the portal through which my mother returned to me, not as a person (that person is forever beyond reach), but as something to be acknowledged. To be brought forth. To be *honoured*.

Some people, in trying to understand why I crossed the desert, assumed that I was doing penance for my mother's death. (As if the journey were not joyous! A stepping into the unknown to find out what you are capable of. In that most exquisite and benign landscape. How odd that something so positive could be seen as a penance.) There is an infinitude of causes behind every action. It's absurd to single one out from along the ramifying chain. However, it is true to say that her death, the manner of her death, was the catalyst of an insight (if I can call it that) which would colour everything in my future.

Twenty-Four

In those vast Malabar afternoons after piano practice, you might skip down into the paddocks, avoiding the bony scrub, and make your way towards the lusher forest along the creek. If you went the narrow paddock way, below the sheds, a patch of cottonweed would have to be inspected for caterpillars – gentle, velvety creatures that stitched themselves into luminous chrysalises before breaking into butterflyhood. My father said they were monarchs, who travelled great distances when they felt like it.

If you chose the horse paddock, you would pass the windmill Dad erected the day I was allowed to take him his lunch from the house. We sat on a stump together and he showed me the proper way to eat an orange. First bash it all up so that the insides get soft. Then, with a very sharp knife (carried in a leather pouch on your belt), you cut a small cone from the top of the orange and suck the juice out. That gives you just the right amount of prickling in the nostrils, without juice running down your chin. That paddock was pink with natal grass.

One more paddock after that and you entered the strip of rainforest where, without thinking, you walked more slowly because the silence struck you, the air hot and still where sun came slanting through the canopy, where it shot shafts of green into the water. Spiders soundlessly skidded on boated feet across the surface of the water, which lay perfectly still beneath fallen trees. Whip birds might crack open the quietness but it quickly closed over.

On the other side of the fogbank separating Malabah from Clontarf, there was a diminished equivalence of Malabah's paddocks, Malabah's forests — the golf course behind our house.

The golf course was like English parkland, sloping down to a line of sighing casuarinas bordering the mudflats and mangrove swamps of the bay. It was full of nothing to do, as if sunlight itself could modulate from major to minor key. But even though it was a poor substitute for Malabah's arcadia, and even though my strolls there were dogged by a melancholy unknown to Malabah strolls, nature still held her ground, and gave me somewhere to go.

It was sometime after my mother died. I must have been twelve or thirteen, perhaps home on a break from boarding school. I was wandering on the golf course as I usually did, in the evening, when all the golfers had gone home.

I was still preoccupied by science, and well understood nature to be different from the way it appeared to us. It was atoms separated by vast amounts of nothing. And the atoms themselves were vast amounts of nothing containing electrical charges which whizzed and spun and came and went and were forever inexplicable, however much we discovered about them. The miracle was that it all somehow constituted itself into the world we knew: our splendid and ever-astonishing home, solidly around us, beneath us, above us, our ground.

I don't know why it was that on that ordinary afternoon there was a sudden shift, or breach, in the appearance of things. Of things-as-they-seem. Not a vision exactly, because nothing changed outwardly. But rather an insight that penetrated the everyday world and caved it in.

I sat down by a tree. But it was no longer a tree, a life form one could feel kinship with, it was a whirlwind of energies streaming into a tree-shaped funnel. These violent energies were ceaselessly flowing into forms – leaf forms, human forms – but the forms were not 'things' at all. They were perpetually changing patterns governed by laws beyond the reach of human understanding.

Nature was not for us, had never been for us. It was not for anything. It was as blind to our presence as we were to its processes. It was in itself devoid of colour or sound or touch or beauty. There was no kindness in it, no love, no purpose, no pity. The agreed-upon world of trees, leaves, people was something we draped over the top of the maelstrom to protect ourselves from that truth.

Continents slammed together, crumpled, melted like cheese. Stars exploded, suns collapsed to the size of fists, oceans froze or boiled away, galaxies collided, ripping each other to wisps, and nothing, nothing at all was solid, nothing held still, reality was this and only this: an apocalypse consuming itself, shitting itself out, eternal, merciless.

And where was 'I' in this tumult? What and where? If the body too was an unstable funnel of energies, then the thing that saw, felt, understood, must be a point of awareness – independent, somehow, of the welter, but embedded within it. I felt that it was lodged in the skull, about an inch behind my left eye.

I lay on the ground, and felt the earth topple through space beneath me. The world fled all around. There was nothing left to trust in, no safety to be found anywhere. Then the thought came to me that all of this frenzy existed only during the instant of the present. The past instant vanished, and spirited everything away with it. The future was another abyss. Everything we experienced, our lives, what we thought of as the past, as the space we moved in, was in fact trapped in this skin of presentness – a membrane of time which hurtled through the dark noiselessly and incalculably fast. I thought of my mother (of all the dead) as having toppled out of this exploding membrane of light.

To escape. To be free of knowing. But how do you escape? Whatever step you take, however fast you run, the ground falls away beneath your feet. The only escape is to dislodge that speck of knowing from its sliver of time. But would it float out into the black, still aware, but without stars, or hope, or any kind of company?

I write about it now with a vocabulary that I did not possess then. Even if there had been a person capable of explaining what had happened to me, I would not have had the language to describe it. I was alone with what I knew, and it would reside inside me like a huge snake.

Once, years before, in the grounds of the Malabah house, my sister and I had stood together, looking up at the sky after a storm. Rays of green-and-gold light poured out between the clouds and a double rainbow braced the two horizons together. I asked my sister if that was heaven. I must have been very young to ask such a question, and I think it took some daring. She looked down at me, as if surprised, and smiled. 'No, rat-head, it's not heaven. It's just the sun.'

This time, too, I went to my sister; it might have been immediately afterwards, or days later. I said that I wanted to die.

I think I was simply reporting a fact, and looking for some kind of explanation, or alternative. I don't imagine that my voice expressed the terror I felt, or that it showed on my face. That in itself was remarkable to me, that a life could turn itself inside out and you looked exactly the same as before. My sister and I were in the kitchen. She went to the cutlery drawer and pulled out Dad's carving knife, handed it to me and said, 'Go ahead, you little shit, let's see if you've got the guts.'

There is the picture, it seems real enough – two girls in a kitchen in, say, 1963, one holding a carving knife, the other backed up against the red Laminex counter top where the electric fry pan is, where the yellow kettle with its Bakelite lid used to be. They are pale with shock or rage or fear.

I describe that scene as if it were as solid as a stage, but it is transparent – an instant isolated from a stream of instants in a thirteen-billion-year backwards trajectory. Like the tree, the two sisters are not 'things'; they are processes, streams of causes beyond comprehension or measure. Where did either of them begin? There is no end to the mystery of who they are, of what anything is. All we can say is that everything they do will reverberate down along each life, and into other lives, like the dominoes they used to play with on rainy days in Malabah. Nor are they as separate as they seem. Each, because of the existence of the other, will have habits of mind that are default perspectives, mental weathers and tendencies that will inform their fates yet lie largely beneath conscious awareness.

In any case, I manifestly did not have the guts, and while her response did not refute the nihilism of my vision, it hardened me against it. In this, my sister may well have saved my life. I do know that she acted out of her own loss and grieving, and that one must never forget the vital significance of point of view.

The revelation on the golf course was one of those pivotal moments around which an existence turns, where the course of a life is disrupted. From that point on, all the ordinary ambitions became irrelevant. Everything achieved would be in relation to what had been revealed – either an attempt to forget it, because forgetting is necessary for the making and maintaining of life, or an effort to pull the world back to solidity, to refute what I had seen – that life is for nothing, and sinks away into nothing, and there is no kinship with the earth, and there is nothing to care for us.

If that day had never been, I might have led a more straightforward kind of life, and I might have loved more conventionally. As it was, love became infused with something like pity – for our shared, unspeakable predicament – and at the same time a terrible need. As if love might defy the heartlessness lying in wait at the root of nature.

Isn't it true that the desire underlying all desires, the love underlying all loves, is the wish to come home, fully, to this world? To be at home, everywhere?

Epilogue

My arrival in this world in a small country not-quite town in the nearly-but-not-quite outback of Australia at the midpoint of the twentieth century, to parents who were neither famous nor prestigious nor important to history, was in no way exceptional. And yet, nothing exactly the same had ever occurred before or will ever occur again.

I live, now, in an old stone house. It has high ceilings, and fireplaces. A corrugated-iron roof, in the Australian manner. In summer the rooms are cool, and in winter the sandstone stores sunlight which pours in through banks of windows. It contains beautiful things, and plenty of room for guests. Many different kinds of people have lived in it before me, each adding or taking away some element, as I have done. The house has lost parts, gained other parts, expanded, fallen into ruin, been partly burnt, recovered, rather like this book, or like my life. But houses, unlike sentences, have a random structure producing all sorts of thoughts like proliferating rooms. They require taxonomy. Its first category, then, is kindliness. It is a kindly house.

I have built a garden around it, which is chaotic and productive. There are vegetables to eat and flowers all year round for the table. Many animals come to share the house

and the garden. Kangaroos up the back. All kinds of birds –
ravens and cockatoos, finches, cuckoos, spinebills, wrens,
thornbills, butcherbirds, magpies chortling for scraps at
the kitchen door … The week I bought it, I found a six-
foot snake in the cellar. Blue-tongue lizards live beneath
the house. I give them blueberries and snails when they
emerge to soak up sunlight.

The house has provided refuge for a number of years,
a sanctuary in which to sort through the scraps, complete
the book. I suppose the house will see me out, but who
knows? In any case, when I die, it will transform again,
and all it contains will tumble through time into new
configurations, with entirely different meanings. We are
not the owners of anything, not even the thoughts that rise
to the surface like deep-water fish …

I am grateful to the house. To the people who come
and go. To the huge oak tree up the back, where I sit and
wonder how the hell I got here. I observe my mind's
dynamics, and try to understand them. I try to get behind
my own act.

I try not to sink into grief at the ruination we have
caused to our planet, to ourselves, to other life forms.
I wonder about my death. How I will be when it comes.
I hope I will find the courage to stay still, face to face with
a universe that has no use for us.

And I think about my fate which seems to have had so
little to do with personal will, but rather is the playing-out
of forces I had no hand in. If the forces had been different –
if my mother had not suicided, let's say – I might have
had a more stable existence, possibly a happier one, almost
certainly a more conventional one. It might have been a

good life, with continuity in it, each phase a predictable florescence of the one before, rather than the discontinuous passages it seems in fact to have been, each present shearing off cleanly from the past, like icebergs from Antarctic cliffs.

As it is, it is just … my life. A very fortunate one.

Sometimes, I will experience a moment like a pause, or an opening. Everything stands still, as if time has opened into space as it did when I was a child in Malabah, when time billowed around us, and held us all safe. My sister unsaddling Prince down by the cowshed; Gwen at the piano, singing; Mark in the paddocks whistling to himself. Everything is unsullied and it is the first day of creation.

As it did in the desert, when the isolated self dissolved into the web of everything. In those moments (vanishingly rare), the wound of severance experienced on the golf course behind our house, after my mother's death, is healed. And I arrive in the only home I could ever have – the ineffable, unfathomable present.

My mother is as close to me, and as hidden from me, as my own face …

A Note on the Author

Robyn Davidson was born on a cattle property in Queensland. She went to Sydney in the late 1960s, then returned to study in Brisbane before going to Alice Springs to prepare for her journey across Australia with camels. Since then, she has travelled extensively and lived in London, New York and India. In the early 1990s she migrated with and wrote about nomads in north-west India. She is now based in regional Victoria, Australia.

A Note on the Text

The text of this book is set in Bembo, which was first used in 1495 by the Venetian printer Aldus Manutius for Cardinal Bembo's De Aetna. The original types were cut for Manutius by Francesco Griffo. Bembo was one of the types used by Claude Garamond (1480–1561) as a model for his Romain de l'Université, and so it was a forerunner of what became the standard European type for the following two centuries. Its modern form follows the original types and was designed for Monotype in 1929.